M I R E I L L E   J O H N S T O N ' S

....

F RENCH
C OOKERY
C OURSE

PART TWO

MIREILLE JOHNSTON'S

*F*RENCH
*C*OOKERY
*C*OURSE

PART TWO

BBC BOOKS

To my daughter Margaret-Brooke, '*fine mouche – fine bouche*',
to my daughter Elizabeth, '*le moineau pensant*', and to my
husband Tom; all of whom have steadily gone, in the course
of these books, from tentative '*petites mains*' to thoughtful
testers and are now reliable partners in our kitchen.

This book is published to accompany the television series
entitled *A Cook's Tour of France 2* which was first broadcast
in September 1993. The series was produced
by Clare Brigstocke.

Published by BBC Books,
a division of BBC Enterprises Limited,
Woodlands, 80 Wood Lane
London W12 0TT

Hardback and paperback first published 1993
© Mireille Johnston 1993
Hardback ISBN 0 563 36760 1
Paperback ISBN 0 563 36767 5
Designed by William Mason
Copy-edited and tested by Wendy Hobson

Photograph credits
Food photography by Graham Kirk. All other photographs by
David South except: Pyrenees by IMP/Marie Louise Avery
and Vallee d'Albertville by Robert Harding Picture Library
Styling by Helen Payne
Home Economist Allyson Birch

Artwork credits
Filler artworks © Sally Launder
Maps © Eugene Fleury

Set in Baskerville by Goodfellow & Egan Ltd
Printed and bound in Great Britain by Clays Ltd, St Ives plc
Colour separation by Technik Ltd, Berkhamsted
Jacket and cover printed by Clays Ltd, St Ives plc

CONTENTS

•••••••••••••••••••••••

INTRODUCTION 8

•••••••••••••••••••••••

REGIONAL INTRODUCTIONS 16

•••••••••••••••••••••••

*Île-de-France; Normandy;
Lanquedoc-Roussillon;
The South-West; Lyonnais,
Savoie, Franche-Comté
and Dauphiné;
Val de Loire*

THE RECIPES

•••••••••••••••••••••••

ACKNOWLEDGEMENTS

This book was prepared in connection with the BBC television series filmed by Clare Brigstocke and her merry crew in six regions of France. I want to express my gratitude to Clare whose indomitable energy and vision kept it and us all together.

Many thanks to Jenny Stevens for her confidence, Diane Hadley for her ever-present support, Tricia Bowker for her infectious good humour, Clare Hughes for her endurance and energy, David South, Eric Fever, Michael Whitehouse, and Mal Maguire for their superb work and their good spirits all along. Working with such a crew transformed hard work into a true pleasure.

I want to thank affectionately Suzanne Webber, my editor who has been constantly generous and attentive, Deborah Taylor for her patience, Frank Phillips for his eye, and Khadija for her grace under pressure. I want to thank Wendy Hobson, it was a delight working with her.

In the making of this series I want to acknowledge all the help we have received from SOPEXA, London and particularly from Gabrielle Allen who provided so many contacts and gave so much of her time. I also want to thank Gillian Green of Air France Holidays and the many regional Chambers of Commerce and Tourist Committees, both regional and departmental, for their invaluable help during the research trips, and most especially the Pont l'Abbé Tourist Office.

I would also like to thank Eric du Chatellier and Patricia Rio at the Château de Kernuz, Quimper, and Carole Handslip and Sarah Pope for their kind cooperation during the demonstration filming.

A C K N O W L E D E M E N T S

And finally I want to thank all the people who during the filming welcomed us so warmly in their restaurants, in their homes, and shared with us their love for their region and its cooking:

JEAN BARDET, *Tours*
MARTINE O'JEANSON, *Tours*
JACQUELINE PILLOY, *Crottes-en-Pithiverais*
MONIQUE LANSARD, *Chambéry*
DANIEL BOUJON, *Thonon-les-Bains*
CLAUDE DUBOULOZ, *Anthy-sur-Léman*
ROYAL CLUB EVIAN, *Evian-les-Bains*
RAYMOND FULCHIRON, *Lyon*
JACQUOTTE BRAZIER, *Lyon*
PIERRE SAUTET, *Paris*
LA COUPOLE, *Paris*
FATMA MAZIANI, *Paris*
PAUL BOCUSE, *Collonges-Mont D'Or*
JOËL ROBUCHON, *Paris*
MONIQUE PIAT, *Pierre Sitte-en-Auge*
THE CAMUT FAMILY, *La Lande St Leger*
DANIEL GASLIN, *Bas-Courtils*
PIERRETTE SARRAN, *St Martin d'Armagnac*
LYDIE DÈCHE, *Nogaro*
MARIE-CLAUDE GRACIA, *Poudenas*
ANDRÉ DAGUIN, *Auch*
BRASSERIE NOAILLES, *Bordeaux*
THE CANO FAMILY, *Fontcouverte*
ELIANE THIBAUT-COMELADE, *Perpignan*
ANN MAJOUREL, *Tornac*
LES TEMPLIERS, *Collioure*

INTRODUCTION

....

I am with my owl-like uncle at the end of a meal. He wets his lips with a sip of armagnac, stares at the ceiling and ponders: 'In life, there are three things that truly count. One is dining well . . . and I can't recall the other two just now.'

The French have always taken their pleasures seriously. Food – earthy, intense, subtle, or simply reassuring – is among those we cherish most. We love to sit together with friends around a steaming *Soupe Gratinée*, contemplating its fragrant broth and the fact that, on the whole, man tends to be a wolf to man except when he prepares a good meal or shares one.

The truth is there are only three basic rules that one needs to know about cooking. It is a civilising force. It must not be intimidating. It is a source of true pleasure.

As for civilisation, there is no question that cooking is among its most vigorous, sustained sources of energy, and in France it is a regional affair. Indeed, French civilisation as a coherent entity does not exist outside bureaucrats' offices. For all their power, Paris officials will never manage to persuade a major French region to renounce its version of civilisation, with its own locally accented culture and cooking. Over the centuries, regional culture and cooking have worked hand in hand as recipes were passed like precious poems from generation to generation until they began to appear in books.

Each region has evolved in step with the times – many enriched by Celtic, Greek, Roman or Moorish invasions – blending together local specialities with what arrived from the Crusades and the rest of the world. Yet much more powerful than external forces in shaping regional character and cooking has been the unique way cooks in each region have responded to their local products.

This is the secret of good French cooking: passionate respect for local products. If you have even the slightest doubt that passion is the right word, please consider this: there are 250 ways to cook chestnuts in Languedoc, over 100 ways to prepare tomatoes in Provence, and apples in Normandy, and at least two dozen ways to use walnuts in Périgord. Each of the six regions we visit in this book – Languedoc-Roussillon, Normandy, Lyonnais and Savoie, the South-west, Val de Loire and Île-de-France – has specific products and individual ways of preparing them. A fish *à la normande*, steak *à la bordelaise*, omelette *à la basquaise* are instantly evocative of their birthplace. The strong affinities between a product, the spirit of its place of origin, and the way it is prepared locally transform each dish into a journey into the region. A pear tart is our quickest link to an orchard in the Loire Valley; a bowl of mussel soup is a breath of air from the ocean in Trouville; a platter of mushrooms transports us to the thick of Rambouillet forest.

But the old suspicions between the various provinces – why so much garlic in Languedoc; why are potatoes sautéed in goose fat in Périgord; why is watercress soup enriched with cream and butter in Normandy; why are meatless *farcis* made in Provence – are less sharply defined than in the past.

The mutual give and take between the scholarly and the sensual, between Paris and provinces, which exists at every level of French life yields more positive results in gastronomy than perhaps in any other area. Most city dwellers in France still visit their relatives in the country regularly and remain in touch not only with their family but also with their village and its ways of cooking. This constant dialogue between local products imaginatively prepared and the influence of classic cooking to sharpen them is often invigorating. A gratin of raspberries may be fresh and delicious, but if we cover it with a pungent *Sabayon* sauce (see page 240) it acquires a new dimension. A fruit tart prepared with *Pâte Sucrée* is delicious, but if *Pâte Sablée* or *Pâte Feuilletée* is used, it rises to another level (see pages 220 and 218).

Although in France fashions and fads – with their litany of truffle or codfish ravioli, the inevitable trendy purslane, rocket, or raw salmon dishes – keep popping up, French cooking remains anchored in a sensible tradition. As Gertrude Stein observed, 'The French change completely, but all the time they know that they are as they were.' *Bon gré, mal gré,* willy nilly, real food reigns supreme!

Yet, if civilisation supports us with the strength of the past, it also bombards us with the future's unsettling changes. To deal with them, we are lost without the second basic rule of cooking: it must not be intimidating. Stores are full of items providing health, slim silhouettes and freedom from time-consuming chores. In this mix of quick fixes, some are sensible, others range from distasteful to dangerous. Trendy food diets, ersatz butter, sugar or chocolate products, manipulated food substitutes, chemically hyped flavours, eggless mayonnaise, crab patties made with fish left-overs and soya

GARDNERS STOCK CONTROL SYSTEM

ACCOUNT NAME   OTTAKAR'S PLC (SALISBURY)

ACCOUNT NO.   OTT001

       RE-ORDER DATE _____

ISBN	0563367695 QUANTITY
TITLE	FRENCH COOKERY COURSE 2
AUTHOR	JOHNSTON, M
PUBLISHER	BBCP01
BINDING	P : 12/11/93 F 320 E
CLASS	304
PRICE	9.99
SUPPLIED	12/11/93

BAR CODE FOR GARDLINK

9 780563 367697

Gardners Books

THE INDEPENDENT WHOLESALER

Eastwood Road,
Bexhill-on-Sea,
East Sussex TN39 3PT
Tel:(0424)224777
Fax:(0424)220560

Unit 13, Commercial Road,
Goldthorpe, Rotherham,
South Yorkshire S63 9BL
Tel:(0709)890661
Fax:(0709) 890668

RE-ORDER SLIP

OTT001
FRENCH COOKERY
0563367695

RE-ORDER QUANTITY _____

Gardners Books

THE INDEPENDENT WHOLESALER

Eastwood Road,
Bexhill-on-Sea,
East Sussex TN39 3PT
Tel:(0424)224777
Fax:(0424)220560

Unit 13, Commercial Road,
Goldthorpe, Rotherham,
South Yorkshire S63 9BL
Tel:(0709)890661
Fax:(0709) 890668

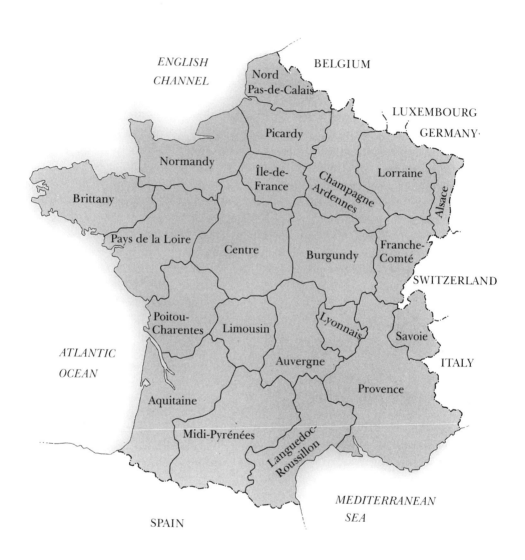

are just a hint of what the future holds for us if nothing changes.

Clearly, we all prefer good food to bad or indifferent food. But what are we prepared to do about it? As we tend to be a little distracted, a bit lazy, often entirely too adaptable, we may, with the best of intentions, find ourselves turned into robots with passive palates, nibbling bland composites from bright containers.

We have marvelled at the variety of exotic fruits and vegetables available throughout the year. We trusted and praised technological progress. Now we are beginning to realise that what was a cause of wonderment may prove to be a threat, as we bite into a perfectly formed, utterly tasteless tomato. Now is the time to choose our products carefully, to take a minute to look, touch, smell and decide which green bean, which potato, which cheese we are buying, to select a fresh whiting rather than a frozen lobster if we can, and a plain but crisp cabbage rather than limp asparagus. No amount of Mornay Sauce is going to transform an inferior industrialised chicken into an acceptable dish.

In France, we now have labels to protect the quality of our cheese, poultry, wines and meats, naming their place of origin and their precise content. This trend is happily developing in Britain. We must use vegetables, fish, meats, cheeses that belong to a recognisable place. If we select a product with care, we can be sure that it will have flavour, be fresh and healthy, and that we are also preserving a rural system and a region.

Today, everybody from home cooks to chefs agrees that as we want lighter dishes, more intense flavours are also what we crave. We use marinades, reductions, herbs and spices to replace unctuosity and quantity. Curiously, all this is as healthy as it is tasty. After a meal with true flavours, pudding binges are few and far between.

The process of cooking need never be intimidating. It is, on the contrary, one of those happy spaces where, with a little effort, our taste and imagination can yield reliably life-enhancing results. Cooking has been for me a solid bridge over turbulent waters. Like an exceptional poem, I find it keeps us close to many things in life that we need to be constantly reminded to see and feel again. That is why a real dish could never appear to us full-blown from outer space. The recipe for a real dish has been nurtured in the soil of past moments of pleasure. It has sustained others who kept it alive for us, and we in turn both take and give life to it as we use it.

After visiting Paul Bocuse, Joël Robuchon and André Daguin in their kitchens recently, it is clear that, as with many of us who cook at home, the rallying cry of these chefs is for food with real taste and texture, food with character. *'Faut de la mache!'* – 'give us something we can get our teeth into!' they say, as they carry a whole fish, or a whole chicken to the table.

Some dishes are more immortal, more irrestible than others. I have gathered in this book a mixture of wholly regional and some more classic recipes, all of which have been adapted for a cook working alone in the kitchen using produce in season. There are variations to many dishes, alternative fillings, choices of accompaniments and garnishes, so each of us can decide what works best for our schedule, budget and what products are available. McDonald may prize itself on the consistency of its Big Mac. We do the very opposite.

As for the preparation of a meal, here too we must free ourselves from any lingering intimidation. As we start to cook we must remember Napoleon's strategy: divide and conquer. A meal is made up of dozens of small victories, and a few decisive steps. Read the recipes you have chosen calmly, and write a reliable shopping list. Choose the products carefully. Then change gear as you transform the kitchen, temporarily, into a battlefield in the spirit of 'fire when you see the whites of their eyes'. You wash, peel, chop and cook many dishes at once. While the stew simmers, and the vegetable gratin and caramel custard bake in the oven, you are free to trim the salad and blend the dressing. But no matter what happens, remember that nothing can go totally wrong. This is not a circus act you are performing in front of a hostile audience. As Julia Child said, bending to scoop a roast chicken accidentally dropped on the floor, 'You are alone in the kitchen!' To make life easier for yourself, cook as many dishes in advance as possible so you can degrease, season and garnish them and be rested and relaxed when it is time to serve them. A stew, a soup, a pâté, a fruit compote, most dressings and many sauces will keep refrigerated for a week, ready to be called upon.

There are no hard and fast rules in the realm of cooking, except perhaps in pastry-making, which does rely on simple chemistry. For the rest, some combinations work better than others, but it's for each of us to choose what we like. We all have our own ideas on how far we can go with shortcuts. One cook will insist on grinding meat by hand for a pâté, another will happily rely on a food processor. One will use a microwave, the other a steamer, the third a pan. A friend recently served me the most fluffy couscous, and I learned that it had been prepared . . . in a microwave. *A chacun sa voie!*

And now, *à table!* In France, some families still sit in a formal way, host and hostess opposite each other, with the honoured guests to their right. Mine is a round table because I find that most convivial. A formal tablecloth may be replaced by mats, a king-size coloured sheet, a light printed bedspread, but cotton napkins give a feeling of comfort and luxury to the table. I use large serving dishes, casseroles, ovenproof dishes wrapped in a tea towel so I can bring them straight from the oven to the centre of the table or stand them on a trolley beside the table. And finally, in our house, everyone is always welcomed as fully-fledged participants in the whole process.

Then there is the question of what is best to prepare for your guests. As it is not easy to answer formally, I would like to quote my great aunt's advice. She was, in fact, talking to me about clothing, but it applies equally well to cooking and entertaining. 'Darling,' she said. 'Three well-chosen outfits are *all* you ever need in a wardrobe. The first – *tout venant* – simple and easy; the second – *pour faire bellotte* – to be your own sweet self; and the third – *pour être triomphante* – to knock them out!'

All we need to entertain at home with no help and a limited budget are a few reliable dishes which fall into the same three categories. There are dishes *à la bonne franquette* when we entertain simply. We may choose to serve *Omelette aux Courgettes* (see page 106), *Soupe aux Légumes* (see page 56), *Salade Lyonnaise* (see page 113) or perhaps *Hachis Parmentier* (see page 134). For a slightly more important occasion, it might be *Mouclade* (see page 72), Cassoulet (see page 146) or *Paupiettes de Boeuf* (see page 132). The dessert will always be something prepared in advance, like *Oeufs à la Neige*, fruit compote or a fine cheese served with fruits. And finally, *pour être triomphante*, for a major event when one needs, as we say, to put 'the little dishes in the big ones' – a large family meal, an important birthday, the return of a special friend – we may prepare *Jambon Persillé* (see page 192), *Bisque de Crabes* (see page 70) or Stuffed Shoulder of Lamb (see page 138). And to crown the meal, *Marquise au Chocolat* (see page 230), *Bavarois* (see page 248), or a fragrant pile of *Crêpes à la Normande* (see page 242).

Finally we have, thank goodness, the third rule, cooking's ultimate obligation: it must be the source of true pleasure. Somehow, anything prepared at home seems fresher, better; *c'est frais, c'est bon, c'est maison*. Seductive aromas floating through the house and the tangible measure of love you have given the preparation of the meal arouses the best in everyone. The dishes are a faithful bridge to palates and hearts. They transmit what at our best we do best: enjoying ourselves together. Give us real food. Bring the garden, the forest, the ocean, the orchard to our plates and, as we say in Provence,

'Régalez vous!' . . . 'Enjoy!'

REGIONAL
INTRODUCTIONS

Above: La Coupole, Paris

Previous page: A water mill in Gers in South West France

ÎLE-DE-FRANCE

It all started with Paris as a privileged centre. Later came Île-de-France, spreading like a rich belt around the city. And then slowly Burgundy, Normandy and all the other autonomous regions joined and gathered in concentric circles. Finally, a little over a hundred years ago, France – as we know her today – was born.

From a forest inhabited by spirits, Île-de-France has developed into one of the most powerful urban regions in the world. Over the centuries, major historical events have taken place in this plain and on these hills, filled with princes' and kings' hunting parties and accompanied by extravagant festivities. Less noticed but no less important to those who pursue them are the region's simpler pleasures. Workers, farmers, shopkeepers, artists and students have long enjoyed fishing along its river banks, dreaming under its majestic trees, picnicking in its woods, hunting for wild strawberries in spring and mushrooms in autumn. In the *guinguettes* of Châtou and Robinson, they danced until they dropped, revived themselves with fried fish and chilled white wine to dance again, and today we have added our own touches to keep this sense of pleasure alive.

This is a painter's country, a region of soft, subtle colours. Corot, Monet, Seurat, all the Impressionists have been inspired by the translucent light, the skies of Bourgival, Barbizon and Argenteuil, and by the innumerable rivers which cross the region, encircling it like an island.

Île-de-France is also Paris's cradle and provider: its market garden, bread basket and dairy farm. Man's sense of order and measure are as tangible here in its perfectly tended gardens, beet fields and orderly rows of corn as they are in Versailles, and Fontainebleau's palaces, Le Nôtre's gardens or its majestic cathedrals.

This fertile plain with its lush valleys and large plateux like Beauce and Brie is an extraordinarily productive region and, despite the overflow from Paris and creeping urbanisation, Île-de-France manages to offer a commuter territory side by side with a pastoral countryside. There are historic towns – St Germain, Versailles, Senlis, Fontainebleau – as well as industrial suburbs and new cities. There are huge forests and peaceful villages, fortified castles and grand manors, formal parks, wood-beamed covered markets, modest vegetable gardens, as well as the formidable Rungis, the largest wholesale food market in the world.

But for some, in spite of its grace and majesty, Île-de-France's size and its diversity translate into blandness, a lack of the specific character that distinguishes other regions in France. And there is a concern about the impact of the area's immense wealth and political power on the rest of the country. Michelet, the historian, worried that Île-de-France, 'the least original part of the country, [had] taken over the rest of the country'. Yet it might be its combination of diversity and gentleness which best explain its success as a political and administrative centre.

In its cooking, Île-de-France reflects the same complexity and profusion. The roasted meats, silky watercress and sorrel soups, velvety sauces enriched with butter and cream – these dishes and many others reflect both the aristocratic and rural traditions of the region as well as a light, modern Parisian touch.

But the very mention of Parisian food raises the issue that concerned Michelet. Has the presence of Paris at its centre destroyed rural Île-de-France's regional dishes? Can one speak of a Parisian cooking? Paris and the provinces have, over the centuries, danced together in a vivacious gastronomic *pas-de-deux*. It is true that Parisian chefs have had a tendency to extrapolate and transpose recipes, but they have always – and today more than ever – drawn their energy and their inspiration from regional cooking. It is a two-way process from the regions to Paris, where a recipe is appreciated for its provincial qualities, then refined and returned to its birthplace with a new twist. Paris's calculated chic and sophisticated appetite makes its own the earthiness of the provinces. Southern herbs – basil, savory, fennel, sage, marjoram and thyme – find themselves mingling with local parsley, chervil and tarragon. Vigorous Provençal, Gascon or Lyonnaise dishes are served along with smooth *grande cuisine* creations. Local dishes revisited by Parisian chefs emerge stronger, more forceful.

Craft, competition, a certain nostalgia and a sincere aim to emulate the best in regional cooking are highly instrumental. Often the best *choucroute*, the best *gratinée*, the best *brandade* are served in the capital. The simple potato purée is elevated to another level

ÎLE-DE-FRANCE

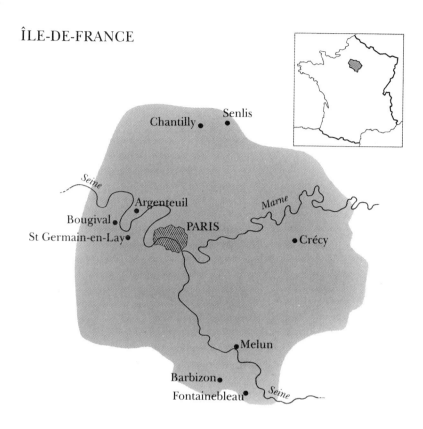

when Joël Robuchon prepares it. Lyonnais or Auvergnat *plats canailles* – rough, potent dishes – still attract the most refined Parisian palates.

Paris and its region are naturally more open to fashions, fads and trends than the rest of the country. Spring rolls, couscous, paella, curry, carpaccios, Indonesian Satay and sushi find their place here easily, but there is still an abundance of room – and appetite – for the patrimony that draws on the Île-de-France's own products. The region's rich orchards, vegetables and dairy products; the Brie, Melun and Fontainebleau cheeses; Chantilly's cream; mushrooms grown in the quarries along the Seine; the bream, perch and minnows in the rivers remain such essential ingredients in all home or professional cooks' repertoires that although a town like Crécy no longer grows carrots, the carrot purée soup named *Potage Crécy* (see page 69) still reflects its roots. The region's split pea soup is called *Potage St Germain*; while Argenteuil means a dish is made with asparagus, and Montmorency one that features local cherries.

When it comes to specifically Île-de-France or Parisian dishes served today, we find few long-simmered dishes, but many that are quickly grilled or sautéed and seasoned with a touch of mustard, lemon juice, or a dot of parsley butter. There is also the traditional roast chicken garnished with a few sprigs of watercress, the always welcome pile of sautéed, fried, puffed or souffléed golden potatoes, the fresh vegetables, with the omnipresent mushrooms sprinkled with parsley. And there is grilled Châteaubriand steak and calves' liver seasoned with shallot-wine-parsley-lemon Bercy Sauce; the *onglet* steak covered with a mellow layer of browned shallots; the generous offering of Robert, Gribiche (see page 85) and Mornay sauces (see page 92) and finally there are the wild duck, partridge, eel and all kinds of traditional Île-de-France pâtés. The baguette is at its crispest in Paris, the brioche its lightest, and the pastries – Saint Honoré, Chantilly tartlets, Opéra, Pithiviers (see page 226) or fluffy fruit mousses – the most refined in France.

Île-de-France has been called a national park of fine living. In fact, its inhabitants – the Franciliens – are realistic. They demand the impossible: the convenience of an urban space and the charm of country life. And if cooking is like music and politics, the art of mingling voices, Île-de-France's happy people can be said to have succeeded in having their cake and eating it, while at the same time expressing what may be the region's true distinctiveness – its pleasure in sharing that pleasure with others.

THE RECIPES OF
ÎLE-DE-FRANCE

• •

NORMANDY

Blessed with green valleys and cliffs overlooking the pounding waves below, Normandy is a province often described by novelists and painted by Impressionists. And yet it is a difficult region to define, for Normandy is quiet and self-effacing, happy to remain among the most discreet of celebrated places. Even its own poets find it hard to encapsulate its charms. When they verge on the edge of definition, they proclaim, 'the fragrance of my country is in an apple', but in the next breath they are questioning themselves: 'is our Normandy a gift from the sea?'

Napoleon used to declare: 'Le Havre, Rouen and Paris are one town, and the Seine river is its main avenue.' This is not the only occasion on which the Emperor's zest for simplifying the complex got the better of him, for Normandy comprises two main regions which have little in character to compare with Paris. Normandy is essentially a rural province along the English Channel coast, divided by the Seine into two quite distinct areas: Upper Normandy, with Rouen as its capital, and Lower Normandy, with Caen as its main city to the west.

From the edge of the Paris basin to Brittany, the rich murmur of the past can be heard throughout this lush, pastoral province. Pink and white blossoms, camellias, hydrangeas . . . for every cloud in the sky, they say in Normandy, there is a flower. They could also add a gallon of milk, since the rain falls gently and regularly, the grass grows faster and thicker throughout the year, and the cows give the richest milk in the greatest quantity in all of France. This region also has a special place in the hearts of gourmets everywhere as the source of Calvados, an elixir some find so divine they claim it should be reserved exclusively for the gods – with a little set aside for them and a few close friends.

Yet Napoleon was at least partly right in his definition of the region, for there are strong links with Paris. Etretat, Honfleur, Trouville and Deauville are today a short enough journey for many Parisians to own cottages, farms and châteaux in the region. Visitors enjoy the casinos, races and film festivals. Nearby, there is the Pays d'Auge with its thoroughbred horse farms, manors, half-timbered houses and thatched cottages – occasionally topped by a line of blue irises.

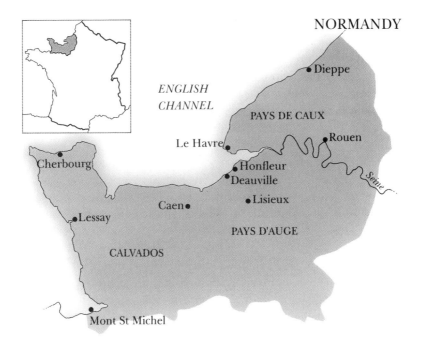

Here also, you will find bustling ports, for Normandy is an important maritime region. High chalky cliffs command wind-swept views of yellow sandy beaches stretching for miles at low tide, and reminding us that this is where sea bathing was invented and first practised. *Les planches* – the wooden plank promenades flanked with brightly coloured tents – invite visitors to stroll along by the shore.

To the west, the Cotentin peninsula marks the boundary with Brittany where you will find the celebrated medieval Mont-Saint-Michel. This 'wonder of the west', visited by multitudes of pilgrims and tourists, rises majestically from the sands or the waves – according to the tides – and for the last 900 years has been protected by the golden Archangel Michel atop his steeple.

Yet the region has not always been so peaceful. Invaded by the war-like Vikings in 911, it was given by King Charles the Simple to the Viking leader Rollo, who was made the first Duke of Normandy. In 1066, Rollo's descendant, William the Conqueror took his forces across the Channel to fight for and win the English crown, thereby uniting Normandy with England. The English and

French fought for supremacy in the region throughout the Middle Ages until the Hundred Years War was finally brought to an end in the mid-fifteenth century by King Charles VII of France, due in no small measure to the intervention of Jeanne d'Arc. Since that time, Normandy has enjoyed a peaceful existence, with the notable exception of World War II, when it played such a vital part both in the evacuation of Allied servicemen, and in their successful return in 1944.

In this now tranquil province, today's descendants of Viking warriors shy away from conflict. They seem content as they greet one another with a generous four kisses. Their traditional response to most queries is a gentle, 'Well, perhaps yes . . . perhaps no . . . who's to say?'

Yet in spite of both its resources and its apparently relaxed demeanour, economic hardship has hit the region, affecting not only dairy farmers but also fishermen and those working in the ports. In an effort to adapt to modern challenges, efficient co-operatives are increasingly replacing the old craft industries. On my last trip I visited, in the most bucolic of settings, a spotless, automated wonder of aluminium and tiles producing 20,000 tons of excellent Camembert each year.

To catch the true flavour of the region, one must sit at a Norman table and observe the magic interaction of food and people. Normans are solid eaters, gourmands by birth who, with their large necks and plump hands, have satisfaction clearly etched in their ruddy faces. Their cooking reflects the region's opulence. It is an honest, no-nonsense exercise that could run the risk of being monotonous, if it were not for that splendid Norman trilogy of cream, butter and apples.

Cream thickens and enhances most dishes from soups to fish and meat dishes, and even salads. Butter, the second secret weapon, makes for the lightest brioches and finest *sablés*. And, of course, the finest cheeses in Normandy – creamy, pungent Camembert, tangy Pont l'Evêque, superb Livarot – are sumptuous and matured to perfection. Some are so potent that no wine or dry cider can be served with them; only Calvados will do.

Apples are to be found everywhere. Unpeeled, browned apples garnish roast meats and sausages. Compotes of onions and apples are flavoured with vinegar or cider to enhance fish and meat dishes. Apples are served instead of vegetables, for which, with the exception of the potato, Normans have little appetite. Apple purée sometimes even replaces the traditional cream to thicken cooking juices.

Apples also yield 'Normandy's sun', the irresistible Calvados. Most inspired cooking uses Calvados – to enhance a dish of tripe, a veal chop, a chicken, a sorbet, or a simple cup of coffee. It is most famous as the *Trou Normand*, when a tiny glass is served between the courses of a rich meal, preferably after a roast, to offer a cleansing pause.

While they use their exceptionally good local fish in many light dishes, Normans are by tradition great meat-eaters. They have splendid beef and pork, fine *charcuterie*, pré-salé lamb, plump chickens and ducks to honour the celebrated *Canard à la Rouen-naise*, with the crushed juices of the carcass stirred into the sauce.

Desserts have a strong presence in Normandy, whether it be a moist *teurgoule* rice pudding, delicate Mirliton almond tart, apple cider fritter or Bourdelot apples. There is an immense variety of apple tarts ranging from thick and creamy to light as a Normandy cloud.

This discreet province conveys a feeling of continuity and well-being in our changing times. Ask the seagull; ask the apple tree.

THE RECIPES OF NORMANDY

● ●

LANGUEDOC-ROUSSILLON

The largest of France's southern regions, Languedoc-Roussillon finds itself contained along a portion of the Spanish border within natural limits imposed by the Pyrenees mountains, the Rhône river and the Mediterranean sea.

Within those limits there is a rich abundance of sights, fragrances and resources, from lagoons and marshes along the coastline to the *garrigues,* scrublands, covered with juniper, lavender and thyme extending north towards the Cévennes mountains, crowned with chestnut trees, and beyond them to the austere Causses plateau where goats and sheep graze as Roquefort cheese matures in rocky caves beneath. Punctuating the landscape are gifts to the region from antiquity: the majestic Roman Pont-du-Gard aqueduct, the Roman theatres of Orange and Nîmes, Romanesque churches, and Carcassonne's medieval fortress.

In the Middle Ages, Languedoc-Roussillon created a world and civilisation of its own as artful as its antique legacy. It is here that the refined, spiritual approach to love known as *amour courtois* was perfected. Troubadours like Jaufré Rudel wrote ballads and *pastourelles* to their ladies, ensconced in the exquisite rituals of medieval court life, as pilgrims streamed into what became a main departure point for the Crusades. These were heady, prosperous times, as described in texts like Bertrand de Bar's, celebrating the large ships loaded with goods in local ports, and the wealth of a city like Narbonne. It was a confident society able to tolerate the forces of dissent, including explosive political satire.

But Languedoc-Roussillon's power and autonomy were seen by those in Paris as threats to the unification of France. For five centuries, northern France tried to impose its rule on this feisty province until it got its way in the sixteenth century and the region joined the entire kingdom of France.

As often in France, a matter of major importance was linked to the outcome of a linguistic dispute. There were two ways of saying 'yes' in medieval France: *oil* and *oc*. It is the victory of the *langue d'oil* – spoken in the northern provinces – as the official written language over the *langue d'oc*, rooted in the Latin traditions of southern Gascony, Limousin, Languedoc and Provence – that confirmed Paris's administrative control throughout France.

This represented a significant setback for the south in general, and for Languedoc-Roussillon in particular. It perhaps explains why this region has traditionally been home to many dissident elements. This is the region where the chaste, vegetarian Cathare religious group settled, converting not only aristocrats but artisans, shopworkers and peasants. It is here that Protestants were offered places of safety, as were other dissidents – Sephardic Jews from Spain, political refugees, rebellious Catalans and, most recently, North African *pieds noirs*. It is a region encumbered by history and familiar with recurrent persecutions from the Catholic clergy as well as the central power from Paris.

Today, the rich and varied elements of the region's cooking are among the most spontaneous and authentic expression of its singularity.

There are large cornfields in Languedoc-Roussillon, corn grown to feed the precious geese and ducks which will become *Confit* (see page 183), *Magrets* (see page 160) and *foie gras* (see page 116). There are orchards of apricots and peaches, and rows of melons, tiny purple antichokes and delicate pink garlic. There is also an abundance of anchovies, squid, red mullet, oysters, mussels, *palourdes* clams, tiny *clovisses*, both wild and farmed.

The vineyards yield the largest quantities of wine in France. In the last twenty years, due to European competition, wine-growers have succeeded in upgrading their table wines. As for the fruity sweet Banyuls and Muscat wines so popular as aperitifs or dessert wines, they are now served as a delicate counterpoint to goose liver, oysters or Roquefort cheese.

The cooking of Languedoc-Roussillon is as remote from elaborate *haute cuisine* as it is from tasteless fast food. It is a rustic cooking with a lot of character, bold and high spirited in Roussillon, milder in Languedoc, bursting with originality. There are 11 ways to cook snails, at least 3 ways to prepare Cassoulet, and 250 ways to use chestnuts in the region. Cooking here is a tool in the fight against the levelling effect of Paris, as it 'gives a rich taste to misery'. Festive dishes like *Cargolade, Bouillinade,* Cassoulet (see page 146), *Gardiane* and *Ouillade* prepare the way for long evenings of dancing and singing.

But the secret weapon of the region is in the light touch – a drop of aniseed liqueur or a square of chocolate in *Civet* (see page

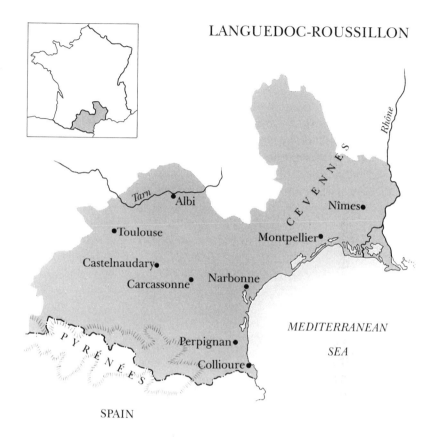

LANGUEDOC-ROUSSILLON

164), a sprig of wild fennel in a snail stew, a sprinkling of *persillade* on a roast chicken, a spoonful of goose fat in a bowl of *Garbure* (see page 60).

As in Mediterranean cooking, *farcis* and *hachis* are all-important here, with a litany of stuffed vegetables, chicken and lamb, meatballs, or a handful of chopped ham, shallots and garlic stirred into a stew, transforming the simplest dish into a redolent delight.

When a dish is *à la languedocienne*, it usually involves a combination of aubergines, tomatoes, and garlic. Sauces are rare, except for the beloved *all y oli (aioli)*, garlic and oil sauce, the *all cremat*, a sauce of sautéed garlic, peppers, saffron and wine, as well as *sauce Catalane* made with garlic and bitter oranges. And finally there is the heady *beurre de Montpellier*, prepared with fresh herbs, greens, olives, capers, anchovies, mustard and lemon juice thickened with . . . both butter and olive oil.

For dessert, we might be offered a piece of Roquefort cheese, a honey and almond pastry or a caramelised *Crème Catalane* custard flavoured with aniseed, lemon and cinnamon.

But if I had to remember my two most cherished meals in the region, I would evoke the *goûter* I shared with little Nicolas on a sunny afternoon after his day at school. We ate warm slices of crisp country bread rubbed with garlic and spread with dribblings of goose fat and, for good measure, we picked a handful of freckled apricots. A far cry from the buttered *tartines* covered with grated chocolate which have always been the fare of my daughters' snacks. It was one of the most heady of afternoon breaks.

The other meal took place on an autumn day when the local *tramontane* wind was blowing on the hilly slopes overlooking the harbour of Collioures. After a morning spent harvesting grapes, we all gathered around a roaring fire of vine trimmings, sipping Banyuls and waiting for strings of sausages and the *cargolade* platters of snails sprinkled with melted goose fat roasting on the barbecue. The table was loaded with dry pork liver sausages and sliced artichoke hearts, red peppers and anchovies, and a large bowl of *all y oli*. We ate, we drank, we danced the *sardane* – hands linked, arms lifted, dainty steps, light jumps – to celebrate this day, this glorious world still at man's measure, the winding lanes leading to the coloured boats under us and the blue and white shifting skies above.

T H E   R E C I P E S   O F   L A N G U E D O C - R O U S S I L L O N

THE SOUTH-WEST

Once upon a time, the Sud-Ouest bore the glorious name of Aquitaine, the 'country of waters'. Blessed with thermal springs, marshes, rivers and an ocean, the presence of Cro-Magnon man's skeleton and the frescoes of Lascaux are eloquent evidence that three million years ago human beings inhabited this vast province.

Myths abound. Some are whimsical, such as powers attributed to bears in the Pyrenees where a notice in front of a church reads: 'Bears have helped build it and will fight for it.' Others mine the region's rich vein of boastfulness, expounding the exploits of Cyrano de Bergerac, Jacquou-le-Croquant, and, of course, d'Artagnan and his Gascon musketeers heedlessly defending the weak against the powerful. The region's passion for the larger-than-life often blurs reality when it comes to the derring-do of local rugby teams, the secret powers of the new Concorde being built by Aérospatiale in Toulouse, or the grand lifestyle of Bordeaux's gentry with their celebrated vineyards.

History has moved forward in fits and starts in this region, which runs from Bordelais, Landes and Pays Basque to Gascony and Périgord, with its two largest cities – Bordeaux and Toulouse – at either end. While all these areas share a common past and future, each views itself first and foremost as Bordelais, Gascon, Périgourdin, Landais or Basque. 'One for all, and all for one!' cry the musketeers, but as each area insists on its individual differences, there is little of the strength that comes from unity, a phenomenon that proved decisive as the region evolved over the centuries.

From the day in the twelfth century when Aliénor of Aquitaine married Henri Plantagenet and he became King of England, the region allied itself with England for 300 years, until it was eventually absorbed into the kingdom of France. When Paris moved to take administrative and political power from the Sud-Ouest, the disorganised region acquiesced and fell into a drowsy somnolence, dropping out of the movement of most of France towards modernisation and the industrial revolution.

Energy and curiosity in the region turned inward with what were often quite interesting results. The contributions of painters,

Mountains, Haute-Savoie

A market-place in Paris

THE SOUTH-WEST

ATLANTIC
OCEAN

Dordogne

Bordeaux

Arcachon

Garonne

Agen

Nogaro

Auch

Toulouse

Biarritz
St Jean de Luz

Pau

SPAIN

PYRÉNÉES

writers, scholars, artisans and farmers made for a satisfying life. There were successful efforts to encourage the planting of new crops, cereals, tobacco, and a vast forest of pine trees in the Landes, which stabilised the dunes and still yield lumber and resin. But by staying out of the mainstream of activity, this least homogeneous of all French regions managed to preserve its unique charm.

And although we smile as we read the words of Henry Miller: 'I believe that Cro-Magnon man settled there because he was extremely intelligent', the genuine quality of life of the region is not exaggerated, nor part of a politician's rhetoric. It is tangible everywhere you turn. Bordeaux, nestling by the estuary of the Garonne river, succeeds with elegance in being both a port and a well-bred city with fine eighteenth century rows of houses, and broad public spaces like the Esplanade de Quinconces – the largest square in France. Here, wine is the blood of the people and the cellars, the wine shops, the glorious Chatrons warehouses, all celebrate proudly the 'blood of the vine'.

Further south, we find the thick pine forests of the Landes, its huge 374 feet high dune, and the well-sheltered triangular Bassin d'Arcachon where oysters and mussels are bred. Just before the Spanish frontier, we reach the Basque country. People there are rather secretive, dour in spite of colourful berets and bright canvas espadrilles. But the region has a pampered, festive air with white-washed houses, fishing villages like Saint Jean-de-Luz, and resorts like Biarritz.

Travelling slowly between Bordeaux and Toulouse through fertile fields of corn, sunflowers, tobacco patches and ranks of legendary wine and armagnac vineyards, we encounter few people, fewer cars, more cows and many ducks and geese. Climbing through the narrow cobblestoned streets of a perched village, bicycling past walnut oil mills and golden-stoned farms, chatting over a glass of Floc d'Armagnac, it is so calm, poised and peaceful that sometimes it all seems too good to be true.

Nearby Périgord – home of Cyrano de Bergerac's descendants – also seems to have been waiting for us for hundreds of years. It stretches along the wild Dordogne river between cliffs scattered with old castles and manors. Towards the Pyrenees, Gascony – whose capital, Auch, still lives under the spell of d'Artagnan – rolls with gentle hills. Perched atop these hills rest about 300 *bastides* – fortified, medieval towns with arcades, shaded squares, churches and cultivated *potagers*, clinging to the top like eagles' nests.

Finally we arrive at the pink city, Toulouse, with its lovely brick buildings, its sumptuous town hall, which has witnessed the ancient grandeur of former counts of Toulouse, and the modern glory of Europe's Aérospatiale.

The cooking throughout the Sud-Ouest is consistently reliable. Kitchens here function under the spell of duck, geese and the magic powers of armagnac. This is hearty regional cooking performed at home by generations of women who have always depended on good local ingredients. Even when some of the recipes are adapted and turned into lighter renditions by chefs like Daguin or Guérard, they retain their essential rustic charm.

Bordeaux is the exception. There are few culinary inventions here. For too long this rich town cut itself off from the neighbouring countryside and its local produce. Things are better today. Shallots and red wine lend a personal touch to the local cooking; shellfish and *Confit* (see page 183) are well used. But still only a few dishes stand out: *Entrecôte Bordelaise* (see page 130), *Lamproie Bordelaise, Pilades,* or *Civelles,* which are eels the size of a matchstick, sautéed *al dente* in garlic and oil. They also make a *beurre rouge* which is a *beurre blanc* variation made with red wine. When a dish is cooked *à la bordelaise,* it may mean several things: served with *cèpes,* sautéed in goose fat with garlic and parsley, or else coated with a bordelaise sauce made from wine and shallots. Another custom of the region, *faire chabrot,* means adding a glass of Bordeaux wine to the last spoonful of soup or broth and drinking it from the dish (see page 50).

In Périgord there are sumptuous dishes based on goose and duck *Confit, foie gras* (see page 116) and the local black truffles. Walnuts enhance salads, main dishes and cakes. Walnut oil is sprinkled on warm *Cassoulet* (see page 146) and tossed greens, cornmeal is used in polenta-like *broye* or *millas* which, once fried in

goose fat, becomes a *Cruchade* to be served with *Civet* (see page 164) or eaten as finger food.

Basque dishes echo Spain's cooking with an abundance of tomatoes, seafood, cured ham, and red and green peppers. There is the spirited *Piperade* (see page 108), the *ttoro* fish soup enriched with mussels, shrimps and red peppers, and squid in all guises including cooked in their ink.

Gascony has imagination in the kitchen; they do wonders with every last bit of duck or goose. They flavour a *gasconnade* leg of lamb with ham, anchovies and garlic. They garnish sautéed *fois gras* and *Magrets* (see page 160) with grapes and armagnac. They fill ethereal, flaky *Croustade* (see page 258) with luscious Agen prunes. But if duck and geese are the pillars of the cooking, armagnac is the local magician. Prunes and walnuts are macerated in it, dry goat cheese and Tourtisseaux pancakes fried in goose fat are sprinkled with it. *Pousse-rapière*, the local aperitif, is made with oranges marinated in armagnac and served with local sparkling wine and, most simply of all, armagnac can turn ice-cream into the most inspiring of desserts (see page 255).

Cookery here begins with exceptional local products. Farmers have learned a lot in the last twenty years about maintaining a steady level of quality in their offerings, whether they are local craftsmen or semi-industrialised. Today the region eloquently sustains its culinary tradition. South-west cuisine may confidently claim to be not only seductive but also, as tradition suggests, part magic and part medicine. We know all about the French paradox: goose and duck products plus wine preventing cardiovascular diseases. Whether or not it turns out to be the case, with the help of pink garlic, savory, verbena, armagnac, brandy, prunes and the gentle, sunny disposition of the people here – by far the most easy-going in France – it is easy to relax with the absolute certainly that we are in good hands.

THE RECIPES OF
THE SOUTH-WEST

•••••••••••••••••••••••••••••••••••

LYONNAIS, SAVOIE, FRANCHE-COMTÉ AND DAUPHINÉ

Lyon is a beautiful, discreet city which spreads along the banks of the Rhône and Saône rivers. The turbulent Rhône – crowded with boats transporting horses, people, grain, olive oil, salt and vegetables – has been tamed here, and is today a peaceful link between the north and the south. The city, standing at the heart of a strategic intersection, commands the roads to the Alps with connections to Switzerland, Italy, northern Europe and the Massif Central, as well as opening the gateway to the Mediterranean.

With its bustling trade fair which has remained active since the Middle Ages, with its silk industry, printing firms and quality craftsmen, Lyon has been a centre of wealth since the time of the Gauls. During the Renaissance, it was a more important city than Paris.

Savoie, Franche-Comté and Dauphiné, the Alpine districts east of Lyon, are fascinatingly diverse, with their thriving valleys, orchards, chestnut and walnut groves, lakes, soaring snow-covered mountains, steep passes and vast skiing and mountain-climbing playgrounds. Much of what used to be cultivated land only a few decades ago is now pasture sprinkled with blue gentian, thistles, silver and yellow flowers, where cows graze to the north, and sheep and goats to the south. Each summer they are joined by Provençal herds in search of good grass and cool air. The region is graced with lovely resort towns like Annecy, Chamonix, Mégève, and thermal baths and health spas like Aix-la-Chapelle and Evian.

The network of communications through this alpine region was started even before the coming of the Romans when donkey tracks wound their way through the mountains. Since that time, roads and tunnels have been carved through the mountains, bridges span the valleys, railways and motorways cross the region, all strengthening the finances of the Counts of Savoie, the original 'gate-keepers of the Alps' who grew rich extracting tolls from alpine travellers.

The Court of Savoie, Lyon's rich notables, the visiting popes, princes, merchants, generals, pilgrims and travellers have for centuries set a high standard of entertaining centred around food.

LYONNAIS, SAVOIE, FRANCHE-COMTÉ & DAUPHINÉ

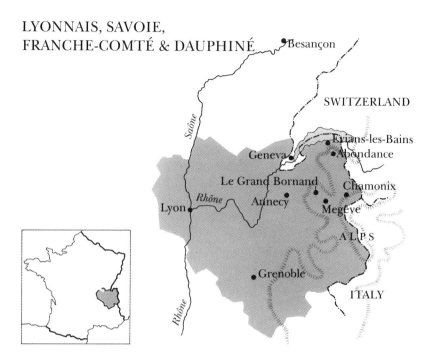

So much so that even today, Lyon is held as the gastronomic capital of France. Local products are consistently of the highest quality. Whereas in Paris, fashionable trends in food come and go, Lyon's chefs remain solidly anchored to their traditions and the products of their soil. They accomplish daily miracles with Bresse chicken, plump pike, a piece of Charolais meat or a handful of morel mushrooms. Celebrated chefs of the past, such as Point or Chapel, and modern chefs such as Troisgros and the indomitable Bocuse, famous *mères* (female chefs), and the chefs at *bouchons* – bustling bistros which offer substantial snacks and wines all day – gastronomic clubs, guilds and *confréries* all work equally hard to perpetuate this tradition of a hearty, spirited, serious cooking. Local wines must not be forgotten, and indeed Lyon is said to be washed by not two but three rivers: the Rhône, the Saône and Beaujolais wine.

Because pigs were traditionally fed on whey left over from cheese-making in Savoie, pork has always been produced in large quantities, and today both the Alpine regions and Lyon still prepare the finest and most abundant *charcuterie* specialities in France. Apart from the wonderful pâtés, terrines and pigs' trotters, the range of sausages is vast. There are sausages enriched with truffles, pistachio nuts or garlic, sausages cooked in brioches, warm *cervelas* served with hot potatoes, and sausages made with tripe.

Savoie, along with Piedmont, Sardinia and Nice, was once part of the Italian states, and as a result many Mediterranean products such as pasta, *morue* (dried salt cod), olive oil – which is used here along with local hazelnut and walnut oil – oranges and candied fruit, have been an intrinsic part of the local cuisine for centuries. The Italian influence remains even today in the small goat cheese and parsley-filled *raviole*, corn dishes including polenta, *crozets* which belong to the gnocchi family, a curious bittersweet jam called green compote, and rosemary blossom jam which has been made here since the twelfth century.

Also from the Rhône valley and Savoie comes an abundant supply of fruit and fresh vegetables, of which potatoes and onions are the local favourites.

The variety of cheeses is superb, whether they are made on farms, in co-operatives or factories. One finds fine goat cheese like Chavignol, creamy Vacherin and St Marcellin, Reblochon, Tommes, and hard mountain cheeses like Beaufort – the prince of Gruyères – Comté and Emmenthal.

There are lake and river fish – trout, pike, crayfish and also the beloved *féra* and *omble chevalier*, members of the salmon family.

At home and in restaurants, cooks prepare invigorating dishes which clearly know and speak their own minds: luscious pumpkin soups and rich onion gratins, pike dumplings, chicken liver *gâteau de foies*, morteau sausage baked with shallots in white wine, sautéed *morue* and onions flavoured with vinegar. Another pungent local dish is *Boeuf à la Marinière*, beef and onions enriched with a paste of anchovy, garlic, mustard and wine. Savoyard and Dauphinois may be the most famous of gratins, but there are all kinds of variations made with onions, *morue*, cardoons, wild mushrooms, leeks or courgettes cooked under a crust of fragrant mountain cheese. Fondue, once eaten by villagers at night as they shelled the walnuts, is now enjoyed by everyone after a day of skiing.

As for desserts, the choice is vast, and the local nuts and fruits feature heavily. Walnut, hazelnut and chestnut cakes delight the palate, bilberry cakes and jam tarts – once made with dried fruits – covered with a lattice of pastry, biscuit de Savoie, *farcement* made with potatoes, raisins, prunes and brandy, Mont Blanc – a fluffy dessert of chestnut purée topped with cream – are to be found in abundance. Finally there is the delicious *Triple Crème*, a rich blend of thick cream, lemon juice, lemon rind and orange water.

Beaujolais is not the only drink to make the region famous. There are all kinds of delicious gentian vermouths, genepi and walnut aperitif wines and, most famous of all, the local green or yellow Chartreuse liqueur made with over a hundred medicinal plants gathered from the nearby hills.

All these invigorating elixirs are glorious reaffirmations of the principle that what tastes good may – if you are lucky – also be good for you. And that is a firmly held conviction here.

THE RECIPES OF LYONNAIS, SAVOIE, FRANCHE-COMTÉ AND DAUPHINÉ

••

Soupe à l'Oignon 66

Salade Lyonnaise 113

Salade au Gruyère et aux Noix 119

Fondue Savoyarde 206

Cervelle de Canut 210

Gâteau de Savoie 237

Gâteau de Foies de Volailles 101

Pâté Chaud Familial 176

VAL DE LOIRE

Le Val de Loire is *la douce France* at its most graceful. Lined with orchards, vineyards, gardens, and rows of poplars and willows, it stretches like a majestic boulevard along the Loire river from Île-de-France to Brittany's border. Blessed by a climate and way of life that are equally gentle, it is here that France's purest French is spoken and its most delicate cuisine prepared.

Scantily populated and with little industry, Val de Loire is a secluded, quiet world of its own dotted with small, lively cities such as Blois, Orléans, Tours, Saumur and Angers. Jeanne d'Arc expressed the feeling of many when she said that if the head of France is Paris, her heart is Orléans.

Val de Loire is also the garden of France, an enclosed place where civilised achievements are visible in the smallest details of espaliered pears and apple orchards trained against trellises, tidy vineyards and beautiful rose gardens. Poets, artists and kings have left their mark on the region, but in the most discreet of ways. People here take life easily. The fishermen who perch along the calm waters look for peace and solitude . . . and eventually a trout, carp, pike, shad, *sandre*, or a few eels. As the hours pass they become one with the peaceful, golden river itself.

In Val de Loire, there are lovely white houses with blue slate roofs, farms, mills, monasteries, churches. Mushrooms are grown and wine is stored in chalky caves in the cool of the earth. A profusion of châteaux is scattered across an elegant pastoral setting: Blois, Chambord, Chenonceaux. Many hunting lodges were built during the Middle Ages when game was abundant, and were later transformed into châteaux. Today, about two thousand châteaux remain in the region. Some have been made into luxury homes, some are hotels, others historical monuments, and some have been abandoned to return to the landscape as ruins.

Val de Loire is the nurturing ground of classic, measured, finely-tuned French cooking. The medieval tradition of festive, courtly extravaganzas – roasted meats, staggering pâtés, every sort of game and elaborate dessert – has left fingerprints here and there, but what prevails is regional bourgeois cooking. Relying on local ingredients, the cuisine steers clear of preciousness and extravagant complications. Refined, confident as it is, its weakness is a tendency to be too tame. However, when we want to enliven dishes from this region, we can simply turn to natural allies such as its spicy grey and golden shallots, fresh sorrel and Orléans' potent wine vinegar.

The only foreign elements date from an Arab presence in the eighth century. Goats and know-how left by the departing *Maures* were assimilated by the locals, yielding the well-named Sainte-Maure goat cheese. Another exotic product is the meaty plum brought back from Damascus after the Crusades. Carefully cultivated and dried, *pruneaux de Damas* are now part of many traditional dishes and, as in the south-west, they perpetuate some of the local medieval sweet and sour dishes. A taste of honey is sometimes added for a stronger, bittersweet effect.

Farmers grow a profusion of traditional vegetables and fruits that include varieties once discarded. Vegetables are prepared in soups, gratins, salads, and as accompaniments. Château Villandry, with its sumptuous formal vegetable garden punctuated by flowers and trimmed trees, embodies the local cult for vegetables. Thanks to the temperate weather and the Loire valley's fertile soil, these *primeurs* are shipped to the markets two weeks before produce from Paris. Vast quantities of wild mushrooms are available all year, including the *rosé des prés*, pink and yellow *pleurottes* and the

VAL DE LOIRE

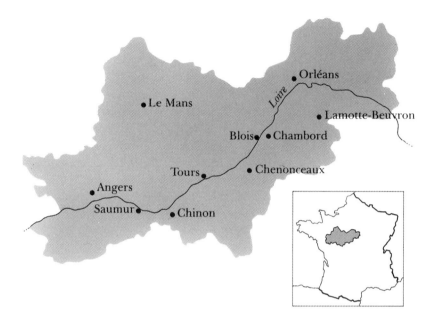

newest arrivals, shiitake mushrooms.

Game – now mostly in Sologne – has long been a favourite of the region. In medieval banquets, they even ate deer's antlers. Today, pheasants, partridges, quails, deer and wild ducks abound. They are sautéed in butter and flavoured with redcurrant jelly, juniper or white grapes if the flesh is tender. Tougher cuts may be braised with wine or turned into fragrant terrines.

Chickens from Loué, fed on grain and running free, are prepared according to one of the region's oldest recipes. Garnished with bacon and onions and cooked with red wine, their sauce is bound with the chicken blood.

Pork is turned into *charcuterie* in small factories that use the traditional techniques that vary from town to town. *Rillettes* are browned first in Tours, while in Le Mans they are simmered and served with fresh walnuts steeped with vinegar for a sharp counter-point of flavour. They also prepare *Rillons* (deep fried meat chunks), tripe sausages – both the soft *andouillettes* and hard *andouilles* – blood pudding made with greens, and white *Boudin* filled with chicken, mushrooms and truffles. And artisans still offer a curious dish of chicken and wild boar legs simmered in red wine to be eaten sliced as a fragrant ham.

River fish are abundant, while trout and salmon are successfully farmed. A treat each year between March and June is the 'springtimes': young salmon served with a spirited *beurre blanc*. *Matelote* – a fish dish made with wine and onions – has been enjoyed here since the days when the Loire was used as an important route and there were inns all along its shores. Among the most popular dishes is *La Petite Friture* – known locally as a *Buisson de Goujons* – a mound of tiny whitebait, none longer than two inches, dipped in milk, coated in seasoned flour and served crisply fried and hot with lemon wedges or warm wine vinegar. You will also find marinated shad, a type of herring, grilled and garnished with a creamy sorrel purée, as well as stuffed bream and carp, and rich stews of eels cooked in wine.

The region's wines find their way into many of the local dishes as they are splendid for cooking and, of course, the perfect accompaniment to the local cuisine.

The traditional habit of sautéeing most dishes in butter remains – whether it be shellfish, meat, potatoes or mushrooms. Even the local *Pot au Feu*'s vegetables and meats are browned in butter before they are cooked in the broth. Just before serving, they are once more sautéed in butter to reinforce their taste. Sauces are few; salad dressings are prepared simply with walnut oil, cider and wine vinegar.

THE   RECIPES   OF THE   LOIRE

•••••••••••••••••••••••••••••••••••••••

Because the region's exceptionally rich land is primarily devoted to fruit and vegetables, there is little pasture and few cattle. Goat cheese prevails and is sold in all degrees of maturity and shapes as small as Crottins de Chavignol, Valençay Pyramids, Pouligny St Pierre, flat and round Chabris and, of course, the father of them all, the cylindrical-shaped Sainte-Maure, pierced by a blade of straw.

Fruits abound in Val de Loire. They appear in the delicate pear crêpes flavoured with local Cointreau, as narrow firm pears cooked in red wine and spices and sprinkled with pear brandy, in exquisite fruit tarts with custard, or simply packed with greengages, cherries, raspberries or peaches and mostly in the irresistible *Tarte Tatin*. Finally, there are the traditional *Crémets d'Angers*, prepared with stiffly beaten cream and egg whites and served with a pile of fresh berries.

Poets have a word for this region, *nonchaloir*, an old term which best describes the cultivated indolence of Val de Loire where nature, man and cooking whisper, contrasts are gentle, opposites are balanced, and harmony prevails. Pleasure is not always in the unexpected.

Above: Lac de Montriond, Haute-Savoie

Previous page: Summer on the Loire river

SOUPS

Les Soupes

France is a country where soup has always been an integral part of the menu, and until recently, soup was the best part of every meal: breakfast, lunch and dinner.

Soups are truly seasonal, made with whatever vegetables, fish or meat are available, and they remain open to everyone's individual ideas and tastes. They are healthy, economical, easy to prepare in advance and invigorating. It sounds like something that should be embroidered on a sampler since most people tend to neglect them these days.

Regional soups like *Bourride*, *Pochouse*, pumpkin soup – in which a whole pumpkin is filled with cream, cheese, garlic and parsley and cooked in the oven – are spectacular productions. Soups like *Bouillabaisse* or *Soupe au Pistou* are a meal in themselves. Some are rich, like onion soup; some are light, like Consommé; some are elegant, like Crab Bisque; some are simple and refreshing, like a vegetable soup. The variety is staggering.

Soups may be thickened with flour, cornflour, cream, egg yolks, *Beurre Manié* (see page 91), a handful of fine vermicelli or the addition of dried or fresh vegetable purées.

Garnishes include grated cheese, Croûtons, fried onions, *persillade* – a pinch of parsley and garlic – finely chopped cured ham, fresh herbs, slivers of bacon and herb omelette, a spoonful of cream or a drop of olive oil. Traditionally, a mixture of butter, parsley and chives makes a subtle soup seasoning while olive oil, basil, thyme, sage and coriander give a more pungent flavour. Sage, bay leaves and parsley enhance the flavour of soups made with duck or goose. But in the end, the choice is individual; there are many regional variations and there are no golden rules.

Here are just two interesting traditions which you may like to try. In south-west France, *faire chabrot* means that when just two spoonfuls of soup are left, diners pour a little red wine into the soup and raise their bowls to drink the invigorating mixture. While in the Alps, a little cold goats' or cows' milk is often added to a thick vegetable soup to enrich the children's portions.

POTAGE À L'OSEILLE
Sorrel soup

The sharpness of the sorrel with its light and cleansing taste makes this *potage* a perfect start to any meal. The chopped sorrel leaves give a more interesting texture to the dish than when they are puréed, but all options are acceptable. You may even like to roll a few sorrel leaves into a cigar shape, slice them into thin ribbons and drop them into the boiling soup before serving.

———————— *Serves 4* ————————

9 oz (250 g) sorrel
2 tablespoons butter
1 large onion, thinly sliced
3 leeks, white parts only, thinly sliced
pinch of freshly grated nutmeg
salt and freshly ground black pepper

2 medium potatoes, thinly sliced
2 pints (1.2 litres) chicken stock or water
pinch of sugar
5 tablespoons single cream
1 tablespoon minced fresh chives or chervil

Discard the sorrel stems and shred the leaves. Melt the butter in a large saucepan and fry the onion over a low heat until soft. Add the leeks and sorrel and season with nutmeg, salt and pepper. Cover and simmer for 5 minutes until the sorrel has softened and the volume diminished. Add the potatoes and simmer for a few minutes. Meanwhile, bring the stock or water to the boil in a separate pan. Add the hot stock or water and a pinch of sugar and salt to the vegetables, cover and simmer for 30 mintues.

Use a wooden spoon to crush the ingredients against the sides of the pan. If you prefer a smoother consistency, purée the soup in a food processor, blender or food mill.

Stir the cream into the soup and return to the boil. Check and adjust seasoning to taste. Serve sprinkled with chives or chervil.

Note
Two egg yolks may be added to the cream and stirred into the hot soup for a richer version, but do not let the soup boil.

SOUPE D'ASPERGES VERTES À L'OSEILLE

Asparagus soup with sorrel

The Loire Valley is known as the garden of France. In spring and summer, both the large market gardens and the small allotments burst forth with a wonderous profusion of vegetables. One of the best places to witness this bounty is at the Château of Villandry near Tours, which has one of the most magnificent kitchen gardens in the world. The vegetables are grown more for their beauty than for their taste, but they show the importance of *potagers* in the intricate garden design of the French Renaissance.

Jean Bardet, the celebrated restaurateur of Tours, is completely enamoured of vegetables. He has a *potager* behind his elegant restaurant, the produce from which inspires his imagination. Although he serves this soup cold, he says you can heat it gently, and if you find the lemony taste of the sorrel too strong, just add a little more cream.

Serves 6

2 lb (900 g) green asparagus	salt and freshly ground black pepper
4 large handfuls of sorrel	4 fl oz (120 ml) double cream
1 oz (25 g) butter	2 egg yolks
2 tablespoons plain flour	juice of ½ lemon
2½ pints (1.5 litres) chicken stock	freshly grated nutmeg

If the asparagus stalks are woody, peel them with a vegetable peeler. Lay them flat on your chopping board with the stalks overlapping the edge of the work surface. Snap the asparagus at the point where they become less rigid, taking care not to break off the tips completely. Put them into a large pan of salted water and bring to the boil. Drain immediately then plunge them into iced water or place them in a colander and hold them under cold running water for a few moments. Cut off the stalks 2 inches (5 cm) from the tips and refrigerate the tips to use as a garnish.

Wash the sorrel carefully and remove and discard the stems.

Reserve 12 small leaves for garnishing and roughly chop the remainder with scissors.

Melt the butter in a large saucepan and add the sorrel; it will reduce down quickly. Add the asparagus stalks and stir well. Sprinkle in the flour and cook over a low heat, stirring continuously, for 3 minutes. Gradually pour in the stock, stirring continuously to avoid any lumps, then season with salt. Bring to the boil, skim off any impurities, then turn down the heat and simmer for 10 minutes until the asparagus is soft. Purée the soup in a food processor or, for a finer texture, force through a *chinois* or a food mill. Leave the soup on a low heat. Whisk together the cream, egg yolks and lemon juice in a small bowl. Pour this into the soup and heat gently for about 3 minutes, whisking all the time, without allowing the soup to boil. Remove from the heat and season to taste with nutmeg, salt and pepper. Cool then refrigerate until ready to serve. To serve, place some of the reserved asparagus tips and two leaves of sorrel into each bowl and pour over the soup.

POTAGE AU CRESSON

Watercress soup

Watercress is a favourite vegetable in the Loire and around Paris, although this soup is also frequently prepared in Normandy. Spring is the best time to serve it as the watercress is not yet bitter. If you have cooked some vegetables, use the cooking water to prepare the soup, or use chicken or beef stock for a stronger flavour.

———————— *Serves 4* ————————

8 oz (225 g) watercress	*2 pints (1.2 litres) water or stock*
4 tablespoons butter	*5 tablespoons single cream*
1 onion, sliced	*pinch of freshly grated nutmeg*
3 leeks, white part only, sliced	*salt and freshly ground black pepper*
3 large potatoes, sliced	*2 tablespoons fresh chervil leaves*

Reserve a handful of watercress leaves for garnish. Discard the stems and coarsely chop the remaining leaves with scissors or a knife.

Melt the butter in a large saucepan and cook the watercress, onions, leeks and potatoes on a low heat for 10 minutes, stirring gently. Meanwhile, heat the water or stock until lukewarm. Add the water or stock to the pan, bring to the boil, cover and simmer for 25 minutes.

Purée the soup in a food processor, blender or food mill. If it is not smooth enough, rub it through a sieve. Return the soup to the heat, stir in the cream and simmer for 2 minutes. Taste and season with nutmeg, salt and pepper. Add the reserved watercress leaves then pour into a warm soup tureen. Serve sprinkled with chervil leaves.

Note

You may like to scatter a handful of Croûtons (see page 68) covered with a little grated Gruyère on top of the soup just as you are ready to serve. When I make watercress salad, I keep the stems with the coarser leaves and use them in the soup.

POTAGE AUX CHAMPIGNONS
Mushroom soup

Whether you choose to serve a homely version, *façon ménagère*, or one in the *grande cuisine* style, a mushroom soup is always delicious. Remember that iron or aluminium tend to discolour mushrooms so choose stainless steel or enamel pans.

———— *Serves 4* ————

3 pints (1.75 litres) water or chicken stock	*1 tablespoon vegetable oil*
1 bay leaf	*2 shallots or 1 onion, coarsely chopped*
1 sprig fresh parsley	*3 tablespoons rice flour*
1 sprig fresh thyme	*3 tablespoons cold water*
salt and freshly ground white pepper	*4 tablespoons single cream*
8 oz (225 g) mushrooms	*2 tablespoons minced fresh chervil or parsley*
4 tablespoons butter	

Place the water or stock in a large saucepan with the bay leaf, parsley, thyme, salt and pepper, cover and bring to the boil.

Meanwhile, slice a handful of mushroom caps. Melt 1 tablespoon of butter in a frying pan and sauté the mushroom caps for about 5 minutes, tossing constantly with a wooden spoon. Sprinkle with salt and pepper then transfer to a side dish. Coarsely chop the remaining mushroom caps and stems. Heat 2 tablespoons of butter with the oil in the frying pan until it foams then add the mushrooms and shallots or onion and cook for about 5 minutes, tossing with a wooden spoon.

Pour the mushrooms into the hot water stock and simmer, stirring, for about 15 minutes. Remove the parsley and thyme. Blend the flour and water to a paste, stir it into the soup and simmer, stirring, for 2 minutes until the soup thickens slightly. Stir in the cream and simmer for 2 minutes. Add the reserved mushrooms, dot with the remaining butter and serve sprinkled with chervil or parsley.

SOUPE AUX LÉGUMES
Vegetable soup

This is France's favourite soup and it varies according to the season and the region. Pumpkin, fennel, garlic, celeriac, turnips, watercress, sorrel, green beans or cabbage can all be used along with the basic trilogy of leek, carrot and potato. I use courgettes, fennel or potatoes to impart a velvety texture to the soup.

In the south of France, the vegetables are often sautéed in olive oil, in central France they use pork fat, while around Paris they use butter. Sometimes for a true *potage de santé*, a healthy soup, the vegetables are simply boiled in water and seasoned with herbs.

The vegetables can be puréed, diced, sliced or coarsely grated. Sliced onions sautéed in butter, minced parsley and garlic, chopped cured ham, fresh basil or chives, grated cheese, a spoonful of cream, a dot of butter or a drop of olive oil can all be added just before serving.

———— *Serves 4* ————

2 onions
1 stalk celery
2 courgettes
1 leek, white part only
2 potatoes
2 tablespoons butter and
   1 tablespoon vegetable oil or
   3 tablespoons olive oil
1½ pints (900 ml) water or
   vegetable stock

1 bouquet garni
salt and freshly ground black pepper
1 tablespoon chopped fresh parsley,
   chives, basil or tarragon

TO SERVE
2 oz (50 g) Gruyère cheese, finely
   grated
1 tablespoon butter or olive oil

Peel and trim the vegetables. If you are going to purée the soup, chop them coarsely. If you don't purée the soup, dice or slice them evenly.

Heat the butter and oil or olive oil in a large saucepan, add the vegetables, cover and cook over a low heat for 10-15 minutes, until soft, stirring occasionally. This will seal in all the flavours.

Meanwhile, bring the water or stock and herbs to the boil in a separate pan. Pour the vegetables into the stock and simmer, uncovered, for 30 minutes at the most. Discard the bouquet garni. Purée in a food processor, blender or food mill or rub through a sieve for a smooth soup. Pour into a warm tureen, season to taste with salt and pepper and serve sprinkled with parsley, chives, basil or tarragon. Grated cheese, butter or a tiny bottle of olive oil can be passed around the table.

— **AUVERGNE AND PROVENCE** —

SOUPE AUX LENTILLES

Lentil soup

Lentil soup is one of winter's pleasures for me. I often sauté a handful of sorrel and add it to the soup just before I bring it to the table.

——————— *Serves 4–6* ———————

1 lb (450 g) lentils
2 tablespoons groundnut or olive oil
2 onions, chopped
1 leek, chopped
2 carrots, chopped
3 cloves garlic, chopped
1 clove
2 teaspoons dried thyme
2 bay leaves

6 pints (3.4 litres) water
salt and freshly ground black pepper

TO SERVE
1 tablespoon chopped fresh parsley,
*   chives or tarragon*
Croûtons (see page 68)
1 tablespoon butter or olive oil

Soak the lentils, if necessary, according to the directions on the packet. Heat the oil in a large saucepan and cook the onions, leek and carrots over a low heat until soft. Add the garlic, clove, thyme, bay leaves, lentils and water, bring to the boil, cover and simmer gently for about 2 hours until the lentils are soft.

Purée the soup in a food processor, blender or food mill and pour into a warm tureen. Season to taste with salt and pepper. Sprinkle with herbs, float a few Croûtons on top, drizzle a little butter or olive oil over the soup and serve.

— **LANGUEDOC AND PROVENCE** —

SOUPE AUX POIS CHICHES

Chickpea soup

This hearty dish is prepared in Provence and also in Languedoc-Roussillon.

——————— *Serves 4–6* ———————

*7 oz (200 g) dried chickpeas or 1 lb
    (450 g) tinned
1 teaspoon bicarbonate of soda (if
    using dried peas)
3 tablespoons olive oil
1 onion, coarsely chopped
2 cloves garlic, coarsely chopped
1 large tomato, skinned, seeded and
    coarsely chopped
1 small lamb's lettuce, coarsely
    chopped*

*2 bay leaves
1 teaspoon dried sage
1 sprig fresh rosemary
salt and freshly ground black pepper
4 oz (100 g) piece of streaky bacon
pinch of ground coriander
2 pints (1.2 litres) chickpea cooking
    liquid, water or stock*

*TO SERVE
Croûtons (see page 68)*

If you are using dried chickpeas, soak them overnight in lukewarm water with the bicarbonate of soda. Drain and rinse, then place in a saucepan and cover with fresh water. Bring to the boil, boil for 10 minutes then cover and simmer for about 2 hours until soft. Leave them to cool in the cooking liquid for 1 hour then drain, reserving 2 pints (1.2 litres) of the liquid. If you are using tinned chickpeas, rinse them in cold water and drain well.

Heat 2 tablespoons of the olive oil in a large saucepan and cook the onion, garlic, tomato, lettuce, bay leaves, sage, rosemary, salt and pepper for 10 minutes over a low heat, stirring occasionally. Add the bacon, coriander and chickpeas. Warm the water or stock and add it to the pan. Bring to the boil, cover and simmer for 1 hour.

Remove the bacon and chop it finely. Discard the bay leaves and rosemary. Purée the soup in a food processor, blender or food mill or rub through a sieve for a thick purée. Return the bacon to the soup, pour into a warm tureen and serve sprinkled with the remaining olive oil and the Croûtons.

VICHYSSOISE

Cold leek and potato soup

Leek is one of the most popular vegetables in France, along with the potato. Vichyssoise soup is, in fact, not a French invention – French soups are always served warm or hot. Many believe it was created by an American chef. However, this celebrated recipe is based on the traditional French leek and potato soup and is served cold, enriched with a little cream.

——————— *Serves 4* ———————

2 oz (50 g) butter
8 oz (225 g) potatoes, chopped
4 leeks, white parts only, sliced
2 shallots, coarsely chopped
2 pints (1.2 litres) chicken stock or water

10 fl oz (300 ml) single cream
salt and freshly ground black or white pepper
2 tablespoons snipped fresh chives or chervil

Heat the butter in a large saucepan and sauté the potatoes, leeks and shallots for about 5 minutes. Meanwhile, heat the stock or water in a separate pan. Add the stock to the vegetables, bring to the boil and simmer over a high heat, uncovered, for 30 minutes.

Purée the soup in a food processor, blender or food mill then pour into a bowl. Stir in the cream and season to taste with salt and pepper. It should be highly seasoned since it will be served cold. Leave to cool, cover and chill for a few hours then serve sprinkled with chives or chervil.

Note

I have eaten Vichyssoise served with a spoonful of salted, whipped cream on top of each portion.

*L*A *G*ARBURE
Cabbage soup

Curnonsky, the scholarly gourmet, once declared there were four great regional dishes in France: *Choucroute garnie, Bouillabaisse, Cassoulet* and *Garbure.*

Like Henry IV, the gallant king, *Garbure* comes from Béarn. Although there are many interpretations, it is always started with onions cooked in goose or duck fat and prepared in a terracotta or enamel casserole. It can then be made with freshly hulled haricot beans, when they are in season, or small, grilled chestnuts and red pepper strips. Cabbage is essential, of course, but a handful of shredded Swiss chard is sometimes included. Goose or duck *Confit* (see page 183) are traditional, and fresh herbs add a lively note to the soup. It may be topped with a thick layer of breadcrumbs and grated cheese seasoned with a sprinkling of parsley, garlic and slivers of streaky bacon.

In her beautiful farm kitchen, Pierrette Sarran, the owner of the Auberge de Bergerayre, St Martin d'Armagnac, prepared a simple *Garbure* for us with just a few ingredients: green cabbage and potatoes in equal quantities, a few garlic cloves and some left-overs she found after she had prepared her *Confit* – a duck carcass, wing tips and necks. She simmered the soup uncovered for 2 hours, stirred in a tablespoon of duck fat at the end and served us a deliciously hearty soup.

Because duck preserve is hard to find, this is my own recipe for *Garbure* which I prepare regularly, especially on wintry evenings. Only a spoonful takes the chill out of adults and children alike and warms their hearts.

——————— *Serves 6* ———————

3 lb (1.4 kg) dried white haricot beans
1 onion stuck with 1 clove
2 lb (900 g) piece of lean streaky bacon
1 thick slice of cured ham
4–5 pints (2.25–2.75 litres) cold water
8 oz (225 g) lima or shelled broad beans (optional)
3 carrots, chopped
1 turnip, chopped
2 leeks, white and pale green parts only, sliced
1 lb (450 g) long green cabbage leaves, shredded

4 oz (100 g) pumpkin, chopped
1 bouquet garni
salt and freshly ground black pepper
1½ lb (675 g) potatoes, diced
5 cloves garlic, crushed
1 ham bone (optional)
a few titbits of meats and bones of preserved duck or goose (see page 183) (optional)
2 tablespoons chopped fresh basil
2 tablespoons chopped fresh mint

TO SERVE
Garlic Croûtons (see page 100)

Soak the beans overnight in cold water. Drain then rinse. Place in a large saucepan, cover with fresh water and add the clove-studded onion. Bring to the boil and boil vigorously for 2 minutes then remove from the heat and leave to cool in the cooking liquid.

Place the bacon and ham in a large saucepan and add the water. Bring to the boil, partially cover and simmer for 1 hour. Add the lima or broad beans, carrots, turnip, leeks, cabbage, pumpkin and bouquet garni and season with salt and pepper. Return to the boil, partially cover and simmer for 30 minutes. Drain the haricot beans and discard the onion. Add the beans to the soup with the potatoes, garlic, and the ham bone and duck or goose, if using. Simmer for a further 40 minutes.

Remove the meats, slice them and discard the bones. Return the meats to the soup, pour it into a warm tureen and season with salt and pepper. Sprinkle with freshly chopped herbs. Place the garlic Croûtons in the bottom of each soup plate and pour the hot soup over them. Or sprinkle with grated cheese and grill briefly.

SOUPE A L'AIL

Garlic-flavoured soup

Whether it is enriched with olive oil or goose fat, called *Aïgo Bouïdo* or *Tourain*, garlic soups are served throughout southern France.

In Provence it is eaten the day after a particularly rich meal since *'l'aigo bouido sauvo la vido'* – garlic soup will save your life. In the centre and the south-west, the *Tourain* is made with onions, tomatoes and garlic seasoned with vinegar and enriched with eggs.

A delightful friend of mine, twelve-year-old Benjamin Cano who lives near the medieval city of Carcassonne, prepared a delicious soup for me. He set soup bowls on a table, placed a Croûton in each and delicately slipped in some fresh egg yolks while he kept an eye on the pan of hot water into which he had thrown a handful of garlic cloves. He energetically whisked some beaten egg whites into the water and poured a little of the hot broth with its delicate egg threads into each bowl as he vigorously stirred the broth into the egg yolks. I felt his was the very best garlic soup I ever tasted and I told him so. More soberly, now that I stand alone in my kitchen, I shall give you what I consider *the two* very best versions I know. Not a word to Benjamin.

LE TOURAIN

Garlic soup

This uses goose or duck fat and it was customary for friends and relatives to bring it to newly-weds about 4 a.m., then go down to the kitchen to share a bowl of *Tourain* and a fresh omelette.

———————— *Serves 4* ————————

1 tablespoon lard, goose or duck fat or groundnut oil	1 sprig fresh thyme or 1 teaspoon dried thyme
2 onions, sliced	1 egg, separated
6 cloves garlic, crushed	1 tablespoon red wine vinegar
2 pints (1.2 litres) water	2 slices stale rye or coarse-grained bread
salt and freshly ground black pepper	

Heat the lard, fat or oil and fry the onions and garlic until soft but not browned. Add the water, thyme, salt and pepper, bring to the boil, cover and simmer for 30 minutes. Strain the soup through a sieve, pushing the garlic and onion against the metal with a wooden spoon. Return to the heat, bring back to the boil and stir in the egg white, whisking steadily for about 2 minutes, then turn the heat to low. Blend the egg yolk with the wine vinegar, stir in a ladleful of the hot broth then stir the mixture into the pan. Remove from the heat and season with salt and pepper. Spread the bread in the bottom of a warm tureen, pour over the hot soup and serve at once.

Note

In Bordeaux, *Tourain* is prepared with tomatoes, onions, garlic and preserved duck and without egg whites. Sometimes, thin noodles are added to the soup, and it is often served with slices of bread spread with goose fat, sprinkled with coarsely ground pepper and grilled until crisp.

AïGO BOUïDO

Provençal garlic soup

———————— *Serves 4* ————————

1 tablespoon olive oil
10 cloves garlic, crushed
2 pints (1.2 litres) water
3 inch (7.5 cm) piece orange rind
2 bay leaves
3 fresh sage leaves or ¹/₂ teaspoon dried sage
1 sprig fresh thyme or 1 teaspoon dried thyme
salt

2 egg yolks (optional)
2 teaspoons red wine vinegar
freshly ground black pepper
2 tablespoons grated Gruyère or Parmesan cheese
1 tablespoon olive oil

TO SERVE
4 thin slices bread made into Croûtons (see page 68)

Heat the oil in a large saucepan and sauté the garlic for 3 minutes until barely golden without letting the garlic burn. Add the water, orange rind, bay leaves, sage, thyme and a pinch of salt, bring to the boil and simmer, uncovered, for 15 minutes.

Beat the egg yolks in a bowl, stir in the wine vinegar and a ladleful of hot broth. Stir the mixture into the pan, lower the heat and simmer for about 2 minutes, stirring gently, until the soup becomes creamy. Do not let the soup boil or the eggs will curdle. Remove the orange rind, bay leaves and herbs and season to taste with salt and pepper. Pour into a warm tureen, sprinkle with the cheese and olive oil and serve with thin, crisp Croûtons.

Note

This soup is sometimes served poured over a few slices of oven-dried bread sprinkled with olive oil.

—— **PROVENCE AND RIVIERA** ——

SOUPE AU PISTOU

*Rich vegetable soup flavoured with a garlic,
basil and cheese paste*

The most exhilarating of soups, *Soupe au Pistou* is also the ultimate *potage de santé*, or health soup. It is generally served as the major part of a meal during the summer when there is an abundance of fresh vegetables; but in autumn or winter, leeks, dried haricot beans, pumpkin or turnips offer interesting alternatives and since the basil and cheese paste can be frozen (I always add the garlic at the last moment), *Soupe au Pistou* makes a fragrant and comforting starter at any time of the year.

In Nice, we like to prepare this soup with most of the vegetables diced into tiny cubes. In fact, in most marketplaces there are piles of freshly shelled white beans and neatly diced vegetables ready-prepared for the busy cook.

Soupe au Pistou can be prepared two or three days in advance. It can be served hot or at room temperature, and the basil mixture is always added to the warm broth at the table so that the heady potent scent of the herb can be enjoyed by all your guests. Remember that the quantity of basil and garlic depend on the quality and freshness of the ingredients and also on your personal taste, so keep tasting and correcting before stirring the *pistou* into the soup. It is always better to gather the basil leaves a few hours in advance so they lose some of their moisture.

Above: Vegetables in Villandry, Loire

Previous page: BISQUE DE CRABES (*see page 70*)

─────────── *Serves 4–6* ───────────

FOR THE SOUP
8 oz (225 g) fresh, dried or semi-
   dried shelled white or red and
   white haricot beans
4 onions
1 leek
1 tomato, skinned
4 potatoes
2 carrots
2 turnips
1 stalk celery
4 courgettes
8 oz (225 g) green beans
3 tablespoons olive oil
2 bay leaves

a few fresh sage leaves
3 pints (1.75 litres) water
salt and freshly ground black pepper

FOR THE PISTOU
2 handfuls fresh basil leaves
3 cloves garlic
4 tablespoons grated Gruyère or
      Parmesan cheese
3 tablespoons olive oil

TO SERVE
grated Gruyère or Parmesan cheese
Crisp slices of bread

If you are using dried beans, soak them overnight in cold water. Drain and rinse. Place in a saucepan, cover with fresh water, bring to the boil and boil vigorously for 10 minutes then reduce the heat and simmer for about 1 hour until soft. Drain well.

Chop all the vegetables into 1 inch (2.5 cm) pieces. Heat 2 tablespoons of the oil in a frying pan and fry the onions and leek for 3 minutes. Add the tomatoes, potatoes, carrots, turnips and celery and cook for 10 minutes, stirring occasionally. Transfer to a large saucepan. Heat the remaining oil in the frying pan and fry the courgettes, green beans, bay leaves and sage for a few minutes. Meanwhile, bring the water to the boil in a separate pan. Add the courgette mixture and the water to the vegetables with bay leaves and sage. Return to the boil and simmer, uncovered, for 30 minutes. Add the cooked haricot beans.

Meanwhile, prepare the *pistou*. Use a mortar and pestle to grind and pound the basil leaves, garlic, salt and pepper to a thick paste then add the cheese and oil. Alternatively, you can use a food processor. Pour the soup into a warm tureen and bring it to the table. Stir in the *pistou* then sprinkle a little cheese on top. Pass a bowl of grated cheese and a basket of crisp slices of bread around the table.

SOUPE À L'OIGNON

Onion soup

There is nothing like a fragrant and invigorating onion soup covered with a golden crust to evoke in an instant a cosy supper after an evening out. But onion soup is not only the privilege of the *noctambules*, the night-owls. Followed by raw oysters or a platter of *charcuterie* and a watercress or chicory tossed salad, it is also the core of many traditional Sunday family meals.

Is onion soup an elaborate Lyonnaise treat, a hearty country dish or a Parisian invention? No one is quite sure. What's more, the purists will argue endlessly over exactly how the soup should be prepared. Should the onions be grated, sliced or puréed? Should one use beef, chicken or veal broth or water? Should it be a light or a thick soup? Should one try to add Camembert, Brie or Roquefort cheese instead of Gruyère? Should there be alternate layers of toasted bread and cheese with the hot broth poured on top before the final baking? Should one stir in a drop of vinegar, cognac, port, milk or white wine before serving the soup? I have no definitive answers to these questions so you must decide for yourselves. The most authentic version I ever tasted was prepared by Pierre Sauvet at Paris' 'intellectual' brasserie, the Brasserie Balzar near the Sorbonne. It contained no beef stock – all the flavour came from the long, slow cooking of the onions. But, here, I have decided to give a more sumptuous recipe that has been my favourite for years.

———— *Serves 4–6* ————

3 pints (1.75 litres) chicken, beef or
*   veal broth or water*
2 teaspoons dried thyme
2 bay leaves
1½ lb (675 g) yellow onions
4 tablespoons butter
1 tablespoon groundnut oil
salt
½ teaspoon sugar
2 tablespoons plain flour

10 fl oz (300 ml) dry white wine
freshly ground black pepper
8 oz (225 g) Gruyère cheese
10 slices baguette cut 1 inch
*   (2.5 cm) thick or large slices cut*
*   into triangles*
2 egg yolks
1–2 tablespoons cognac (optional)
2 tablespoons port, sherry or
*   Madeira*

Bring the stock or water, thyme and bay leaves to the boil while you peel and slice the onions under water to avoid tears. Heat 2 tablespoons of the butter with the oil in a large saucepan and cook the onions on a low heat until soft. Sprinkle with salt, sugar and flour and cook for 5 minutes, uncovered, until the mixture turns brown. Stir the mixture occasionally and add a little stock if it sticks to the pan. Stir in the wine then pour in the hot stock and simmer, uncovered for 30 minutes. Season with salt and pepper. You can cool, cover and refrigerate the soup at this point if you wish then re-heat and garnish it later.

Meanwhile, grate half the cheese and thinly slice the other half. Toast the bread slices on one side, turn them and sprinkle with grated cheese and then grill for a few seconds until the cheese has softened.

Pre-heat the oven to gas mark 4, 350°F (180°C).

Arrange the slices of cheese at the bottom of a large ovenproof tureen or in individual tureens or soufflé dishes. Pour over the hot soup, top with the bread and cheese and dot with the remaining butter. Bake in the oven for about 20 minutes until the cheese is browned. If it is not, flash it under a hot grill for a minute until browned.

Beat the egg yolks with the cognac, if using, and the port, sherry or Madeira and sprinkle with pepper.

Bring the soup to the table. Lift a bit of the cheese and bread crust with a fork, pour in the egg mixture and blend gently. This blending is called *touiller* and is a ritual needed to ensure a truly perfect Onion Soup. Serve at once.

Note

In parts of the south-west, the onion is sautéed in goose fat and Roquefort blue cheese is added to the Gruyère for a spirited version of the dish. Some cooks like to add a pinch of grated raw onion on crisp toast or a few poached eggs to the soup just before serving.

BREADS

Of the breads available in France, these are the most popular.

Baguette: Made with flour, salt, water and yeast. A baguette *à l'ancienne* is made with slightly sour dough.

Ficelle: Thin, short baguettes about 1½ inch (4 cm) wide.

Pain de Campagne: Made with rye or wholewheat flour, they may be hearty or disappointingly bland.

Pain de Mie: Dense sandwich bread made with butter, flour, sugar and milk.

Fougasse: A large, brown loaf covered with sea salt or herbs and made with flour, salt, yeast and olive oil, and sometimes herbs or crispy bacon.

Pain Viennois: Made with flour, sugar and milk, these are shaped like a plump baguette and dusted with flour on the top.

Pain aux Noix: Wholewheat or rye breads made with walnuts.

Bread as a Garnish: *Chapons* are slivers of French bread crust left to dry for 2 days then rubbed with cut garlic cloves until they are sticky and shiny and drizzled with a little oil. They are served with salads, such as *Salade Niçoise*, or, as in the southwest, sautéed in duck, goose or chicken fat until golden then sprinkled over hot greens with chopped fresh herbs and tossed together gently.

Panure or *chapelure*, breadcrumbs, are best made with 2–3 day old bread finely grated or chopped in a food processor. They can be used to top gratins, soups, stews or stuffed vegetables.

To make perfect *croûtons*, pre-heat the oven to gas mark 6, 400°F (200°C). Cut a baguette into ½ inch (1 cm) slices. Quarter the slices if the loaf is large, or cut them into triangles for tiny *croûtons*. Arrange on a baking sheet and bake for 10–20 minutes until dried and lightly brown. Then sprinkle with a little oil or a dot of butter and bake for a further 1 minute.

Mouillettes are long, narrow strips of fresh bread used to dip into poached eggs.

Tartines are rounds of bread, or baguettes cut lengthwise, buttered and spread with jam, honey or grated chocolate and served with hot chocolate or *café au lait*.

POTAGE CRÉCY

Light carrot soup

Crécy is a town near Paris where the best carrots in France are grown and they use them to prepare this smooth, fragrant, puréed soup. You can make it either with fresh, tender spring carrots or large winter ones. It needs a thickening agent, and you can use rice, potato or wheat flour. I like to garnish *Potage Crécy* with Croûtons or diced potatoes sautéed in butter, added to the soup just as it is brought to the table.

————————— *Serves 4* —————————

3 oz (75 g) butter
3 lb (1.4 kg) carrots, sliced
1 onion, sliced
3 potatoes, sliced
1 tablespoon chopped fresh thyme
2 pints (1.2 litres) vegetable,
  chicken or beef stock or water
1 teaspoon sugar

1 tablespoon chopped fresh chervil
salt and freshly ground black pepper

TO SERVE
4 slices bread made into Croûtons
  (see page 68) or 1 large diced
  potato sautéed in butter

Melt a little of the butter in a large saucepan and cook the carrots and onion over a low heat until soft. Add the potatoes, thyme and stock or water, bring to the boil, cover and simmer for 35 minutes until the vegetables are soft.

Purée the soup in a food processor, blender or food mill or rub through a sieve. Stir in the remaining butter with the sugar and chervil. Taste and season with salt and pepper. Pour into a warm tureen and serve sprinkled with Croûtons or diced sautéed potatoes.

BISQUE DE CRABES

Crab Bisque

Once, bisques were thick stew-like soups prepared with beef, pigeons, or game. Today they are only made with crayfish, lobsters, prawns or crabs. They are considered immensely elegant and so complicated and expensive to prepare that few sensible home cooks would venture to try them. Considering the number of utensils needed – mortar, sieve, saucepans – it seems like a true labour of endurance and love. Considering the price of lobster, crayfish and even prawns, it would seem that bisques are out of reach for most of us today. However, this recipe for an unctuous, velvety and spirited Crab Bisque is one that I often prepare and is really worth trying. Crabs are richly flavoured and quite inexpensive, while the help of a friendly food processor makes the whole procedure very straightforward.

In France, the *live* shellfish would be cooked in hot butter. I found this too difficult to face and I cook the crabs separately in boiling water, using the cooking broth later for the soup. Bisques are traditionally thickened with rice, cream of rice, potato flour or arrowroot.

In colloquial French, *bisquer* means to get angry. I suppose this comes from the fact that the dish is as coloured as an angry face.

———— *Serves 4–6* ————

2 × 1½ lb (675 g) crabs
salt
5 bay leaves
2 tablespoons butter
1 tablespoon vegetable oil
1 carrot, diced
1 onion, diced
1 stalk celery, diced
1 clove garlic, crushed
1 sprig fresh thyme
2 pints (1.2 litres) crab cooking
 liquid or water

10 fl oz (300 ml) dry white wine
pinch of cayenne pepper
4 egg yolks
5 tablespoons single cream
1 tablespoon arrowroot or cornflour
1 tablespoon brandy
2 tablespoon chopped fresh chervil,
 parsley or tarragon

TO SERVE
4 slices bread made into Croûtons
 (see page 68)

If you buy live crabs, bring a large saucepan of salted water to the boil, add 2 of the bay leaves and simmer for 5 minutes. Add the live crabs, cover and cook for 30 minutes. Leave to cool in the cooking liquid then strain, reserving the liquid.

Now you can start the soup. Place the cooked, cold crabs, back down, on a wooden board or strong work surface. Twist and break off the legs and claws from the body. Cut along each side of the leg shell with scissors and remove as much meat as possible with a skewer or knitting needle. Crack the claws and remove the meat with a knitting needle. Twist off and discard the tail from the body then crack the central section of the shell under the tail and prise it apart. Remove the meat from the shell and discard the grey, spongy gills, the 'dead men's fingers', the head sac and the coral-coloured roe. Prise out the meat, discarding any membrane. The left-over pieces and the broken shell will flavour the broth. Dice the crab meat and put it to one side for later use.

With a heavy mallet, pound the shells until they are crushed. Place them in a food processor with a little cooking stock or water and switch on and off for a few minutes until they are finely crushed. It will make a great deal of noise.

Heat 1 tablespoon of the butter with the oil in a very large saucepan and sauté the carrot, onion and celery for about 10 minutes until soft. Add the remaining bay leaves, the garlic and thyme then stir in the crushed shells and stir with a wooden spoon over a low heat for 5 minutes. Add the cooking stock or water and the wine, bring to the boil, cover and simmer for 30 minutes. Stir well with a wooden spoon. Cover again and simmer for a further 30 minutes. Leave to cool.

Scrape the shell and vegetable mixture into a coarse metal sieve and strain the broth into a pan, mashing the shell mixture with a spoon. Bring the broth to the boil and season with cayenne pepper. Mix the egg yolks, cream and arrowroot or cornflour in a bowl, stir in a little of the hot broth, then stir the mixture into the pan and simmer over a low heat, stirring, for 5-10 minutes until the broth thickens. Do not let the soup boil or the egg will curdle.

Heat the remaining butter in a separate pan and sauté the crab meat for a few minutes. Stir in the brandy then add the mixture to the soup. Pour into a warm tureen and serve sprinkled with fresh herbs with the Croûtons passed separately.

— **CHARENTES AND NORMANDY** —

MOUCLADE

Creamy mussel dish

Every region along the Mediterranean, Atlantic or Channel coasts has its own recipe for mussel soup. But *Mouclade* comes from Charentes, where mussels have been farmed for the last seven centuries, either flat in parks, hanging on ropes or on wooden posts, *bouchots*, driven into the sea bed. Ships have sailed to La Rochelle from the Orient for hundreds of years, bringing curry powder, cayenne pepper and saffron; while cognac, butter and cream abound in the region.

——————— *Serves 4–6* ———————

4 lb (1.8 kg) mussels	*juice of 1 lemon*
1 pint (600 ml) dry white wine	*2 egg yolks*
1 bay leaf	*7 fl oz (200 ml) double cream*
2 onions, chopped	*1 tablespoon cognac (optional)*
3 tablespoons butter	*pinch of cayenne pepper*
2 shallots, coarsely chopped	*salt and freshly ground black pepper*
2 cloves garlic, finely chopped	*2 teaspoons chopped fresh parsley*
½ teaspoon curry powder or ground saffron	

Soak the mussels in cold water for 30 minutes then drain and rinse. Scrub the shells with a hard brush and cut off the beards. Discard any open ones. Rinse the mussels in several changes of cold water.

Heat the wine, bay leaf and onions in a large pan then add the mussels. Cover and cook for about 5 minutes, shaking the pan from time to time, until the mussels have opened. Discard any that remain closed. Remove the mussels from the liquid with a slotted spoon and place them in a bowl. Wearing oven gloves to protect your hands, discard the top shells and half the bottom shells. Cover the mussels with kitchen foil or a thick towel and keep warm in a warm, turned-off oven. Strain the cooking liquor through a muslin-lined sieve.

Heat the butter in a large saucepan and sauté the shallots for 5 minutes until soft. Add the garlic, curry powder or saffron, lemon juice and the strained cooking liquor. Bring to the boil over a medium heat.

Beat the egg yolks and cream in a bowl, stir in a ladleful of the hot broth then pour into the pan and simmer over a low heat for 5 minutes, stirring. Do not let the mixture boil. Add the cognac, if using, and taste the soup; it should be highly seasoned. Season to taste with cayenne, salt and pepper.

Place the mussels and the remaining shells on a warm, large shallow dish, pour the hot, fragrant, creamy broth over and serve sprinkled with parsley using a ladle or two large spoons. Place spoons, paper towels and finger bowls on the table for each guest.

—— **THROUGHOUT FRANCE** ——

CONSOMMÉ DE VIANDE

Beef consommé

Consommé is not only for invalids, new mothers or elderly people, it is a truly sophisticated dish. But it must be intensely flavoured and be thoroughly degreased. A Consommé is basically the broth of a *Pot au Feu* made with twice the amount of meat. It used to take eight hours to prepare a Consommé so that all the juices would be extracted and the liquid would be reduced to its essence. Today we add a little uncooked meat to the bone and vegetables in order to flavour the broth.

You can make Consommé with beef and veal, or you may add chicken wings, necks, carcass or giblets. I like to prepare the following recipe because it is richly flavoured and only uses easily available ingredients. If you cannot buy bones at your local supermarket, you will certainly be able to obtain them from the butcher.

Beating egg whites into the cold Consommé then re-heating it causes the cloudy bits to rise to the surface so that they can be easily discarded to give a sparkling clear Consommé.

A little Madeira or sherry can be added just before serving. Each person is usually served about 10 fl oz (300 ml) of Consommé. You may like to add a few bits of shredded, raw carrot as you serve.

—————— *Serves 4* ——————

2 lb (900 g) beef shank, brisket or
   shin
4 lb (1.8 kg) beef bones, cracked
5 pints (2.75 litres) water
8 oz (225 g) carrots, quartered
5 oz (150 g) turnips, quartered
4 oz (100 g) leeks, halved
1 stalk celery
1 onion studded with 4 cloves
1 head garlic
2 sprigs fresh thyme

3 bay leaves
2 sprigs fresh parsley
1 teaspoon salt
8 black peppercorns
2 egg whites

TO SERVE
2 tablespoons Madeira, port, cognac
   or dry Sherry
4 slices bread made into Croûtons
   (see page 68)

Place the meat, bones and water in a large pan and bring slowly to the boil. Add the vegetables and herbs, salt and peppercorns, return to the boil, partially cover and simmer gently for 3–4 hours, skimming as necessary. Leave broth to cool then strain and refrigerate.

Skim the fat from the surface with a large spoon. Re-heat the broth until liquid. Taste and correct the seasoning. Whisk the egg whites in a bowl until they hold soft peaks. Add to the broth, whisking until thoroughly mixed. Bring gently to the boil, whisking all the time so that you incorporate all the impurities. Be sure to stop whisking before the broth reaches boiling point. At boiling point the albumen in the egg white coagulates and forms a crust which holds all the impurities. Do not whisk once this has happened. Let the crust rise to the top of the pan then turn off the heat and let it subside. Repeat, allowing the top of the crust to rise to the top of the pan again then let it subside.

Line a colander with 2 layers of muslin and stand it over a large bowl. Gently ladle the crust into the colander and pour in the broth. The clear, sparkling broth will drain into the bowl and the egg whites, meat and bone particles will remain in the colander and can be discarded. Strain again, through the egg white, if necessary.

Re-heat the Consommé and stir in the Madeira, port, cognac or dry Sherry just before serving. Serve with a basket of Croûtons.

S AUCES

L e s   S a u c e s

••••••••••••••••••••••••••••••

In classic cuisine, the ruling principle used to be: sauces and more sauces! But of the 400 sauces which are supposed to be part of the French patrimony, few today are still prepared at home, and few are used in most restaurants.

With the new appetite for fresh, healthy food and carefully chosen ingredients, we no longer follow the old saying, '*C'est la sauce qui fait passer le poisson*', 'It is the sauce which makes the fish edible'. We now want to taste the fish itself – and the vegetables, the chicken and the lamb – and we don't enjoy cloying sauces. Many of the rich – or in the case of the south, crisp and fragrant – sauces which we do still enjoy come from regional dishes. Here, the sauces are an integral part of the dish and have absorbed all the juices and seasonings during cooking.

Nouvelle cuisine introduced the idea of coating plates with a sauce then placing a portion of the cooked meat, fish or cake on top so that its appearance and texture, whether crunchy or moist, would not be masked by the sauce. I believe this custom is here to stay.

Sauces should never be used lightly or as a second thought. Whatever the ingredients and cooking method, and whether a sauce is thickened with eggs, cream, butter, goose fat, flour or vegetable purées, it does modify both the texture and appearance of a dish. Today, when we choose a sauce we want its flavour to speak loud and clear and we want it to be an integral part of the final dish; neither a mask nor a distraction. A sauce without a sharp, decisive personality which does not relate to its base is like clothes without . . . an emperor.

Sauce Hollandaise

Egg yolk and butter sauce

Hollandaise Sauce is a grand old lady of French cuisine. Today, few people dare to prepare it at home, and yet once the basic principles are understood this is a simple sauce to master. Since this rich and delicate sauce has no thickening agent, it is very sensitive to heat so if you use the traditional method, a double boiler is a must to heat the egg yolks very gently as the butter is gradually added and absorbed. I will propose here two simpler ways: the cold butter method and the blender method. Stainless steel pans should be used because aluminium will give an unappetising grey tone to the sauce.

It is served with steamed fish, vegetables and poached eggs. The sauce can be refrigerated for up to two days.

— *Makes about 10 fl oz (300 ml)* —

2 tablespoons white wine vinegar
1 tablespoon water
1 teaspoon crushed white
 peppercorns
3 egg yolks
salt and freshly ground white pepper

6 oz (175 g) butter, cut into
 walnut-sized pieces
1 tablespoon cold water (optional)
juice of 1 small lemon, warmed
pinch of cayenne pepper (optional)

Place the wine vinegar, water and peppercorns in a heavy-based pan, bring to the boil and boil over a high heat until reduced to 1 tablespoon. Place the egg yolks in a heatproof bowl, stir in the reduced wine with a wooden spoon and season with salt and pepper. Place the bowl over a pan of simmering water over a low heat and whisk until the sauce becomes frothy and thickens. Add the pieces of butter one at a time, whisking constantly as you would to make Mayonnaise (see page 92) and waiting until one piece has melted into the sauce before adding the next. The sauce should be thick enough to coat the back of a spoon. The sauce must not become too hot or it will curdle; you must always be able to touch the bowl with your bare hands. If the sauce becomes too thick, slowly whisk in a teaspoonful of water. When all the butter has been absorbed, remove from the heat, add the lemon juice and season to taste with salt and cayenne pepper. To keep the sauce warm, cover the bowl and stand it over a pan of warm but not boiling water. If the sauce starts to curdle, pour it into a cold bowl, add a little warm water or an egg yolk and stir well before returning the sauce to the double boiler.

COLD BUTTER METHOD

This is a much quicker method, but remember that the saucepan and the butter must be chilled.

— *Makes about 10 fl oz (300 ml)* —

4 egg yolks
2–3 teaspoons lemon juice
1/4 teaspoon salt

1/8 teaspoon white pepper
8 oz (225 g) butter, chilled

Cool a saucepan briefly in the refrigerator. Whisk the egg yolks, lemon juice, salt and pepper in the saucepan until blended. Cut the cold butter into cubes. Place the saucepan over a low heat add the butter a piece at a time, whisking continuously until the sauce thickens. Keep in warm container until ready to serve.

BLENDER METHOD

A blender makes this sauce child's play. The proportions are a little different from hand-made Hollandaise as you use less butter.

— *Makes about 10 fl oz (300 ml)* —

3 egg yolks
1/4 teaspoon salt
1/2 teaspoon freshly ground white
   pepper

juice of 1 lemon
4 oz (100 g) butter

Place the egg yolks, salt and pepper in a blender and blend at top speed for a few seonds until well mixed. Warm the lemon juice, pour into the blender and blend again until the mixture thickens slightly. Melt the butter. With the blender running at low speed, gradually pour in the hot butter. The sauce will thicken as you add the butter. Pour into a bowl, cover and place over a pan of lukewarm water until ready to use.

Note

To serve the sauce with boiled fish, stir in a teaspoon of well-drained capers. Chopped fresh herbs or a little orange juice and grated orange rind may also be added to the Hollandaise.

I will share a well-kept secret here: if the meal lingers or the guests are late and you must keep this sauce thick and smooth, whip one or two tablespoons of Béchamel Sauce (see page 83) into the pan of Hollandaise and your sauce will remain perfect. Restaurants would never admit to it, but most of them do it!

──── **THROUGHOUT FRANCE** ────

SAUCE MOUSSELINE

Creamy Hollandaise sauce

There are two *Sauces Mousseline*: a cold one made with whipped cream or egg whites gently blended into a bowl of Mayonnaise and this warm one made with a Hollandaise Sauce which is lovely with soufflés, steamed asparagus and steamed fish.

— *Makes about 14 fl oz (400 ml)* —

10 fl oz (300 ml) Hollandaise Sauce (see page 77)

4 fl oz (120 ml) whipping cream, chilled

Prepare the Hollandaise. Beat the cream in a chilled bowl until stiff. Fold the cream into the warm Hollandaise just before serving, whipping until it is frothy. Keep the sauce warm over a pan of warm water until ready to serve.

SAUCE BORDELAISE

Wine, herb and shallot sauce

Sauce Bordelaise used to be prepared with a *fond brun* – a rich stock made from bones, meat and bacon rinds which was simmered for hours – with shallots and white wine. But times have changed even in Bordeaux. *Sauce Bordelaise* is now prepared with a reduction of shallots, herbs and red wine and without a stock base. It is served with grilled meats, but also with poached eggs. In Paris, a variation of this sauce is called *À la Marchand de Vin*, in the style of a wine merchant. This pungent version of the sauce, made with or without bone marrow, is one I use with beef.

— *Makes about 8 fl oz (250 ml)* —

10 fl oz (300 ml) Bordeaux red
   wine
3 shallots, coarsely chopped
3 tablespoons beef stock
1 clove garlic, crushed
½ teaspoon freshly grated nutmeg
2 teaspoons dried thyme
2 bay leaves

pinch of cayenne pepper
salt and coarsely ground black
   pepper
4 oz (100 g) beef marrow bones
   (optional)
1 tablespoon brandy
3 tablespoons butter

Heat the wine then add the shallots, stock, garlic, nutmeg, thyme, bay leaves, cayenne pepper, salt and pepper. Bring to the boil then simmer, uncovered, until reduced to one-third of the original amount.

Meanwhile, wrap the marrow bones, if using, in a piece of muslin and plunge them into a pan of boiling water. Simmer for 15 minutes then drain.

Add the brandy to the sauce and remove it from the heat. Swirl in the butter a little at a time then place the sauce back over a low heat, stirring for a few minutes. Just before serving, slide the marrow out of the bone, finely chop the marrow and stir it into the sauce.

Opposite: MOUCLADE (*see page 72*)

Vallée d'Alberville, Haute-Savoie

SAUCE RAÏTO

Wine, tomato and herb sauce

This spirited sauce has such fragrance, that spooned over chicken, veal, fried or baked fish, *morue*, pasta, vegetables, fritters or even poached eggs, it transforms them instantly into a Provençal treat. Traditionally, *Sauce Raïto* was made at Christmas time with *vin cuit*, a fortified home-made wine, but a red vermouth, a sweet wine, even a hearty red wine will make an honourable *Sauce Raïto* any time.

— *Makes about 1 pint (600 ml)* —

2 tablespoons olive oil
3 medium onions, finely chopped
1 pint (600 ml) sweet red vermouth, sweet Banyuls, red Muscat or a good hearty red wine
10 fl oz (300 ml) water
2 cloves garlic, crushed
4 plump ripe tomatoes, skinned, seeded and chopped
2 cloves
2 teaspoons dried thyme
2 teaspoons dried savory
2 bay leaves

1 teaspoon fennel seeds or aniseeds (optional)
salt and freshly ground black pepper
2 tablespoons purple or black olives in brine or plump black oil-cured olives from Nyons, Italy or Greece, stoned and coarsely chopped
3 teaspoons capers, chopped
3 teaspoons chopped gherkins (optional)
2 tablespoons chopped fresh flat-leaved parsley

Heat the oil and fry the onions for about 15 minutes until soft. Add the wine and water and simmer for a few minutes, uncovered. Add the garlic, tomatoes, cloves, thyme, savory, bay leaves, fennel, if using, salt and pepper and simmer for 1 hour, uncovered, until the sauce is quite thick. Discard the bay leaves. Purée the sauce in a food processor, blender or food mill or rub it through a sieve. Stir in the olives, capers, gherkins and parsley. Pour over warm meat, fish or vegetables.

Note

Sometimes a few pounded walnuts are added to the *Sauce Raïto* at the end of cooking to thicken the sauce.

Sauce Meurette

Wine sauce

This Burgundian sauce makes the most of Burgundy's favourite ingredients. It is used to coat poached eggs served on garlic toasts, but it is also served with freshwater fish.

There is no need to use a great wine, a good hearty one will do. *Meurette* is made with red wine in Burgundy, but is prepared with white wine elsewhere in France. It is an unctuous, rich sauce. Lately, experimental chefs are serving it as a single reduction of wine and herbs. Their *Meurette* is fresh and light but it lacks the explosive flavours and the velvety texture we like in this sauce. This makes enough for four people.

—— Makes about 1½ pints (900 ml) ——

2 tablespoons butter
3 oz (75 g) streaky bacon, cut into
    small slivers
1 large onion, chopped
2 carrots, chopped
2 cloves garlic, chopped
1 leek, white part only, chopped
2 pints (1.2 litres) hearty red wine
2 bay leaves
1 sprig fresh thyme
1 clove
5 peppercorns

1 teaspoon butter kneaded with 1
    teaspoon plain flour (Beurre
    Manié) *(see page 91)* or 1
    teaspoon arrowroot (optional)
1 teaspoon sugar (optional)
salt and freshly ground black pepper
1 tablespoon marc brandy (optional)

FOR THE GARNISH
2 slices bread made into garlic
    Croûtons *(see page 100)*

Heat the butter in a frying pan and sauté the bacon for 1 minute. Add the onion and cook for 5 minutes. Add the carrots, garlic and leek and cook over a low heat until soft. Add the wine, herbs, clove and peppercorns, bring to the boil then simmer, uncovered, for about 30 minutes until reduced by half. Rub the sauce through a sieve, pounding the vegetables with a wooden spoon. Return the sauce to a low heat.

If you are using the sauce for *Oeufs en Meurette* (see page 100), it is ready to serve. If you are using the sauce with meat or fish, whisk in the *Beurre Manié* or arrowroot to thicken the sauce and simmer for 5 minutes. Add a little sugar if the sauce is too acid. Season to taste with salt and pepper then add the brandy. Serve with garlic Croûtons.

—— **THROUGHOUT FRANCE** ——

SAUCE *B*ÉCHAMEL

White sauce

Béchamel Sauce is indeed the most versatile of sauces. It can be prepared in only a few minutes using milk, cream or broth, and is not only used with fish, chicken, veal, eggs and vegetables, but also provides the base for many soups, gratins and soufflés.

Cream, egg yolks and spices can all be used to improve on a basic Béchamel Sauce. Grated cheese, tomato purée, chopped mushrooms, all kinds of spices such as curry or saffron and a great variety of other ingredients can be added to create a range of different sauces.

For a delicate *Sauce Parisienne* or *Sauce Poulette*, prepare a pan of Béchamel. Blend 2 egg yolks and 8 tablespoons of single cream in a bowl then blend in a little of the Béchamel Sauce. Stir for a few minutes then pour the smooth mixture into the rest of the warm Béchamel, stirring until it just reaches boiling point. Remove from the heat immediately, stir in the juice of a lemon and serve at once.

— *Makes about 10 fl oz (300 ml)* —

1 tablespoon butter	*salt*
1½ tablespoons plain flour	*pinch of freshly grated nutmeg*
10 fl oz (300 ml) milk or beef,	*pinch of cayenne pepper*
chicken or vegetable stock	

Slowly melt the butter in a heavy-based saucepan. Stir in the flour and cook on a low heat for 3–4 minutes, stirring with a wooden spoon, until the mixture froths without turning brown. Meanwhile, heat the milk or stock in a separate pan just to boiling point. Remove the butter and flour from the heat and stir for a few seconds until cooled slightly. Add the hot milk or stock and whisk vigorously until smooth. Season to taste with salt, nutmeg and cayenne pepper. Return the sauce to a low heat and bring to the boil. Reduce the heat and simmer for 5–10 minutes, stirring steadily, until smooth and velvety. Check and adjust the seasoning to taste.

You can keep the sauce on a low heat for immediate use or pour it into a bowl, add a little milk or a dot of butter on top to prevent a skin forming then re-heat gently when required.

For a richer sauce, add a tablespoon of butter or a few tablespoons of single cream to the sauce, stirring for a few minutes. If you do find a few lumps, rub the sauce through a metal sieve. You can thin your Béchamel Sauce with either milk or stock.

—— **THROUGHOUT FRANCE** ——

Sauce Soubise

Onion sauce

This is prepared with a Béchamel base flavoured with an onion purée. I use lots of onions for a stronger flavour, but half the quantity would still make a tasty sauce. Serve *Sauce Soubise* with eggs, chicken, lamb or vegetables.

— *Makes about 10 fl oz (300 ml)* —

3 tablespoons butter
8 oz (225 g) onions, sliced
1 quantity Béchamel Sauce (see
  page 83)

2 tablespoons double cream
pinch of freshly grated nutmeg
pinch of sugar
salt and freshly ground black pepper

Heat 2 tablespoons of the butter, add the onions, cover and cook over a medium heat for about 15 minutes, stirring occasionally, until they are soft but not brown. Purée in a food processor, blender or food mill or rub through a sieve.

Prepare the Béchamel Sauce. Stir in the onions and whisk vigorously until smooth. When you are ready to serve, stir in the remaining butter and cream and season to taste with nutmeg, sugar, salt and pepper.

Note

Sometimes a little white wine or beef broth is added to the onion purée and the mixture is reduced for a few minutes before adding it to the Béchamel Sauce.

—— **THROUGHOUT FRANCE** ——

SAUCE MORNAY

Cheese sauce

This delicate sauce made with a Béchamel base is perfect for poached eggs, grilled fish or veal, poached chicken, steamed vegetables and also to coat crêpes and gratins. Don't let it reach boiling point. Only stir in the cheese at the last moment or the sauce will become rubbery.

If the sauce is used with fish, add 2 tablespoons of the fish cooking liquid. If it is served with poultry, add a little of the cooking juices. If you use Mornay Sauce to cover crêpes or gratins, use only 2 oz (50 g) of cheese to prevent it from becoming stringy.

— *Makes about 10 fl oz (300 ml)* —

1 quantity Béchamel Sauce (see page 83)
3 egg yolks
3 tablespoons single cream (or more for a thinner sauce)
2–4 oz (50–100 g) Gruyère cheese or Gruyère and Parmesan cheese, grated

salt
pinch of cayenne pepper
pinch of freshly grated nutmeg
1 teaspoon butter

Prepare the Béchamel Sauce. Beat the egg yolks and cream together. Add the hot Béchamel Sauce, stirring vigorously. Pour the mixture into a saucepan and simmer over a low heat for a few minutes, stirring continuously. Stir in the cheese and let it melt. When the sauce is smooth, season to taste with salt, cayenne pepper and nutmeg and remove it from the heat. Spread a little butter on the top to prevent a skin forming.

SAUCE *B*ÉARNAISE

Egg yolk and butter sauce flavoured with shallots,
wine and herbs

This wonderful sauce is another grand old lady so intimidating that few ever dare make it at home without qualms. It is a more concentrated cousin of the Hollandaise, using vinegar instead of lemon juice and flavoured with lively tarragon.

It should be prepared in a stainless steel or copper saucepan, not aluminium as this will give a grey colouring to the sauce. It tastes delicious with grilled meat or fish, egg dishes, steamed vegetables and vegetable flans. This recipe makes about ½ pint (300 ml) of sauce.

If you are nervous of trying this traditional method, experiment with the quicker technique.

— *Makes about 8 fl oz (250 ml)* —

6 oz (175 g) butter	*salt*
2 tablespoons red wine vinegar	*2 small egg yolks*
2 tablespoons dry white wine	*1 tablespoon water*
3 tablespoons finely chopped shallots	*1 tablespoon chopped fresh chives,*
(about 3 small shallots)	*parsley or tarragon*
1 tablespoon chopped fresh tarragon	*pinch of cayenne pepper*
½ teaspoon coarsely ground	
peppercorns	

Melt the butter over a low heat or in the top of a double boiler over gently simmering water. Skim and discard the white particles from the top and keep the butter lukewarm.

Heat the wine vinegar, wine, shallots, tarragon, peppercorns and a pinch of salt in a stainless steel pan and let the mixture simmer, uncovered, for about 5 minutes until reduced to about 1 large tablespoon. Rub the mixture through a sieve and let it cool.

Stir the egg yolks into the shallot-vinegar mixture in a heat-proof bowl or the top of a double boiler. Add a pinch of salt, 1 tablespoon of the melted butter and the water and beat vigorously with a whisk. Place the bowl over a pan of hot water over a gentle heat and continue to beat vigorously. When the mixture starts to thicken, add the remaining melted butter a little at a time, stirring continuously until the sauce has the consistency of a custard. Remove from the heat, stir in the herbs and season to taste with salt and cayenne pepper. Keep the sauce covered with a plate on top of the pan of lukewarm water until ready to use. It is served lukewarm, never hot.

QUICK BÉARNAISE SAUCE

— Makes about 8 fl oz (250 ml) —

2 tablespoons red wine vinegar
2 tablespoons dry white wine
3 tablespoons finely chopped shallots
1 tablespoon chopped fresh tarragon

salt and freshly ground black pepper
2 egg yolks
4 oz (100 g) butter

Heat the wine vinegar, wine, shallots, tarragon and seasoning in a stainless steel saucepan and simmer, uncovered, for about 5 minutes until reduced to about 1 large tablespoon. Rub the mixture through a sieve into a cold bowl, add the egg yolks and whisk until blended.

Melt the butter until liquid and bubbling. Pour the hot butter gradually into the egg yolk mixture while beating on medium speed with an electric hand whisk. The sauce will thicken with the heat of the butter. Pour into a warm sauce boat and serve.

Note
To rescue the sauce if it does not blend, add 1 to 2 teaspoons of water and whisk vigorously. Alternatively, pour 2 teaspoons of water into a cold bowl and gradually whisk in the sauce.

———————— **SOUTH-WEST** ————————

SAUCE DE SORGES

Cooked egg sauce with shallots and herbs

A favourite in the south-west, this sauce is often served with a poached chicken.

— *Makes about 8 fl oz (250 ml)* —

2 eggs
4½ fl oz (135 ml) groundnut oil,
    olive and groundnut oil or
    groundnut and walnut oil

3 tablespoons red wine vinegar
3 tablespoons chopped fresh herbs
1 tablespoon finely chopped shallot
salt and freshly ground black pepper

Place the eggs in a pan of water, bring to the boil and boil for 2 minutes. Remove from the pan and dip in cold water. Peel the eggs and separate them carefully. The yolks should be soft. If the whites are still runny, return them to the boiling water for a further 1 minute. Whisk together the oil, wine vinegar, herbs and shallot and season with salt and pepper. Stir in the soft egg yolks. Chop the egg whites and stir them gently into the sauce.

———————— **THROUGHOUT FRANCE** ————————

SAUCE FLEURETTE À L'ESTRAGON

Tarragon cream sauce

A delicate, cold sauce used for green and mixed salads.

— *Makes about 10 fl oz (300 ml)* —

½ teaspoon Dijon mustard
1 teaspoon red wine vinegar
10 fl oz (300 ml) single cream

1 teaspoon chopped fresh tarragon
    leaves
salt and freshly ground black pepper

Stir the mustard into the vinegar then add the cream, tarragon, salt and pepper. When the mixture is well blended, correct the seasoning and serve.

SAUCE AILLADE

Walnut and garlic sauce

A speciality of Languedoc, *Sauce Aillade* is often served with *Magrets de Canard* (see page 160). The proportions vary considerably from household to household so experiment and choose whatever quantities of walnuts and garlic you prefer. Bottles of walnut oil should be refrigerated after opening. This is a thick sauce.

— *Makes about 10 fl oz (300 ml)* —

3 cloves garlic, crushed	5 fl oz (150 ml) walnut oil or
handful of walnuts, peeled	walnut and groundnut oil
¼ teaspoon salt	2 tablespoons red wine vinegar
freshly ground black pepper	1 soft-boiled egg yolk
	1 tablespoon chopped fresh parsley

Pound the garlic and walnuts to a paste in a mortar. Blend in the salt, pepper, oil and wine vinegar. Add the egg yolk and when it is well blended, add the parsley.

Note

In the eastern part of Provence and in Savoie, a similar sauce made with walnuts, garlic and olive oil is used to top hot pasta and tiny cheese ravioli.

COULIS DE TOMATES

Tomato sauce

In the south-west and Provence, *Coulis* is a cooked sauce prepared with ripe tomatoes and herbs. It is traditionally used either as the base for or the accompaniment to many dishes such as *Potées* (see page 158), *Pot au Feu*, pasta, boiled rice, grilled fish, sautéed squid, stuffed lamb and poached or fried eggs. It is also used to deglaze chicken, fish or meat cooking juices in the bottom of their cooking pan. Sprinkled with a handful of chopped fresh herbs, it can turn into a last-minute, fragrant soup.

Today we still love this traditional *Coulis*, but we also prepare another version with raw tomatoes for a fresher flavour. Raw *Coulis* is served lukewarm or cold with poached eggs, stuffed vegetables, grilled peppers, cold beef or poached fish. For a healthy snack, rub a piece of toast with a cut garlic clove then spread a little raw *Coulis* on top.

Store *Coulis* in sterilised screw-top jars for 3 to 4 days in the refrigerator since tomatoes ferment easily. The oil will float to the top to protect the *Coulis*.

COOKED COULIS

— *Makes about 1 pint (600 ml)* —

2 tablespoons olive oil
2 onions, chopped
2 cloves garlic, chopped
2 lb (900 g) ripe tomatoes, skinned, seeded and coarsely chopped
2 bay leaves
2 teaspoons dried thyme

2 inch (5 cm) piece of orange peel, dried in a low oven for 15 minutes
1 teaspoon sugar
handful of basil leaves (optional)
3 tablespoons chopped fresh flat-leaved parsley
1/2 teaspoon cayenne pepper
salt

Heat the oil and fry the onions and 1 of the cloves of garlic over a low heat for 10 minutes until soft. Add the tomatoes, bay leaves, thyme, orange peel and sugar, bring to the boil and simmer, uncovered, for 20 minutes on a fairly high heat so that most of the water evaporates. Rub through a sieve for a smooth consistency. Add the remaining garlic, the basil and parsley and season to taste with cayenne pepper and salt. If the sauce is too thin, cook it for a further 10 minutes, uncovered. Add a drop of olive oil; it will rise to the surface and protect the sauce. Leave to cool then refrigerate in tightly-closed sterilised jars or freeze.

Re-heat the sauce on a low heat as needed.

Raw Coulis

— *Makes about 1 pint (600 ml)* —

2 lb (900 g) ripe tomatoes
1 tablespoon chopped fresh basil
pinch of ground coriander
1 tablespoon chopped fresh parsley

2 spring onions or tiny fresh onions,
* finely chopped*
salt and freshly ground black pepper
3 tablespoons olive oil

There are two ways to prepare raw *Coulis*.

The first way is to dip the tomatoes in a pan of hot water then skin them with a sharp knife. Seed and chop them into small dice then mix them with the remaining ingredients.

The second way is to prepare the sauce in a food processor or blender. Prepare the tomatoes as above, then place all the ingredients in the blender and process for about 3 minutes.

—— **THROUGHOUT FRANCE** ——

Beurre Manié

Kneaded butter

Sauces can be thickened by slow simmering; by whisking in butter, cream or egg yolks; by adding tomato, onion or carrot purées; or by stirring a little arrowroot or potato flour, diluted in cold water, into the hot sauce. But *Beurre Manié* remains the quickest and safest way to turn a sauce or broth into a velvety mixture. Keep the sauce simmering and do not let it reach boiling point.

FOR 10 FL OZ (300 ML) HOT LIQUID
2 tablespoons butter
2 tablespoons plain flour

Knead the butter and flour with a fork or between your fingers to a paste. Divide it into pea-sized balls for easy cooking. Toss a piece of *Beurre Manié* into the pan of hot stock or sauce and shake the pan a few times. Simmer the sauce for a few minutes, whisking gently and adding the *Beurre Manié* a little at a time until the sauce reaches the desired consistency.

Note

A *roux* is an alternative to *Beurre Manié* made with equal quantities of butter and flour kneaded and heated together, and is used at the beginning of cooking a sauce. It can be made in advance for later use. Melt the butter in a pan over a low heat, add the flour and stir or whisk constantly for about 2 minutes for a white roux, and up to 10 minutes for a deeper brown colour. Add the liquid, remove the roux from the heat and whisk constantly until all the liquid has been absorbed. Return the sauce to the heat and stir until it reaches boiling point.

—— **THROUGHOUT FRANCE** ——

MAYONNAISE

Mayonnaise is one of the most useful of sauces, and it is one of the easiest to prepare despite what some people believe. All the ingredients should be at room temperature, a tea towel should be placed under the bowl to prevent it from sliding as you beat the sauce with a whisk or fork, and the oil must be added slowly. If the Mayonnaise separates, place a fresh egg yolk in a clean bowl, add a little mustard and start stirring, slowly adding the curdled mixture until the sauce is silky and firm. You can use all groundnut oil if you prefer.

— *Makes about 10 fl oz (300 ml)* —

1 large egg yolk
1 teaspoon Dijon mustard
4 fl oz (120 ml) olive oil
4 fl oz (120 ml) groundnut oil

1 ½ teaspoons white or red wine
vinegar or the juice of a lemon
salt and freshly ground black pepper

Beat the egg yolk and mustard with a hand whisk for 1 minute, then beat in about a quarter of the oil, a drop at a time, until it is incorporated into the sauce. When there is a tablespoon or so of firm Mayonnaise you can proceed a little more quickly but always with an attentive eye and a steady hand. When all the oil has been absorbed, add the wine vinegar or lemon juice to taste and season with salt and pepper.

SAUCE GRIBICHE

Piquant hard-boiled eggs 'mayonnaise'

This spirited sauce, made with hard-boiled eggs, is used with cold fish, shellfish, cuts of meat and chicken.

— *Makes about 10 fl oz (300 ml)* —

2 hard-boiled eggs with crumbly yolks, separated	1 tablespoon red wine vinegar
2 teaspoons Dijon mustard	2 teaspoons finely chopped gherkins
salt and freshly ground black pepper	2 teaspoons capers, chopped
300 ml (10 fl oz) olive oil or groundnut oil	2 teaspoons chopped fresh parsley or chervil

Press the egg yolks through a sieve into a bowl then stir in the mustard and season with salt and pepper. Blend the ingredients to a paste; only when it is very silky and smooth will it absorb the oil. Slowly pour in the oil and whisk with a wire whisk as you would for Mayonnaise (see page 92) until the mixture thickens. Slowly add the wine vinegar. Place the chopped gherkins with the capers in a little piece of muslin and squeeze to extract the excess moisture then stir them into the sauce with the parsley or chervil. Press the egg whites through a sieve and stir them into the sauce. Check and correct the seasoning with oil, wine vinegar, salt or pepper.

Note

Sauce Ravigote is a cousin of *Sauce Gribiche* and *Sauce Tartare*. It is prepared in the same way but without the eggs and with the addition of a minced onion.

SAUCE VERTE

Green mayonnaise

There are two equally interesting versions of *Sauce Verte.*

SAUCE VERTE 1

This is served with cold fish, meat or poultry, shellfish, or grilled fish. It is a Mayonnaise sauce enriched with herbs. It is sometimes called *Sauce Vincent* after a famous eighteenth-century cook Vincent Lachapelle.

— *Makes about 10 fl oz (300 ml)* —

10 fl oz (300 ml) Mayonnaise (see page 92)
2 tablespoons chopped fresh chives, chervil, tarragon, sorrel or parsley (or a mixture of 2 or 3 herbs)

1 tablespoon chopped fresh spinach or watercress
salt and freshly ground black or white pepper

Prepare the Mayonnaise. Plunge the herbs and spinach or watercress into a pan of boiling water and leave to stand for 3 minutes. Drain, rinse under cold water and drain again. Purée in a food processor or crush in a mortar. Whisk this green purée into the Mayonnaise then season to taste with salt and pepper. Cover and refrigerate until ready to serve.

Note

I sometimes use blanched spinach and fresh *uncooked* herbs for a more pungent version of Sauce Verte.

SAUCE VERTE 2

Makes about 10 fl oz (300 ml)

4 oz (100 g) frozen leaf spinach,
*   thawed and drained thoroughly*
1 hard-boiled egg, peeled
5 anchovy fillets
1 slice white bread, crusts removed
*   and moistened*

5 fl oz (150 ml) olive oil
2 tablespoons red wine vinegar
3 teaspoons chopped gherkins
1 teaspoon chopped capers
salt and freshly ground black
*   pepper*

Place the spinach, egg, anchovies, bread, oil and wine vinegar in a food processor or blender and blend until smooth. Pour into a bowl, stir in the gherkins and capers and season to taste with salt and pepper.

—— **THROUGHOUT FRANCE** ——

SAUCE *RÉMOULADE*

Mayonnaise flavoured with anchovies, shallots and herbs

This lively, cold sauce based on Mayonnaise is easy to make and instantly transforms a bowl of steamed shellfish or left-over poultry, fish or vegetables into an interesting starter.

—   *Makes about 12 fl oz (350 ml)*   —

10 fl oz (300 ml) Mayonnaise (see
*   page 92)*
1 tablespoon chopped gherkins
2 teaspoons Dijon mustard
2 shallots, finely chopped
1 tablespoon capers (optional)

1 tablespoon chopped fresh,
*   preferably flat-leaved, parsley*
1 tablespoon chopped fresh tarragon
*   or chervil*
2 anchovy fillets, chopped (optional)

Prepare the Mayonnaise. Stir all the ingredients gently into the Mayonnaise. The sauce will keep for a few days in a screw-top jar in the refrigerator.

E G G S

L e s   O e u f s

Above: Chefs enjoying their break in Paris

Previous page: PIPERADE (*see page 108*)

Eggs are the symbols of life; the richest and the simplest of foods. When I was a child, this idea was taken literally, and whenever we felt tired or listless at school we had to swallow the yolk of a raw egg beaten with orange water and sugar; or worse, to suck the pierced shell of a raw egg for instant energy. Now the thought of an uncooked egg gives me the shivers. But we do have an enormous repertoire of recipes for frying, stuffing and baking eggs, and for transforming them into a rich variety of omelettes, sauces, custards and soufflés. The possibilities of egg preparation in French cooking are a measure of one's imagination – limitless.

There are a few points to remember: freshness is all-important. Eggs must be free-range, dated, and kept refrigerated. A fresh egg has a plump yolk covered with some of the white, the rest of the white is more liquid. There should be no microbes within an egg, so always rinse the shell of an egg before using it. Always add a drop of vinegar to the boiling water when you cook eggs and remember they must be at room temperature before you boil them so the shell will not crack. Wine and eggs don't get along, so serve water or at best a dry white wine or a light rosé.

OEUFS POCHÉS

Poached eggs

Break the eggs into a bowl so that you can check that the yolks are firm and the eggs are very fresh. Add ½ a teaspoon of vinegar for each egg but no salt as it will prevent the whites from coagulating. Bring a wide saucepan of water to a rolling boil. Carefully slide the eggs into the boiling water so that the bubbles shape the whites neatly. Don't cook too many eggs at once or they will reduce the temperature of the water. Simmer for about 4 minutes so that the yolks remain soft when lightly pressed. Remove the eggs from the pan with a slotted spoon and trim the whites with scissors before serving.

You can keep the eggs warm in a pan of warm salted water. If you wish to re-heat a poached egg, place it in a bowl and carefully pour over some boiling water. Leave it to stand for 2 minutes. Snip off the loose bits of egg white with scissors.

You can serve poached eggs on toast, on a bed of warm ratatouille or a layer of warm watercress purée. You can place each egg in a hollow scooped out of a baked jacket potato or of a cooked, trimmed artichoke and spoon some sauce over the top. A variety of sauces can be served: Béarnaise (see page 86), Hollandaise (see page 77) to make Eggs Benedict, Mornay (see page 85), Mousseline (see page 79), Meurette (see page 82), Béchamel (see page 83) or *Coulis de Tomates* (see page 89).

OEUFS MOLLETS
Eggs Mollets

These are soft-boiled eggs cooked in their shells until the white is firm but the yolk soft. Bring a pan of water to the boil then gently lower the eggs into the water and simmer for 5–6 minutes. Remove the egg from the pan with a slotted spoon and plunge them into a bowl of cold water for a minute. Tap them lightly with the back of a knife to make them easier to shell, then rinse under cold water.

Re-heat in a pan of hot water for 3–5 minutes before using. They can be arranged on a bed of cooked spinach, covered with Béchamel Sauce (see page 83) and then baked.

OEUFS FRITS
Fried eggs

Fried eggs are usually cooked gently in a lightly greased frying pan until the whites are firm and lightly browned underneath. Alternatively, pre-heat the oven to gas mark 4, 350°F (180°C) and separate the eggs. For each person, add ½ teaspoon butter and ½ teaspoon water (to prevent the whites from browning) to a small round cast iron or enamel dish and sprinkle with a little salt. Heat over a medium heat then add the egg whites and place in the oven for about 2 minutes; the top should remain soft. Sprinkle with a few drops of red wine vinegar then slide in the egg yolks on top. Return to the oven for a further 2 minutes. Season to taste.

OEUFS MIROIR
Shirred eggs

Also known as *Oeufs au Plat* and *Oeufs sur le Plat*, shirred eggs are broken into a buttered flameproof dish then basted with either plain butter or browned cooked butter, herbs, cream or cheese, or they can be broken on to a bed of softly cooked vegetables. Cook them under a hot grill for about 3½ minutes until the white is just softly set and the yolk still liquid.

Note
A more sophisticated version is prepared when you separate yolks and white. Pour a little butter and a drop of oil into a flameproof dish, sprinkle with salt and heat on top of the stove for a minute. Add the egg whites then bake in a medium oven for 1½ minutes. Sprinkle with salt and wine vinegar then add the egg yolks and bake for 2 minutes. Serve with *Mouillettes* of bread sprinkled with chopped herbs (see page 68). It is complicated, but you are sure that the egg white is firm and that the egg yolk is moist but warm.

OEUFS BROUILLÉS
Scrambled eggs

Scrambled eggs are made by beating whole eggs with salt and pepper and just enough water to blend. Pour most of the mixture into a lightly buttered pan and cook over a low heat for about 5 minutes, stirring slowly and continuously with a wooden spoon. When the eggs begin to scramble and thicken, pour in the reserved egg with your chosen seasonings: cream, butter, chopped fresh herbs, chopped ham, grated cheese or chopped mushrooms and heat through gently. Remove from the heat and keep stirring until the mixture is slightly thinner than you prefer, as the eggs will continue to cook off the heat. Scrambled eggs can be prepared 15-20 minutes in advance, covered and kept in a warm place. They should be highly seasoned and remain creamy.

The regional version is called *Brouillade* (see page 110).

---------- **BURGUNDY** ----------

OEUFS EN MEURETTE

Eggs in wine sauce

A potent Burgundian dish, this makes a spirited lunch if you serve it with an endive or dandelion tossed salad. It also makes a lovely starter for dinner. The sauce improves if it is prepared in advance and re-heated.

------------ *Serves 4* ------------

FOR THE SAUCE
1 quantity Sauce Meurette (see page 82)
1 teaspoon sugar
salt and freshly ground black pepper

FOR THE CROÛTONS
2 tablespoons butter
1 tablespoon oil
3 slices bread, cut into triangles
2 cloves garlic, halved

FOR THE EGGS
1 tablespoon red wine vinegar
4 eggs

TO SERVE
3 tablespoons chopped fresh flat-leaved parsley

Prepare the Sauce Meurette. Season to taste with sugar, salt and pepper.

Bring a wide saucepan of water to the boil and add the vinegar. Do not add salt as this will prevent the whites from coagulating. When the water is boiling vigorously, break each egg into a ladle and slide it into the hot water in one quick movement so that the white coagulates at once around the yolk. When all the eggs are in the water, lower the heat and simmer for 3 minutes.

Meanwhile, prepare the Croûtons. Heat the butter and oil in a frying pan and sauté the bread on both sides until crisp. Remove from the pan and rub on both sides with the garlic.

Remove the poached eggs from the pan with a slotted spoon and trim any extra bits of egg white with scissors. Place the eggs on a warmed serving dish, spoon over the hot sauce and garnish with the Croûtons. Serve sprinkled with the parsley. Or else place the eggs on top of the Croûtons and spoon the sauce over.

GÂTEAU DE FOIES DE VOLAILLES

Chicken liver custard

One of the great traditions of Lyon is that of the *mères*: those formidable women who helped create the city's reputation for gastronomy. In the late nineteenth and early twentieth century, women used to take in paying guests. Little by little, these *mères* started restaurants which served the same hearty home cooking but with a definite touch of refinement. The names of the women are still reflected in the names of Lyonnais restaurants – *Mère Guy*, *Mère Fillioux*, *Chez Lea*, *Chez Paulette* and, one of the last great *mère* restaurants which still has a woman at the helm, *Mère Brazier*. Jacquotte Brazier keeps up the traditional dishes – *poularde demideuil*, *fonds d'artichauts au fois gras* and *gâteau de foies de volailles*. In Lyon, these custards are often cooked in individual ramekins and turned out on a small plate with the tomato sauce poured round.

———— *Serves 6–8* ————

1 lb 2 oz (500 g) chicken livers
5 eggs
17 fl oz (500 ml) single cream
a pinch of freshly grated nutmeg

a few sprigs of fresh parsley, finely
  chopped
salt and freshly ground black pepper
1 quantity Coulis de Tomates (see
  page 89)

Pre-heat the oven to gas mark 4, 350°F (180°C) and butter a 2½ pint (1.5 litre) soufflé dish.

Put all the ingredients, except the *Coulis de Tomates*, in a food processor, seasoning generously, and process until smooth. If you do not have a food processor, mince or chop the livers as finely as possible. Beat the eggs, add the cream then add the livers and the remaining ingredients. Pour the mixture into the prepared soufflé dish and stand the dish in a baking tray filled with 1 inch (2.5 cm) of water. Cook in the oven for about 50 minutes until the custard is firm and a skewer inserted in the centre comes out clean. Serve it warm but not piping hot, with the *Coulis de Tomates*.

OEUFS EN COCOTTE

Baked eggs

For the simplest of starters, you can break one or two eggs per person into a little buttered *cocotte* – an individual pottery or china ramekin – and cover the top with cream before baking until the yolks are lukewarm and creamy and the whites lightly set. You may also like to spread cooked shallots, mushrooms or thinly sliced Gruyère cheese in the bottom before you add the egg and sprinkle the tops with minced fresh herbs, or a little cream, or any of the following sauces before baking: *Soubise* (see page 84), *Coulis de Tomates* (see page 89), Béchamel (see page 83) or Mornay (see page 85).

——————— *Serves 4* ———————

2 tablespoons butter
4 tablespoons single cream
4 eggs

salt and freshly ground black pepper
a pinch of freshly grated nutmeg
2 tablespoons minced fresh chives

Pre-heat the oven to gas mark 5, 375°F (190°C) and use a little of the butter to grease 4 ramekin dishes. Place them in a deep ovenproof dish and add enough water to come half way up the dishes. Bake in the oven for 5 minutes.

Warm the cream. Pour it into the ramekins and break the eggs carefully on top. Sprinkle with salt, pepper, nutmeg and chives and dot with the remaining butter. Bake in the oven for about 15 minutes until the egg whites are milky-coloured.

OMELETTES

Rolled omelettes

There are many types of omelettes. The flat, thick vegetable omelettes are served in the country. Soufflé omelettes are generally only eaten for dessert. They are stuffed with jam, fruits, ice-cream or custard. The creamy, *baveuse*, 'rolled' omelette is a dish served mainly in restaurants and by the Parisians.

A rolled omelette is a quick dish to prepare. The eggs must not be beaten for too long; just enough for the yolks and whites to be lightly blended. The frying pan must be smooth with round edges so it is easy to roll the omelette on to the plate. It must be light so you can handle it easily and it should not be sticky, so it is better not washed but rubbed clean with kitchen paper and rough salt. If you must wash it, it should be dried carefully then lightly oiled.

——————— *Serves 2* ———————

1 tablespoon butter	*2 tablespoons cream, milk or water*
2 teaspoons oil	*salt and freshly ground black pepper*
4 eggs	

This soft, creamy rolled omelette is easy to prepare once you have done two or three. The size is important. The best rolled omelettes are made with a 7 inch (23 cm) frying pan with 3 to 4 eggs or a 10 inch (25 cm) frying pan with 6 to 8 eggs. It is always better to make several rolled omelettes rather than one large one, since cooking an omelette takes only a few minutes. The trick is to cook the omelette over a high heat and to use a frying pan made of stainless steel, enamel, treated aluminium or the old ⅛ inch (5 mm) thick French type of black plain iron. In a good pan, the omelette will slide easily without sticking to the bottom.

Heat the butter and the oil over a high heat and tilt the pan so that the bottom and sides of the pan are well coated. Break the eggs into a bowl, whisk in the cream, milk or water and season with salt and pepper. When the butter begins to foam, pour the eggs into the pan. They should seize immediately and make few bubbles. Stir with the flat of a fork for about 10 seconds until the egg begins to set. Pull the set edges to the centre, tipping the uncooked egg to the sides for about 30 seconds until lightly set. Hold the handle of the pan in one hand, flip over the side of the omelette closest to you with a fork, and tip the pan away from you. Place the lip of the pan on the serving plate, tilt both the pan and plate then turn the frying pan upside down so that the omelette rolls on to the plate with the seam underneath. Serve at once. The rolled omelette is never prepared for more than 2 or 3 persons.

Note

Omelettes may be stuffed with anchovies; asparagus tips; cubes of stale bread sautéed in butter; leftover rice; grated cheese; thick cream; diced, cooked or cured raw ham; sautéed and sliced goose or chicken livers; mushrooms; steamed mussels; cooked onions; diced, sautéed potatoes and herbs; prawns; poached scallops; cooked sorrel; truffles; chopped tomatoes; chopped walnuts and herbs.

OMELETTE AUX FINES HERBES

Herb omelette

The most popular of rolled omelettes.

2 eggs	*1 tablespoon groundnut oil*
pinch salt	*2 teaspoons fresh chervil, parsley,*
freshly ground black pepper	*tarragon and chives, cut finely*
1 tablespoon butter	*with scissors*

—————— *Serves 1* ——————

Mix the eggs, salt and pepper and beat together for a few seconds. Melt the butter and oil over a high heat and tilt the pan so that the bottom and sides of the pan are well coated. When the butter begins to foam, pour the eggs into the pan. They should seize immediately and make few bubbles. Stir with the flat of a fork for about 10 seconds until the egg begins to set. Add half the minced herbs and cook until the omelette is lightly browned on the base and lightly set and creamy on the inside. Hold the handle of the pan in one hand, flip over the side of the omelette closest to you with a fork, and tip the pan away from you. Place the lip of the pan on the serving plate, tilt both the pan and plate then turn the frying pan upside down so that the omelette rolls on to the plate with the seam underneath. Sprinkle with the remaining herbs and serve at once.

OMELETTES DE CAMPAGNE
Flat omelettes

Flat, open-faced omelettes look like plump pancakes. Prepared in the morning, they used to be given to school children and farm workers for their lunch. I find flat omelettes fresher and lighter – not least because they use half the number of eggs – than the classical rolled omelettes and they are wonderful when a great number of guests are expected. They can be made very large, and can be served warm or cold.

They are prepared with grated courgettes; chopped leeks; slivered peppers; drained tomatoes; sliced onions; chopped olives; capers and anchovies; sliced artichoke hearts; peas; chopped spinach; sorrel; or Swiss chard. And for a more substantial dish, use grated potatoes or potatoes mixed with onions and diced bacon. *Omelettes de Campagne* are a must for picnics and buffets in the summer.

SPINACH OMELETTE

I usually use frozen leaf spinach for this omelette. It's a great saving of time and I find both the texture and taste very good.

———— *Serves 4* ————

2 tablespoons oil
1 tablespoon butter
1 small onion, grated
3 eggs
10 oz (275 g) frozen leaf spinach,
  squeezed
2 tablespoons chopped fresh parsley

2 oz (50 g) Gruyère or Parmesan
  cheese, grated
pinch freshly grated nutmeg
salt and freshly ground black pepper

TO SERVE
olive oil or softened butter

Heat the oil and butter and fry the onion for 1 minute. Pour the eggs, spinach, parsley, cheese, nutmeg, salt and pepper into a bowl and beat lightly. Pour the mixture on top of the onion in the hot frying pan. Cook for about 5 minutes over a medium heat, stirring lightly from the sides to the centre, until the base is set and golden.

Place a plate on top of the pan and, holding it firmly against the pan, invert it so that the omelette falls upside-down on to the plate. Add a little more oil to the pan, if needed. Slide the raw side of the omelette into the frying pan and cook for 1–2 minutes. Sprinkle with a drop of olive oil or a dot of softened butter to serve.

Note

You may like to fry 2 oz (50 g) diced streaky bacon or cured ham until crisp, drain it then add it to the egg and spinach mixture.

COURGETTE OMELETTE

You need to use firm courgettes for this recipe.

———————— *Serves 4* ————————

2 tablespoons oil
1 tablespoon butter
5 courgettes, unpeeled, coarsely
    grated
1 clove garlic, chopped
5 eggs

salt and freshly ground black pepper

TO SERVE
1 tablespoon chopped fresh parsley
    or mint (optional)
softened butter or olive oil (optional)

Heat 1 tablespoon of the oil and the butter and cook the courgettes and garlic for about 10 minutes until soft, stirring with a wooden spoon. Drain them carefully. Put the eggs, salt and pepper together in a bowl and beat lightly then add the cooked courgette mixture. Heat the remaining tablespoon of oil, pour in the egg and courgette mixture and cook over a low heat for 4 minutes. Place a plate on top of the pan and, holding it firmly against the pan, invert it so that the omelette falls upside-down on to the plate. Add a little more oil to the pan, if needed. Slide the raw side of the omelette into the frying pan and cook for a further 2 minutes. Alternatively, cook the first side of the omelette then place the omelette under a grill to cook the top before sliding on to a plate to serve. Sprinkle with the chopped parsley or mint and a dot of softened butter or olive oil, if liked.

TOMATO OMELETTE

I never peel tomatoes because I like the crunchy skin, but you may prefer to do so.

———————— *Serves 4* ————————

1 tablespoon groundnut oil
1 onion, peeled and grated
1 clove garlic, peeled and sliced
3 ripe tomatoes, seeded and diced
1 teaspoon plain flour
1 teaspoon dried or 2 teaspoons
  chopped fresh thyme
salt and freshly ground black pepper

5 eggs, beaten
1 tablespoon olive oil

TO SERVE
1 tablespoon chopped fresh parsley
  or basil
few drops olive oil

Heat the groundnut oil in a frying pan. Add the onion, garlic and tomatoes, and sprinkle with the flour, thyme, salt and pepper. Cook over a medium heat for 10 minutes. Beat the eggs in a bowl then add the hot mixture to the eggs. Then proceed as for the previous recipe.

Note

With firm, fleshy tomatoes, there is no need to cook them. You can add raw, seeded and thinly sliced tomatoes to finely grated raw onion and eggs and proceed as above.

ONION OMELETTE

Follow the recipe above, replacing the tomatoes with 3 sliced onions and 2 cloves cooked until soft. Discard the cloves and add the onions to the beaten eggs with a little salt and pepper.

POTATO OMELETTE

Diced potatoes, diced pieces of streaky bacon and grated onion should be sautéed until crisp then flavoured with 2 tablespoons of chopped fresh chives or parsley and added to the beaten eggs for a plump, hearty flat omelette.

──────── **BASQUE COUNTRY** ────────

PIPERADE

Basque pepper omelette

This is *the* Basque omelette. The word *piperade* comes from the dialect word for red pepper, *piper*. Generally it is a flat pepper and tomato omelette, but sometimes Piperade is a soft scrambled egg mixture which is served with warm cured ham. I have also seen it prepared like a moist rolled omelette stuffed with cooked peppers and tomatoes. The following creamy egg and vegetable purée is supposed to be the authentic recipe.

──────── *Serves 4* ────────

4 tablespoons olive and groundnut oil or half goose fat and half oil
2 lb (900 g) large tomatoes, skinned, seeded and chopped
1 large red pepper, seeded and chopped
1 green pepper, seeded and chopped
a pinch of cayenne pepper or 1 tiny chilli pepper, seeded and chopped
2 onions, chopped
2 cloves garlic, crushed

1 sprig fresh thyme or 2 teaspoons dried thyme
2 bay leaves
1 tablespoon chopped fresh parsley
salt and freshly ground black pepper
7 eggs, beaten
1 tablespoon butter
2 tablespoons goose fat or 3 tablespoons olive oil
4 thin slices cured Bayonne or prosciutto ham, cut into thin slivers.

Heat 3 tablespoons of the oil in a frying pan and sauté the tomatoes, peppers, cayenne pepper or chilli pepper, onions, garlic and herbs. Simmer gently for about 45 minutes to 1 hour until most of the liquid has evaporated and the mixture becomes thick and unctuous. Season with salt and a little cayenne pepper to taste.

Purée in a food processor or blender or rub through a sieve. Return the mixture to the pan and simmer gently, uncovered, until reduced to about 1¼ pints (750 ml). Leave to cool.

Heat the remaining oil in a frying pan. Pour in the vegetable mixture and bring to the boil over a medium heat, stirring. Add the eggs and stir the mixture in a circular motion with a wooden spoon, working from the edges of the pan to the centre until the eggs are creamy but firm. Taste and season to taste with salt and pepper and stir in the butter.

Meanwhile, heat the goose fat or oil and fry the ham.

Arrange the creamy Piperade in a shallow, warm serving platter and place the ham on top.

Note
Stoned black olives are sometimes added at the last minute. The ham can also be served on a separate plate, sliced or cut into slivers and sautéed.

*B*ROUILLADE AUX *C*ÈPES

Creamy mushroom scrambled eggs

A *Brouillade* is a southern version of scrambled eggs. It should be creamy yet thick enough to be eaten with a fork. I like to prepare *Brouillade* with chopped olives or *Tapenade*, or finely chopped anchovy fillets. In Poudenas, Gascony, Marie-Claude Gracia prepared a luscious *Brouillade* with *cèpes*, using the finely chopped stems to make the *Brouillade* and the sliced caps to decorate it. I have added garlic and parsley to her recipe, since we usually have to use plain button or creamy field musrooms which are more readily available and less expensive than *cèpes*.

——————— *Serves 4* ———————

8 eggs
2 tablespoons single cream
salt and freshly ground black or
  white pepper
2 tablespoons butter
1 tablespoon groundnut oil
8 mushrooms, diced

2 mushrooms, sliced
1 small clove garlic, crushed
2 teaspoons chopped fresh parsley

TO SERVE
thin slices of toast

Break the eggs into a bowl and beat them with a fork for 1 minute. Add the cream, season and beat for a further 1 minute.

Melt ½ tablespoon of the butter and the oil and fry the diced mushrooms for 1 minute then transfer them into a side dish and reserve. Sauté the sliced mushrooms then transfer them into a side dish and reserve.

Heat the remaining butter in a frying pan and pour in the beaten eggs. Whisk them in a steady movement from the edges of the pan to the centre over a medium heat for a few minutes until the mixture is smooth and creamy but still fairly liquid. Remove from the heat. Stir in the diced mushrooms, garlic and parsley and return to a high heat for a few seconds, stirring until the mixture has the consistency of a thick custard. Pour into a warm shallow dish or individual dishes, arrange the sliced mushrooms on top in a star pattern and serve at once with thinly sliced toast.

SALADS

Les Salades

• •

Whether it is in the provinces or in Paris, at home or in restaurants, most meals in France have always included salads, and today more than ever, green tossed salads and mixed salads are very much part of the scene. Mixed salads, in particular, have become immensely fashionable in the last few years because of their imaginative and playful mingling of ingredients. In fact, they have been named *salades folles*, mad salads, for the unlimited variety of ingredients which were tossed together.

Whether they are wildly inventive or sensibly down to earth and prepared with whatever ingredients are to hand, mixed salads, *salades composées*, are reliable friends that can be served as starters or as a meal in themselves.

In the best restaurants and at elegant dinner parties, you will find elaborate affairs enriched with preserved goose or duck livers, lobster, scallops, raw or smoked salmon or truffles. For a more simple dish, you may find they include country sausages, smoked herrings, haddock, ham or cheese. Warm or cold slivers of meat fish or shellfish, all trimmed to perfection, make tasty additions, and there is no end to the range of vegetables or pulses you can include: potatoes, leeks, green beans, raw spinach, beetroot, cour-gettes, mushrooms, peppers, shredded cabbage, raw purple arti-chokes or cooked globe artichokes, crisp spring onions, sliced red onions, fennel roots, celery stalks, lentils or chickpeas. Even fruits find their way into the repertoire to offer a surprising counter-point.

I have selected a few exciting mixed salads, all based on well-proven combinations of flavours and textures. I hope they will inspire you to create your own personal versions.

Above: A farm in the Pyrenees

Overleaf: SALADE LYONNAIS (*see page 113*)

SALADE LYONNAISE

Rich mixed salad from Lyon

An excellent *Salade Lyonnaise* was served to me by the owner of one of Lyon's best-loved establishments. Café des Fédérations. Raymond Fulchiron explained that his *Salade* was the essence of simplicity: just salad, lardons, croûtons, vinaigrette and a perfectly poached egg. It can be enriched with chicken livers, Croûtons, shredded bacon, pieces of herring, anchovy fillets, beef tongue, country sausages, boiled potatoes, poached or hard-boiled eggs, pickled herrings or fresh herbs. An exuberant dish, it is always highly seasoned.

——————— *Serves 4* ———————

6 handfuls of fresh greens such as
*   curly endives, lamb's lettuce,*
*   young dandelion leaves, romaine*
*   lettuce*
6 oz (175 g) streaky bacon
2 slices country bread
2 cloves garlic, halved
1 tablespoon red wine vinegar
4 eggs

FOR THE VINAIGRETTE
2 tablespoons red wine vinegar
5 tablespoons olive oil
1 tablespoon Dijon mustard
1 tablespoon chopped fresh chives,
*   tarragon, parsley or chervil*
salt and freshly ground black pepper

Wash and trim the greens and tear them into bite-sized pieces.

Cut the bacon into pieces about 1 × 2 inches (2.5 × 5 cm) and grill until crisp. Toast the bread then rub it lightly with the garlic on both sides and cut it into 1 inch (2.5 cm) strips. Whisk together all the vinaigrette ingredients until well blended.

Bring a saucepan of water with the wine vinegar to a rolling boil. Break the eggs into a bowl then carefully slide them into the boiling water so that the bubbles shape the whites neatly. Simmer for about 4 minutes so the whites are firm and the yolks still runny. Remove from the water and trim away any untidy bits of white.

Arrange greens in a salad bowl, add the bacon and Croûtons, pour over the vinaigrette and toss. Arrange the eggs on top. Serve.

Salade aux Foies Chauds

Green tossed salad with sautéed chicken or duck livers

Marie-Claude Gracia lives in Poudenas, a tiny village in the Gers, in a house fronted by a bed of fresh herbs and a large verbena. The village has a church, a castle and a small town hall where Marie-Claude's husband works as the mayor. A singing creek rushes through the mill which has been converted into a charming hotel. Surrounding the village are fields of corn, which is grown partly to feed the ducks and geese which are the pride of the region, next to fields of large cows with thick, bent horns.

Marie-Claude prepares duck in every possible way: duck stew with crisp *Cruchade*, corn pudding; crunchy *Confit*; grilled pieces of duck carcass, *Demoiselles*; and *Frittons Pâtés*. Her desserts are equally interesting: luscious *Millas*, a custard flavoured with armagnac and prunes; silky *Pots à la Crème* flavoured with verbena leaves; and light crêpes flavoured with aniseed and bitter orange.

When I asked her for a truly simple dish she prepared the following recipe with gusto. Whether it is done with duck, goose or chicken livers it makes a delicious dish. Marie-Claude uses her own fragrant Prune Vinegar for the recipe. It is delicious and keeps indefinitely. The prunes can be used to accompany a stuffed, boiled chicken or a *pot au feu*.

———— *Serves 4* ————

FOR THE PRUNE VINEGAR
10 fl oz (300 ml) good red wine
   vinegar
4 oz (100 g) sugar
freshly grated nutmeg
few peppercorns
pinch of ground cinnamon
8 oz (225 g) prunes, stoned

FOR THE SALAD
8 chicken livers or 2 duck livers
1 tablespoon butter (optional)

salt and freshly ground black pepper
1 batavia or escarole lettuce
few chervil leaves
1 tablespoon groundnut oil
1 pear, peeled, cored and thickly
   sliced
1 shallot, coarsely chopped
1 tablespoon armagnac
1 tablespoon Prune Vinegar or red
   wine vinegar
2 tablespoons olive oil

To make the Prune Vinegar, place all the ingredients in a saucepan and bring to the boil. Remove from the heat and leave to cool. Bring back to the boil 4 times. Strain the vinegar through a sieve into a screw-top bottle.

Trim the livers and pat them dry. If you are using duck livers, you do not need any fat. If you are using chicken livers, melt the butter in a frying pan. Sauté the livers for 4–5 minutes, turning them gently with a wooden spoon until they are golden brown on all sides but remain pink inside. Remove from the heat and sprinkle with salt and coarsely ground pepper. Discard the fat.

Wash, trim and dry the lettuce and tear it into bite-sized pieces. Place little piles of lettuce on individual plates and sprinkle with chervil leaves.

Heat a frying pan, add the groundnut oil and cook the pear slices for 1–2 minutes until soft. Add the shallot and the livers and cook for a further 2 minutes. Pour the armagnac into the pan and stir so that the livers are coated with the juices. Remove the livers from the pan, cut them into thick slices and arrange them on top of the greens. Arrange the pears around the edge and scatter the shallots on top. Add the Prune or wine vinegar to the hot pan, stir well, then pour it over the salad. Sprinkle with the olive oil, salt and pepper and serve.

Note
Thin slivers of cured Bayonne ham or sliced duck breast can be added to the salad and walnut oil can be used instead of olive oil.

FOIE GRAS

In 2500 BC, Egyptians were already busy force-feeding geese with figs, and Ancient Romans, too, enjoyed fattened geese and their livers. But the idea of force-feeding is even older. Geese preparing for their long migration flight south, have always eaten as much as they can gorge.

Force-fed ducks and geese are turned into *Confit* (see page 183), *Magrets* (see page 160), *Grillons* (see page 178), and mostly silky smooth and exquisite *foie gras* – duck or goose liver.

Regional Variations

Although the south-west and Alsace remain the centre of production for *foie gras*, it is preserved in different ways in different regions. In Alsace, they prefer to season goose liver with spices. In the south-west, they use duck liver and marinate it with salt, pepper and brandy – preferably armagnac – giving a sweeter and nuttier taste. Many other regions, such as Burgundy and the Auvergne, are now raising ducks and geese and preparing their own *foie gras*. Even in Brittany, where lambs used to nibble the left-over apples after the cider-making season, duck and geese have now taken their place.

Buying and Storing *Foie Gras*

In the last few years, *foie gras* has become immensely popular. It is sold uncooked (*frais*) and half-cooked (*mi-cuit*), but mostly preserved in sterilised jars (*en conserve*). It is expensive because breeding is a long process and because *foie gras* loses half of its weight when it is cooked.

A *foie gras cru, or frais*, fresh uncooked liver, weighs about 1–1½ lb (450–675 g) for a goose, a little less for a duck, and may be sold vacuum packed. It can be refrigerated for 3 weeks.

A *foie gras mi-cuit*, or *semi-conserve*, barely cooked, is always of the finest quality and has been pasteurised at 200°C (400°F). It is sold vacuum packed, in a terrine or jar, or wrapped in foil and shaped as a roll. It can be refrigerated for up to 8 months.

Preserved *foie gras* can be prepared in a variety of ways, all governed by strict rules. A perfect slice of *foie gras* should be of a uniform colour since it must come from the same liver and must have been gently cooked. Today, *foie gras* is sold in a number of different categories which cover a range of both prices and quality. The labels must indicate all the ingredients and you should read them carefully so that you know what you are buying.

Foie gras d'oie on a label indicates that the jar contains liver from force-fed, fattened geese. It is a much finer quality of liver than *foie d'oie* which comes from ordinary goose livers.

Foie gras entier is a raw, whole force-fed goose liver – including both the large and small lobes of the liver in one piece – lightly seasoned and sold fresh or *en conserve*, preserved in a jar or a terrine. Only truffles may be added to this.

Foie gras de canard ou d'oie is 100 per cent liver made of agglomerated entire lobes of liver.

Bloc de foie gras is made of 50 per cent fattened duck liver or 35 per cent goose liver in chunks mixed with blended liver.

Parfait de foie is lesser quality, made with unfattened and imperfect livers. It is 50 per cent *foie gras* wrapped with forcemeat made with ordinary chicken, veal or pork liver.

Mousse or purée de foie are made with ordinary duck or goose livers rather than force-fed duck or goose livers.

Galantine, *médaillon* and *pâté* are prepared with veal, chicken or pork forcemeat wrapped around 35 per cent of real goose or duck liver, not necessarily liver from force-fed birds.

Serving *Foie Gras*

Cold *foie gras* can be sliced or cut into chunks and scattered over a green salad. Don't use plain red wine vinegar for a dressing as it will ruin the *foie gras*'s delicate flavour. Make a fruit vinegar with a fine red wine vinegar, nutmeg, clove, sugar and fresh fruits all slowly reduced. It will taste sweet and just a little acid.

Preserved *foie gras* itself is traditionally served as a starter with warm toast, sliced brioche or baguette which should *not* be buttered. It is accompanied by a sweet dessert wine, a Pineau de Charentes or champagne. In the south-west, many people go against the grain and choose a vigorous Bordeaux red or a hearty Madiran wine, while in Alsace they like to serve a mellow Alsatian wine. *Foie gras* is *the* festive treat in France.

SYMPHONIE DE CHAMPIGNONS DE COUCHE

Symphony of cultivated mushrooms

Champignons de Paris, white mushrooms, acquired their name because they used to be cultivated in the Paris area. Now, a large proportion of them are grown deep in the dark, mysterious tunnels that connect the tufa caves scattered throughout the Loire valley.

Monsieur Robert Meyer of Meyerchampi in St Paterne Racan supplies one of the best restaurateurs in the region, who in turn created this dish in honour of the magestic fungi. Jean Bardet usually uses red oyster mushrooms as well as grey ones, but as they are not readily available, I've substituted chestnut mushrooms. The important thing is to have a variety of flavours and textures which contrast with the peppery taste of the rocket.

Serves 6

8 oz (225 g) grey oyster mushrooms
8 oz (225 g) shiitake mushrooms
8 oz (225 g) chestnut mushrooms
8 oz (225 g) white mushrooms
4 oz (100 g) butter
salt and freshly ground black pepper

2 shallots, finely chopped
7 fl oz (200 ml) chicken stock
1 handful small celery leaves,
*   coarsely chopped*
1 bunch rocket

Wipe or wash the mushrooms carefully, making sure you do not soak them in water. Melt half the butter in a large frying pan. When it starts to foam, throw in the mushrooms in the following order: oyster, shiitake, chestnut and finally white. Sauté them until golden, stirring continuously. Season with salt and pepper, add the shallots and stir until well coated. Pour in the stock, bring to the boil then add the celery leaves. Reduce the heat and add the remaining butter a little at a time, making sure the sauce does not boil. Adjust the seasoning if necessary. Divide the rocket between individual plates, spoon the mushrooms and sauce over the top and serve warm.

──── **SAVOIE AND DAUPHINE** ────

SALADE AU GRUYÈRE ET AUX NOIX

Green salad with Gruyère cheese and walnuts

This dish is from Savoie, where Gruyère cheese, cream, country ham and superb walnuts abound. The quality of the cheese, the freshness of the walnuts and the crispness of the greens are all-important. It is often served as a main course for a 'ladies' luncheon' or a light summer dinner.

──────── *Serves 4* ────────

FOR THE DRESSING
2 tablespoons red wine vinegar
1 tablespoon Dijon mustard
4 tablespoons olive oil
2 tablespoons single cream
salt and freshly ground black pepper

FOR THE SALAD
1 lb (450 g) Gruyère cheese

1 curly endive, romaine, or escarole lettuce
4 shallots, finely chopped
2 tablespoons chopped fresh flat-leaved parsley, chives or tarragon
8 walnuts, halved
3 oz (75 g) cured ham such as Bayonne or prosciutto, slivered

Blend together the dressing ingredients in a bowl. Cut the cheese into thin sticks about 1 inch (1.5 cm) long, add to the bowl, stir and leave to stand for 30 minutes.

Wash and trim the greens and tear them into bite-sized pieces. Place in a large serving bowl and add the shallots, herbs, walnuts, ham, cheese and dressing. Toss well so that all the greens are well coated in the dressing. Serve with country bread.

Note

In the south-west, an interesting variation is made with Roquefort cheese and crisp slivers of chicory.

LES SALADES VERTES

Green salads

GREENS

The French eat a bowl of tossed green salad at least once a day throughout the year. Whether it is a simple lunch, an elegant dinner or a festive meal, a green salad is a healthy way of creating a pause after the main course to refresh the palate.

At home for an informal meal, the salad is often served on the same plate as the main meat or fish dish, or it may be served on a separate plate. Cheese usually comes later on its own plate. Recently, cheese and tossed lettuce are sometimes served together, although most people think the vinegar in the dressing kills the subtlety of the cheese.

The variety of greens is vast, and often several kinds are chosen for one salad, Little Gem, Webb's Wonder, radicchio, escarole, romaine, oak leaf, lamb's or long-leafed cos; rocket, watercress, young dandelion leaves, endive, tender spinach leaves, young Swiss chard are all popular. With its tasty, fleshy leaves, purslaine has become very fashionable. When chicory leaves are used, they are cut into small slices, seasoned and arranged standing up round the dish so that the other greens can be placed in the centre.

Trim and carefully rinse the greens twice under cold water then tear them into bite-sized pieces (one never uses a knife to prepare salad leaves). Wrap them in a tea towel and store them at the bottom of the refrigerator until you are ready to use them. (If they are to be kept longer than a day, store them in a punctured plastic bag.)

Serve green salads in a large, wide glass or china bowl so that you can toss them easily without bruising the leaves. The dressing and its garnish are poured into the bottom of the bowl with the serving fork and spoon crossed on top and the greens placed on them so that they do not touch the dressing. Bring the bowl to the table and toss lightly but thoroughly. We call this *fatiguer la salade*. A tossed salad cannot be kept for more than 30 minutes or it will turn soggy so discard any left-overs.

Dressings

You will need a little more than a tablespoon of dressing per person. The most common dressing in France is Vinaigrette. It can be prepared using olive oil, groundnut oil or walnut oil and a variety of vinegars. There are also other popular dressings: olive oil, lemon juice, Dijon mustard and freshly minced herbs tastes delicious with endive, chicory or watercress. In Provence, *mesclun*, a mixture of very young wild greens, is served with olive oil, vinegar and garlic *Chapons* (see page 68). Bitter greens such as endive, rocket, tender spinach leaves and dandelion leaves are best seasoned with warm red wine vinegar, crisp bacon and garlic-flavoured bread crusts (*Chapons*). Single cream seasoned with lemon juice, salt and pepper makes a delicate dressing.

Garnishes

Choose a few from this list:

1 tablespoon coarsely chopped walnut halves;

2 hard-boiled egg whites, minced;

2 hard-boiled egg yolks, crumbled;

4 anchovy fillets, crushed;

3 cloves garlic, crushed;

3 shallots, finely chopped;

3 teaspoons Dijon mustard;

3 teaspoons crumbled Roquefort cheese;

3 teaspoons crumbled Roquefort cheese mashed with a little brandy and 3 teaspoons single cream;

a few Chapons (see page 68) rubbed with garlic;

Croûtons, oven-dried slivers of bread crust or bread rounds sprinkled with olive oil or fried in butter or oil and rubbed with garlic, if liked;

2 or 3 teaspoons of any of the following finely chopped fresh herb leaves: flat-leaved parsley, basil, mint, coriander, chives, savory, chervil, tarragon, dill, fennel leaves;

if you only have dried herbs, mix them with oil and vinegar at least 30 minutes before serving.

With any salad dressing, proportions of vinegar, garlic and oil depend on personal taste.

ROUSSILLON

Salade de Poivrons Rouges aux Anchois

Red pepper and anchovy salad

Collioure is a pretty Catalan harbour town on the threshold of Spain. Surrounded by green hills, it boasts a beautiful castle, dark cliffs overlooking the sea and terraced vineyards sloping down towards the water. There are two factories where the freshly-caught anchovies are cleaned and prepared in vinegar, brine or olive oil, hence most of the local dishes include anchovies in some form.

In Collioure, I met a family which symbolised the Catalan heritage. Monsieur Joseph Pous officiates at *Les Templiers*, a beautiful restaurant which was run by his parents before him. The bar is a splendid wooden carved boat shell, and the walls are covered with oil paintings and watercolours. Around the heavy wooden tables, *habitués* play cards and sip the velvety, local Banyuls wine. Monsieur Pous's son is a musician and plays the *sardane*, the slow local dance, while his wife runs a shop selling local crafts and also leads the *sardane* dance once a week. As I sat with him beneath the beamed ceiling of his beautiful bar, with a plate in front of us piled with sautéed *cèpes* and prawns, he recalled *pêle-mêle*, when Spanish Catalan resistance fighters walked across the border; the colony of painters, Matisse, Picasso, Dali, Marquet, Durain and Dufy, who lived in Collioure around the turn of the century; and mostly what it means in all aspects of life – politically, musically, gastronomically and emotionally – to be a Catalan today.

Later in the day we sat on his terrace overlooking the sea and ate this wonderful red pepper and anchovy salad. It was a lovely, warm evening and a couple of guitarists were playing and singing. They began with a native song, Charles Trénet's *sardane* about lazy evenings, then moved on to Gilbert Bécaud's song about Provençal marketplaces and finally to Louis Armstrong's melody about summertime in Dixieland. Somehow it all fitted together.

———————— *Serves 4* ————————

4 large fleshy red peppers
4 oz (100 g) fresh or tinned
   anchovy fillets in oil or vinegar
red wine vinegar or Banyuls wine
   vinegar (if using fresh
   anchovies)
2 hard-boiled eggs, peeled and
   quartered
8 black or green olives, stoned

FOR THE GARNISH
3 tablespoons finely chopped fresh
   flat-leaved parsley
2 garlic cloves, crushed
3 teaspoons olive oil
2 teaspoons red wine vinegar
salt and freshly ground black pepper

Pre-heat the oven to gas mark 6, 400°F (200°C).

Place the peppers on a baking sheet and cook in the oven for about 20 minutes, turning once or twice, until the skins are charred. Place in a plastic bag, close the top and leave for about 5 minutes. Remove from the bag, slide off the skins and remove the stem and seeds. Cut the flesh into triangles about 2 inches (5 cm) wide and 3 inches (7.5 cm) tall or into slivers.

If you are using fresh anchovies, marinate them in red wine vinegar or Banyuls wine vinegar for 24 hours. If you are using tinned fillets, drain, rinse and pat dry.

Arrange the anchovies and peppers on individual plates, alternating them so that they form a spiked pattern. Arrange the hard-boiled eggs and olives attractively on the plates.

To make the *persillade*, mix the parsley and garlic together, stir in the oil and wine vinegar and season with salt and pepper. Sprinkle over the salad and serve at room temperature with toasted bread.

Note
You can try adding a handful of sliced fennel bulb to this salad for a lovely texture.

Oysters

They have no mouth, no eyes, no nose. They start life as a male, turn female, then become male again if they live long enough. We have enjoyed these strange creatures for thousands of years. In 55 BC, after the Romans discovered the oysters in Brittany, they created oyster beds on the shores of Italy and offered as many as six dozen to each guest at their banquets. The latest modern record had the champion eating thirty-two dozen at one sitting.

The people of Brittany, Normandy, the Atlantic coast, Languedoc-Roussillon and Corsica have a love of oysters that has led to a prosperous oyster-farming industry in France, now Europe's foremost producer.

The quality of an oyster depends on where it flourishes, which is why oysters of a similar type often have different names, being called after the region from which they came. In fact, there are only two kinds of oyster: the round, flat Belon, which is by far the most exquisite today, and the hollow, craggier Portuguese or Japanese type. Bigger oysters are not tastier than small ones, yet they are priced according to their size. For cooking, it is better not to use the smaller ones since they will shrink a little under the heat.

Oyster Farms

It takes about four years of continuous care to develop a good oyster. The oyster farms are situated in calm waters where the sea bed is firm. Various supports made with shells, clay tiles and hollow tiles are created beneath the water so that the tiny *spat*, as small as a grain of sand, can cling to them and grow for about ten months into baby oysters. These are then stripped out and placed in basins where they are fed on plankton from the sea. Every year for four years they are moved to a new basin which supplies fresh water and protects them from predatory fish. During this time, each oyster filters from 2 to 12 pints (9 to 7 litres) of water a day. After four years the oysters are transferred to *claires*, huge clay oyster beds, from whence they are shipped to the markets. They can survive for about ten days out of water.

Choosing Oysters

Once, oysters were not eaten in the months without an 'r' – May to August, which is their breeding season. Summer Oyster are now available, but they tend not to have much flavour.

Oysters are graded according to size. In France, Portuguese oysters are graded as P (*petites*, or small), M (*moyennes*, or medium), G (*grosses*, or large) and TG (*très grosses*, or very large) while flat Belon oysters are graded from 000 (the largest) to 6 (the smallest). *Spéciales* are rich, meaty oysters. *Claires* have been reared in clay basins. In Britain, they are graded from 1 (the largest) to 4 (the smallest); tiny ones are known as 'buttons'.

Opening Oysters

To open oysters, use an oyster knife or a strong, short, pointed knife. Hold the oyster in your left hand wrapped in a thick oven glove or cloth. Insert the point of the knife blade between the shells next to the hinge and twist to prise the shell open. Cut the muscle of the animal from the shell and discard the top shell. Use the knife to loosen the muscle in the lower hollow shell. If removing the meat, tip it, with the juice, into a bowl. If serving on the half shell, leave the oysters on the bottom shell.

Serving Oysters

If you are serving oysters raw, only open them fifteen minutes before you serve them and place them on a bed of ice sprinkled with coarse salt or seaweed to prevent them slipping. Pepper and buttered bread are the ideal accompaniments; vinegar or shallots will kill the delicate flavours.

SALADE AU CHÈVRE

Goat cheese salad

This easy-to-prepare salad is prettier if served on individual plates.

———————— *Serves 4* ————————

FOR THE MARINATED CHEESE
3 × 4 oz (100 g) round goat cheeses
3–5 dried red chilli peppers
2–3 cloves garlic, peeled
3 bay leaves
2 sprigs fresh thyme
olive oil

FOR THE SALAD
4 handfuls romaine, batavia, lamb's
lettuce, endive, chicory or
watercress, or a mixture

FOR THE VINAIGRETTE
5 tablespoons olive or groundnut oil
or a mixture of walnut and
groundnut oils
1 tablespoon red wine vinegar
salt and freshly ground black pepper

If you like marinated cheese, you must prepare it in advance so you have it ready whenever you need it. Place a few ripe, firm, little round goat cheeses in a jar and sprinkle with the peppers, garlic, bay leaves and thyme. Cover with olive oil, seal the jar and keep in the refrigerator for a few days, a few weeks, up to 3 or 4 months, stirring delicately once or twice to make sure the herbs and oil coat the cheese thoroughly.

When you are ready to serve your *Salade au Chèvre*, wash, trim and dry the greens, tear them into bite-sized pieces and arrange on individual serving plates.

Drain the cheese, if you are using marinated cheese, reserving the flavoured oil, or use fresh cheese. Cut it horizontally into thick slices. Arrange on a buttered flameproof dish and place under a hot grill for a few minutes until soft (or place on a round of bread before cooking).

Whisk together all the vinaigrette ingredients. If you are using marinated cheese, stir in 1 or 2 tablespoons of the fragrant oil. Sprinkle the vinaigrette over the salad. Use a spatula to transfer the grilled cheese into the centre of the greens and serve at once.

MEATS

Les Viandes

• •

In France, butchers are educators. Their shop walls display the 'labels of quality', the varius grades of meats, the medals and prizes won by Charolais, Salers and Limousin cattle, and by Sisteron, Paulliac or pré-salé lamb. There are large coloured charts showing the various cuts of meat. What's more, butchers take time to explain why meat must be 'parsleyed' or 'marbled' – when the ivory fat and cherry red lean meat intermingle for a full flavour and a rich texture – and why lamb and beef need to be aged in a cold place to become *bien rassis,* to improve the taste and tenderness. They will explain why 'a good rest' after cooking is essential for a roast before carving so that all the juices will spread evenly. They emphasize how coarse sea salt (preferably from Brittany) and freshly crushed pepper (preferably coarse) must be sprinkled lightly before cooking and more generously after cooking. Appropriate recipes are offered, and ingenious advice given on what to do with left-overs. They may also offer very special gifts to improve a dish: a large veal bone for the *Sauté de Veau,* a piece of beef cheek for the stew, a few sprigs of parsley for the boiled beef. Chatty and dependable, butchers are pillars of society. And this is why, although we eat vast amounts of fresh vegetables, we remain a nation of meat-lovers. Meat in small quantities – a paper-thin slice of beef, a tiny lamb chop, a chicken wing – remain part of our daily diet.

Visitors are frequently baffled by the most popular dish in France, *le steak frites:* a pan-grilled steak served with potato chips. They are equally puzzled when they observe that rare meat remains a regular dish in the form of *Boeuf Tartare* or *Carpaccio,* and when they notice that Tournedos and fillet steaks are served simply pan-fried (so that none of the pan juices are lost), flavoured with a little parsley butter or a spoonful of a shallot-white wine (*Bercy*) or red wine (*Bordelaise*) sauce and sit happily alongside *Plats Mijotes,* the traditional long-simmered dishes.

For centuries, meat was rare and expensive and only the very rich could afford the prime cuts. Imagination and patience came to the rescue of the home cook: a pinch of herbs, a drop of wine, a teaspoon of brandy, a shallot or two, a leek, a carrot, a few soft

Opposite: SALADE AU CHÈVRE (*see page 126*)

A fisherman on the Loire

prunes, a handful of unpeeled garlic cloves would help this tough little piece of meat taste good and go a long way. And since cheap cuts were also the most flavoursome, miracles appeared in the form of pungent *daubes*, plump *paupiettes*, hearty *potées* and herb-stuffed lamb shoulder. Every last cut of the meat was treated with respect. While *foie gras* and puff pastry-covered *filet mignon* or truffle-studded leg of lamb were reserved for the most opulent tables, the rest of the nation was busy braising, stewing, stuffing, boiling and enjoying cheaper cuts.

Today, when robust flavours and serious food are back in fashion, every bistro boasts about its *morceaux du boucher* – the cheaper but tastier pieces butchers often keep for themselves: *onglet, poire, araignée, bavette*. These thin steaks are simply pan-fried with a few shallots and deglazed with a drop of wine to make an inexpensive but delicious treat. Starred restaurant chefs and home cooks both go back to traditional recipes, interpreted with a new choice of vegetables, of fresh herbs, home-made pasta or tiny Ratte or Charlotte potatoes. Luscious *blanquettes*, fresh *navarins*, sumptuous *parmentiers* remain popular but are now lighter and more pungent than in the past.

The following pages include a selection of my favourite meat dishes. I hope you will enjoy them and they will become yours.

*E*NTRECÔTE *B*ORDELAISE
Steak with marrow, shallots and wine

Bordeaux is an elegant city and an important port. The wines are clearly all-important, but I also tasted piles of fragrant *cèpes* seasoned with garlic and parsley, crisp *ventrèche* – and dainty caramelised *canelés* cakes.

The most famous speciality, however, remains *Entrecôte Bord-elaise*. The dish started with steak cooked on a fire of old wine barrels or grape vine cuttings, then garnished with shallots and wine. Simply prepared with wine and shallots, it is called *Marchand de Vin*; with marrow it becomes *Bordelais*. Some add a tablespoon of *Beurre Manié* and some redcurrant jelly to thicken the wine sauce. In the *Brasserie de Noailles*, Martial Dehaut was thickening his sauce with a piece of bitter chocolate and said that a great Bordeaux wine was not essential to the dish; what was needed was a good, natural wine with a high alcohol content. Since it is barely cooked, the meat must be of the best quality and the sauce short, pungent and powerful. I never prepare this dish for more than five or six guests and tend to use less butter than in classic recipes since I find the addition of marrow rich enough for the sauce. The shallot-herb-wine sauce can be prepared in advance and spooned over the steaks just before serving.

Serves 4

*4 lean steaks, each weighing 8 oz
    (225 g), trimmed*
3 tablespoons groundnut oil
salt and freshly ground black pepper

FOR THE SAUCE
3 oz (75 g) shallots, finely chopped
4 cloves garlic, chopped
*1 pint (600 ml) full-bodied, hearty
    red wine*
1 tablespoon cognac (optional)
1 bay leaf

1 sprig fresh thyme
pinch of freshly grated nutmeg
2 tablespoons red wine vinegar
5 fl oz (150 ml) beef stock or water
*2 teaspoons coarsely ground black
    pepper*
pinch of cayenne pepper
1 tablespoon cold butter

FOR THE MARROW
2–3 veal or beef marrow bones
   (optional)
coarse salt
5 teaspoons red wine vinegar

TO GARNISH
4 tablespoons fresh parsley or
   parsley and chives cut up with
   scissors

Rub the surface of the steaks with a little oil and season lightly with salt and pepper. Place on a plate, cover with cling film and refrigerate for a few hours.

Remove the steaks from the refrigerator an hour before you cook. Pat them dry with kitchen paper. Mix together the shallots, garlic, wine, cognac if using, bay leaf, thyme and nutmeg in a saucepan. Bring to the boil and boil, uncovered, for about 15 minutes until reduced by two-thirds. Strain, reserving both the shallot mixture and the liquid. Discard the herbs.

If you are using marrow bones, dip the ends of the bones into rough salt, wrap them in a piece of muslin and place in a pan of cold water with the wine vinegar. Bring to the boil then simmer for 10 minutes. Drain well and remove the muslin. Slide the blade of a knife inside the marrow bones and the marrow will slip out. Dice or slice the marrow.

Heat 1 tablespoon of the oil in a heavy-based frying pan until very hot then add the steaks and cook for 2 minutes on one side. Season with salt and pepper then turn on the other side and cook for a further 5 minutes. They should still be rare inside. Remove the steaks from the pan, spread half the shallot mixture over the steaks and cover with a lid.

Pour the wine vinegar into the hot pan, bring to the boil and boil for 2 minutes, scraping up the juices in the pan. Add the stock or water, return to the boil and simmer for a few minutes. Add the remaining shallot mixture and the cooking liquid, the pepper and cayenne, stir well and boil until reduced to about 10 fl oz (300 ml). Stir in the butter.

Heat the remaining oil in a separate pan and cook the steaks for about 3 minutes on each side. Sprinkle the diced marrow on top of the steaks and grill under a hot grill for 1 minute. Arrange the steaks on a warm serving platter, spoon over the sauce and serve at once, sprinkled with the parsley or parsley and chives.

PAUPIETTES DE BOEUF

Beef slices stuffed with vegetables and herbs

These stuffed beef rolls are often called *Alouettes sans Têtes* or 'headless larks' because of their plump shape. Each slice of beef is flattened, wrapped around a very fragrant filling and cooked in wine, herbs and vegetables. In the south-west, a few pine nuts, a pinch of saffron and cinnamon is added to give a Catalan touch.

Paupiettes are usually cooked in advance and kept in the refrigerator. The fat rises to the top and can easily be lifted off and discarded. Then you can remove the string and slowly re-heat them for about 20 minutes so they are easy to serve. They can be served with rice, noodles, sautéed mushrooms or glazed carrots.

Serves 4

10 × 10 cm (4 in) square thin
    slices lean chuck steak, eye of
    silverside or top round

FOR THE FILLING
2 tablespoons groundnut oil,
    groundnut and olive oil or goose
    fat
1 small onion, chopped
2 oz (50 g) lean streaky bacon or
    cured ham, chopped
2 oz (50 g) mushrooms, chopped
2 cloves garlic, crushed
1 teaspoon dried thyme
1 egg yolk, size 3
1/2 teaspoon ground bay leaves
pinch ground coriander
2 tablespoons finely chopped fresh
    parsley
1 teaspoon dried savory
2 oz (50 g) Gruyère cheese, grated

2 oz (50 g) frozen leaf spinach,
    thawed, chopped and drained
    thoroughly
salt and freshly ground black pepper
2 tablespoons groundnut oil
1 tablespoon unsalted butter
2 tablespoons plain flour
8 fl oz (250 ml) dry white wine
10 fl oz (300 ml) beef stock
a few coriander seeds, ground
pinch dried thyme
1 × 2 in (5 cm) strip orange rind
1 tomato, skinned and chopped
1 clove star anise
1 bouquet garni
5 carrots, sliced
2 onions, sliced
1 tablespoon Dijon mustard

TO SERVE
2 tablespoons chopped fresh parsley
    or basil

Place each slice of meat between 2 sheets of waxed paper and flatten it to about ⅛ in (3 mm) with a wooden mallet or rolling pin.

Heat the oil or fat and fry the onion over a moderate heat until softened. Add the bacon or ham and mushrooms and fry gently for a few minutes. Remove from the heat and stir in the garlic, thyme, egg yolk, ground bay leaves, coriander, parsley, savory, cheese and spinach and season with salt and pepper. Chop the mixture with a heavy knife or process in a food processor, blender or food mill.

Season the beef slices with salt and pepper. Spread a small spoonful of the filling on each slice, roll them up into neat cylinders about 1½ in (4 cm) wide and tie with string.

Heat the oil and butter until hot then add the *Paupiettes*, a few at a time if necessary, and fry for about 2 minutes until browned on all sides. Remove from the pan. Lower the heat, sprinkle with the flour and mix together. Pour in the wine and stock and stir until blended. Sprinkle with coriander and thyme, add the orange rind, tomato, star anise and bouquet garni. The liquid should just cover the meat. Bring to a simmer, cover and simmer for 1 hour.

Add the carrots and onions, cover and simmer for a further 30 minutes until the meat is tender. Discard the orange rind and bouquet garni, remove the string from the *Paupiettes* and stir in the mustard. Sprinkle with the chopped parsley or basil to serve.

Variation

Paupiettes may also be filled with a mixture of chopped ham, gherkins, tarragon, anchovies and diced pork cooked in goose fat with shallots, carrots and wine and sprinkled with fresh basil.

HACHIS PARMENTIER

Beef, parsley and garlic potato gratin

André Parmentier brought the potato plant from America in the eighteenth century and was a zealous promoter of the potato in French cuisine. *Hachis Parmentier* is usually made with the left-overs from *Pot au Feu* coarsely chopped, moistened with cooked onions, tomatoes, white wine and chopped parsley, covered with a light potato purée. *Hachis Parmentier* is an irresistible family dish: inexpensive and easy to prepare in advance. It is placed in the oven half an hour before sitting down to the meal and is welcomed by everyone from seven months to seventy-seven years.

I prepare *Hachis Parmentier* often and never wait for left-overs to appear. Ironically, I make it in vast quantities so it might itself make interesting left-overs to add to omelettes, to stuff courgettes or aubergines or to make into crisp croquettes.

In my version of the dish my secret weapon is an inordinate amount of parsley. Whether the top is covered with breadcrumbs, dotted with butter or olive oil, grated cheese or a beaten egg, there must be plenty of fragrant crust for everyone, so use one or two wide dishes for the *Hachis*. Serve with an endive, dandelion, watercress or chicory tossed salad.

———————— *Serves 4* ————————

FOR THE TOPPING
2 lb (900 g) potatoes
1 tablespoon butter
1 pint (600 ml) milk
salt and freshly ground black pepper
pinch freshly grated nutmeg

FOR THE FILLING
2 teaspoons groundnut oil
4 oz (100 g) lean streaky bacon,
   chopped
2 onions, chopped
2 bay leaves

2 teaspoons dried thyme
1 large bunch fresh flat-leaved
   parsley, basil or chives, chopped
2 cloves garlic, crushed
1½ lb (675 g) lean beef or left-over
   beef, chopped

TO FINISH
4 oz (100 g) Gruyère or Parmesan
   cheese, grated
2 tablespoons breadcrumbs
2 tablespoons butter

Wash the unpeeled potatoes, place them in a saucepan and cover with salted water. Bring to the boil and simmer for about 25 minutes until tender. Using a thick tea towel or oven gloves, peel the warm potatoes. Mash or purée them with the butter, gradually adding enough milk to make the mixture moist but not sticky. Season to taste with salt, pepper and nutmeg.

Pre-heat the oven to gas mark 4, 350°F (180°C). Butter one or two shallow ovenproof dishes.

Heat half the oil in a large frying pan and sauté the bacon for a few minutes until crisp. Add the onions, bay leaves and thyme and stir over a low heat for a few minutes. Add the parsley and garlic, stir well, then remove from the pan, discard the bay leaves and set aside.

Heat the remaining oil and sauté the beef for a few minutes, stirring it evenly so that it breaks up as it cooks. Stir in the bacon and onion mixture.

Spoon a thin layer of the potato purée into the prepared dish then add the meat and vegetable mixture. Spoon the rest of the potatoes on top and spread evenly with a fork. Sprinkle with grated cheese and breadcrumbs, dot with butter and bake in the oven for 30 minutes. If the top begins to brown too much, lower the oven temperature. Serve in the cooking dish wrapped in a tea towel and accompanied by a tossed green salad.

──── **THROUGHOUT FRANCE** ────

POCHE DE VEAU FARCIE

Stuffed veal breast

This is a lovely dish, quite inexpensive and easy to prepare. If you find veal breast hard to come by, you can use lamb's breast instead. Ask your butcher to remove all the bones and reserve them for the broth. The meat will look like a large pocket waiting to be stuffed. The filling can include fresh or frozen peas or tiny butter beans, Swiss chard or cabbage. Make sure there is plenty of flat-leaved parsley and garlic in your filling so that it is highly flavoured.

Poche de Veau looks a plump cusion and is served either warm or cold. Steamed vegetables, sautéed, diced potatoes, glazed carrots, plain rice, buttered noodles or a gratin of tomatoes and aubergines all make splendid accompaniments.

──────── *Serves 4–6* ────────

1 veal or lamb breast (about
    2 lb/900 g), boned

FOR THE STUFFING
2 tablespoons groundnut oil
2 spring onions or 1 onion, chopped
8 oz (225 g) lean streaky bacon,
    chopped
½ oz (15 g) frozen leaf spinach,
    chopped
7 tablespoons chopped fresh flat-
    leaved parsley
3 cloves garlic, chopped
1 egg
pinch of freshly grated nutmeg
4 tablespoons cold cooked rice
2 tablespoons grated Gruyère or
    Parmesan cheese (optional)
10 black, green or purple olives,
    stoned
2–3 tablespoons brandy

FOR THE BROTH
few veal bones
3 bay leaves
1 clove
green part of 1 spring onion or leek

FOR THE VEGETABLES
1 tablespoon groundnut oil
1 tablespoon butter
3 onions, sliced
5 carrots, sliced
3 spring onions
1 large fennel bulb, quartered
2 leeks, white part only, sliced
1 clove garlic, crushed

TO FINISH
1 tablespoon groundnut oil
1 tablespoon butter
4 fl oz (120 ml) dry white wine

FOR THE COLD SAUCE
2 tablespoons chopped fresh parsley
   or basil
1 teaspoon ground coriander
6 tablespoons olive oil
1 large tomato, skinned, seeded and
   chopped

salt and freshly ground black pepper

TO SERVE
chopped fresh parsley, basil or
   tarragon

First, make the stuffing. Heat the oil and sauté the spring onions or onion and bacon for a few minutes until soft. Stir in the remaining stuffing ingredients. Fill, but do not overstuff, the veal or lamb breast, fold over and sew up the opening with a large needle and cook's string. Prick the surface with a fork. Bring a large saucepan of salted water to the boil with the veal bones, bay leaves, clove and green part of a spring onion or leek. Cover and simmer for 30 minutes. Add the veal, return to the boil, lower the heat, cover and simmer for 1½ hours. Leave to cool in the broth.

Heat the oil and butter and sauté the onions until soft. Add the carrots, spring onions, fennel and leeks and sauté for 5 minutes. Stir in the garlic. Remove from the heat and reserve.

Half an hour before the meal, remove the veal from the broth, drain it and pat dry on kitchen paper. Heat the oil and butter and brown the veal on all sides. Add the wine and scrape the coagulated juices in the pan. Add the cooked vegetables, cover and heat through for about 20 minutes.

To prepare the sauce, mix the parsley or basil and coriander in a bowl then whisk in the olive oil. Add the tomato and season.

Transfer the meat to a chopping board and discard the string. Using a sharp knife and holding a plate against the stuffing to hold it together, cut the meat into thick slices and arrange them on a warm serving plate. Sprinkle with salt and pepper. Surround the meat with the vegetables and spoon a little broth over the top. Skim the fat off the pan juices and strain over the meat. Sprinkle with parsley, basil or tarragon. Pass the sauce separately.

Note

If you serve this cold, it will be much easier to slice. If using lamb add afew prunes or raisins and a tablespoons of marc brandy to the filling. Serve it with potatoes sautéed in olive oil.

GIGOT RÔTI AUX HARICOTS BLANCS

Roast leg of lamb with haricot beans, tomatoes and shallots

Lamb is very popular throughout France. In Provence, they graze on scant grasses but many fragrant herbs and are cooked with thyme, rosemary, olive oil and a handful of unpeeled garlic cloves. In the south-west, they feed on richer grass, and may be stuffed with prunes, anchovies or fruits.

But it is in Normandy that I have tasted the most interesting lamb dishes. Near Mont-Saint-Michel I saw the famous pré-salé lambs grazing on pastures which are swept by the tides, the sea winds and spindrifts. Gulls soared overhead, while the golden steeple of Saint Michel glimmered in the distance. Pré-salé lambs, which means lambs raised on salted pastures, are bold and determined. They leave their barn unaccompanied at eight o'clock each morning, walk some 4 or 5 kilometres to graze on verdant grasses cleared of weeds by the tides and frequent showers, then return at six o'clock every night. Only the high tides in early autumn or spring may force them to stay indoors for a few days in the year. Because they eat fragrant, slightly salty grass, walk a lot and spend their time mostly outdoors, they have a distinctive flavour and texture. The best lambs are those raised in the summer, for a lamb feeding on dune grasses will not taste the same as a lamb raised on lush summer grass. The taste, however, is always delicate, with a slightly gamey flavour. The flesh is red with a firm texture. It is never fat nor bland, and in Normandy they insist that it needs neither herbs nor garlic. In fact, I noticed that they do not even use salt or pepper for fear of smothering the subtle fragrance of the meat. The lambs have naturally long legs (to prevent their bellies dragging in the water), and *gigots* of pré-salé are compared to a ballerina's leg: pink, firm, lean flesh under a thin net of white fat, *la glinette*. Although it sells for twice the price of ordinary lamb, the production of pré-salé cannot fill local demand.

We tasted pré-salé lamb in the lovely home of Daniel Gaslin, looking out over pastures enclosed by the sea. Most of the meals in his house are shared by three generations and, although Normans are known to be cautious and not prone to enthusiasm, all the guests were sipping their cider with anticipation, for they knew we had a treat in store; a pré-salé never disappoints.

Daniel was in charge of the fire but everyone volunteered their advice. He was cooking the lamb on a grill 10 inches (25 cm) above the embers to 'seize it', then he wrapped it in foil so that none of the juices would escape. He used no herbs, no mustard, not even a pinch of salt or pepper.

When the meal was served, the part near the shank called 'the muse', which is considered the tastiest part, was given to the eldest cousin. The children shared the centre and all the adults begged for the crisp, tasty bits near the bone at both ends. It was served with a plain dish of lightly buttered green beans.

Since pré-salé is not available for most people, I have created this recipe which will transform a good leg of lamb into a sumptuous dish. If you cook the vegetables while the lamb is in the oven, they should be ready at about the same time. A few tablespoons of fresh cream are often added just before serving.

——————— *Serves 8* ———————

FOR THE VEGETABLES
1 lb (450 g) dried white haricot
    beans
1 large onion studded with 2 cloves
1 bouquet garni
salt and freshly ground black pepper
3 tablespoons butter
1 teaspoon groundnut oil
1 carrot, chopped
2 onions, chopped
3 shallots, coarsely chopped
4 cloves garlic, chopped
3 tomatoes, skinned and chopped
1 tablespoon chopped fresh thyme

3 tablespoons finely chopped fresh
    parsley

FOR THE MEAT
4 lb (1.8 kg) leg of lamb with bone,
    trimmed
4 cloves garlic, cut into slivers
2 oz (50 g) butter
1 tablespoon dried thyme or
    2 teaspoons dried rosemary
4 fl oz (120 ml) dry cider or dry
    white wine
3 tablespoons single cream
    (optional)

Soak the beans overnight in cold water according to the instructions on the packet.

Drain the beans, place them in a saucepan and cover with

boiling water. Cover and leave to stand for 1 hour. Drain the beans and return to the pan. Cover with cold water and bring to the boil. Lower the heat and add the clove-studded onion and bouquet garni. Cover and simmer for 1 hour or until the beans are soft, skimming the foam from time to time. The cooking time will depend on the quality and freshness of the beans. Season with salt and pepper and drain.

Meanwhile, pre-heat the oven to gas mark 8, 450°F (230°C).

Prepare the meat. Make a few incisions in the lamb with the point of a sharp knife and insert the slivers of garlic. Rub the lamb with the butter, sprinkle with thyme or rosemary and press the herbs over the surface. I never add salt to lamb before cooking since it makes the cooking juices run freely. Place the lamb in a roasting tin, add a little water so the juices do not burn and bake in the oven for 10 minutes. Reduce the oven temperature to gas mark 6, 400°F (200°C) and cook for about 1¼ hours for medium or 2 hours for well-cooked meat, basting occasionally.

Half an hour before the lamb is ready, start to cook the vegetables. Heat the butter and oil in a large frying pan and add the carrot, onions, shallots, garlic and tomatoes. Cook for about 15 minutes until most of the moisture has evaporated then crush the vegetables coarsely with a fork and add them to the cooked beans. Sprinkle with thyme and parsley, cover and keep warm.

Transfer the lamb to warm platter, cover with kitchen foil and keep in a warm place. Add the cider or wine to the roasting tin and bring to the boil, scraping the bottom vigorously to mix in all the cooking juices. Simmer for 5 minutes. Skim as much fat as you can from the top then stir in the cream, if using, and season with salt and pepper.

Carve the lamb and arrange it on a warm serving platter. Sprinkle with salt and pepper and spoon a little of the warm sauce over each slice. The remaining sauce can be served separately. The beans and vegetables can be arrange around the meat or served in a separate dish.

SALT

Where there is salt, there is life. Salt is essential to mankind; it is sacred, a symbol of purity and wisdom. For centuries it was also a means of trading. Roman soldiers were paid with salt, hence the word 'salary'. In France, *la gabelle*, a tax on salt imposed in the Middle Ages which continued until the Revolution, gradually crept back into the tax system in other guises and was not finally dismissed until after 1945. Even today, one cannot take a litre of salty sea water without the permission of the Ministry of Finance.

Salt is gathered both from mines, *sel gemme*, which is of lesser quality, and from the sea, *sel de mer*, along the Mediterranean and the Atlantic. Since the fourteenth century, the salt marshes along the Atlantic coast have provided the best salt, receiving no chemical purification treatment. It is rich in magnesium, potassium and calcium.

The coarse bluish-grey salt, *le sel gris*, coloured by the clay in the soil, and the coarse sea salt, *le gros sel*, are used for cooking; they awake and enhance all the natural flavours. The fine, delicate *fine fleur* or *fleur de l'eau* salt that is gathered on the surface of the water is kept for seasoning at the table.

Salt has been used as a preservative for centuries. It turns plain cod fish into the fragrant *morue*. In charcuterie, hams, sausages and *petit salé* are rubbed by hand with rough sea salt to preserve them and impart flavour and colour. The splendid *jambon de Bayonne* from the south-west is cured with two salts, one from Salies de Bearn and one from Bayonne.

Cooks love sea salt. They bake a whole fish, a chicken or some duck breasts under a thick layer of sea salt with thyme to seal in all the flavour (see page 161). *Potées* (see page 158), *Pot au Feu*, fresh radishes, spring onions and raw, tender butter beans are always served with a tiny pot of *gros sel* as a condiment.

In cooking, it is impossible to give precise quantities of salt. Some salts are more pungent than others, some palates require more salt than others, people are accustomed to a different levels of saltiness in the cuisine of their particular region. That elusive dose is called *le grain de sel*. It is that pinch of magic which enhances all the flavours of the dish.

ÎLE DE FRANCE

NAVARIN D'AGNEAU

Lamb and vegetable stew

The best Navarins are prepared in spring when young, tender carrots and turnips are available. The variety of lamb is important: shoulder or leg because they are lean and meaty, breast, ribs and neck because they give flavour and texture. Navarin must be prepared in advance. The pieces of meat are sautéed then simmered and refrigerated. An hour before the meal, the fat can be lifted off the top of the pan and the bones discarded. The vegetables are steamed separately so that they remain crisp and provide a fresh counterpoint. Frozen peas or green beans can be added at the last minute, otherwise fresh vegetables are essential.

———— *Serves 6* ————

FOR THE MEATS
3 lb lamb (shoulder, leg, neck, ribs)
3 tablespoons groundnut oil
1 tablespoon sugar
salt and coarsely ground black pepper
1 tablespoon plain flour
1 large onion, chopped
3 cloves garlic, whole
1½ pints (900 ml) beef stock or water
3 bay leaves
1 sprig fresh thyme
4 tomatoes, skinned and chopped

FOR THE VEGETABLES
Choose a selection from the following vegetables:
6 small carrots with 1 inch (2.5 cm) green stem or carrots cut into sticks

6 small turnips
4 oz (100 g) green beans
12 tiny spring onions with 1 inch (2.5 cm) green stem
1 fennel bulb, cut into 1 inch (2.5 cm) pieces
6 oz (175 g) fresh peas or small frozen peas
2 oz (50 g) mangetout
2 lb (900 g) potatoes, cut into 2 inch (5 cm) pieces

TO GARNISH
pinch of ground coriander
2 tablespoons chopped fresh thyme, chives, chervil or flat-leaved parsley
1 tablespoon fresh parsley cut up with scissors

Trim the meats, remove the bone from the shoulder and reserve. Cut the meat into 2 inch (5 cm) cubes and pat dry on kitchen paper. Choose a large, heavy-based frying pan and cook the meat in batches so it has room to brown easily. Heat a little oil over a medium heat and sauté the pieces of meat for about 10 minutes until golden brown on all sides. Sprinkle with a little sugar; it will caramelise in a minute. Sprinkle with salt and pepper and stir until crisp and brown. Sprinkle with a little flour, lower the heat and stir so the flour turns golden and the meat is coated. Transfer the meat and bones to a large flameproof casserole dish and keep them warm while you sauté the remaining batches of meat.

Add a little more oil to the pan and fry the onion and garlic for 2 minutes. Pour in a little broth or water and stir well to scrape up the meat juices. Pour over the meat and add enough stock or water to cover the meat. Bring to the boil, stirring occasionally, then lower the heat, cover and simmer for 30 minutes. Add the bay leaves, thyme and tomatoes and cook for a further 1 hour, uncovered, until the meat is very tender. Leave to cool then cover and refrigerate overnight.

An hour before the meal, remove the fat congealed on the top of the pan and lift the meat out of the broth. Trim away any gristle or fat and discard the bones and herbs. Heat the broth over a high heat for a few minutes to reduce it a little. Add the pieces of meat to the broth and simmer for about 30 minutes. Taste and season with salt and pepper.

Meanwhile, cook your chosen vegetables in a steamer or a large pan of salted water for about 30 minutes, adding them one type at a time so that they all complete cooking together. They should remain quite firm and almost crunchy. Place the carrots and turnips in first, then add green beans, spring onions and fennel and finally the peas and mangetout. The potatoes can be cooked separately in boiling salted water until tender.

Arrange half the steamed vegetables on a warm serving platter and spoon the meat on top. Add the rest of the vegetables and spoon over most of the meat cooking juices. Sprinkle with the coriander and herbs. Arrange the potatoes in a separate dish and sprinkle with salt and parsley.

*T*AGINE D'*A*GNEAU *A*UX *O*IGNONS

Lamb and onion stew

One of the legacies of France's colonial history has been the development of North African – Maghreb – communities in French cities. Moroccans, Tunisians and Algerians have all imported their highly flavoured cuisine, which has enlivened native French palates. Couscous and *tagines* are among the most popular dishes for the French to cook at home.

Fatma Maziani came to Paris from Casablanca in 1983. An office cleaner by day, after work she's in great demand as an informal caterer. Fatma makes her delicious stews, salads and couscous – perfumed with coriander and cumin, ginger and cinnamon – for people to serve at home. This *tagine* is typically Moroccan: meat and vegetables in a salty-sweet sauce. It is best made with Moroccan saffron powder, if you can find it, and served with rice or plain couscous.

———————— *Serves 6* ————————

2 lb (900 g) lean lamb
4 teaspoons cinnamon
1 teaspoon ground ginger
3¹/₂ tablespoons sugar
1 small bunch fresh parsley,
   chopped
1 small bunch fresh coriander,
   chopped
a pinch of saffron powder
salt and freshly ground black pepper

2 tablespoons olive oil
2 tablespoons peanut oil
1 clove garlic, finely chopped
1 onion, chopped
1 tomato, skinned, seeded and
   chopped
3 teaspoons ground cumin
3 oz (75 g) raisins, soaked in warm
   water and then drained

Opposite: EPAULE D'AGNEAU FARCIE AUX LEGUMES ET AUX
FRUITS (*see page 152*)

Paul Bocuse in Lyon

Cut the lamb into 2 inch (5 cm) squares. Heat half the olive and peanut oils in a deep, heavy-based flameproof casserole dish. Add the meat. Add 1 teaspoon cinnamon, the ginger, 2 tablespoons sugar, parsley, coriander, a pinch of saffron and salt and pepper. Fry over a fairly high heat until brown. Turn the heat low. Add water to cover the meat, then add the garlic and tomato. Cover and simmer gently for about 1 hour, checking and stirring occasionally and adding a little water if the meat starts to stick.

Meanwhile, heat the remaining oil in a separate pan and add the onions and the remaining cinnamon, sugar, and cumin. Cook for about 15 minutes, stirring, until the onion is light golden. After the meat has cooked for 1 hour, spoon the onions on top of the lamb, without stirring them in. Cover and simmer for a further 20 minutes. Stir in the raisins just before serving.

CASSOULET

*A rich bean, pork, lamb, duck, onion, tomato and herb stew
baked under a breadcrumb crust*

The word *Cassoulet* comes from casserole, the earthenware pot in
which *Cassoulet* is baked, and it is a *plat mijoté* – a simmered dish –
par excellence. It should be cooked at least one day in advance so that
all the flavours successfully mingle. It is prepared with many
different ingredients and takes a little time but is not difficult and is
relatively inexpensive.

Cassoulet is often served at political banquets, family meals and
village festivals. Prepared in advance, baked and served in its
cooking dish, it needs little attention. Monsieur André Bonnaure
remembers a *Cassoulet* served to 400 guests on a national road
which went through the centre of his village where local gendarmes
had to divert the traffic for hours so that the beloved *Cassoulet*
could be enjoyed peacefully outdoors by the whole community.

This glorious stew may have been invented by the Arabs and
originally prepared with butter beans and dried goose, but it has
been part of southern French repertoire for about ten centuries.
With its golden crust and its aromatic, creamy juices, *Cassoulet* is a
superb sight. However, I must confess I often find it too heavy, too
greasy and also too bland. I remember days of lots of mineral
water, vegetable broth and sage teas in my grandparents' house the
day after ' a genuine' *Cassoulet* was served!

The three most celebrated versions of *Cassoulet* today are those
of Carcassone, Toulouse and Castelnaudary – the Mecca of *Cassoulet*. In medieval Carcassonne, lamb, and even an occasional partridge, may be included. In Toulouse, the city of *Aérospatiale* where
Concorde and the European Airbus are assembled, pieces of
preserved duck or goose and local pork sausages enrich the bean
stew. In Castelnaudary, preserved duck, onions, garlic, bacon and
pork rind are added to the beans.

I have cooked a great many versions of *Cassoulet* over the years
and have finally settled on this recipe as the one I prefer. The
melting beans are redolent with rich flavours but it is – and I know
the choice of word may seem strange – light. Lightness in a

Cassoulet may sound like a hopeless challenge but this is how it goes. I use this year's crop of beans if possible, blanch the beans to make them more digestible then cook them with streaky bacon, ham and tomatoes in a very fragrant broth made with wine, herbs, meats and vegetables. The lamb is always cooked separately, with more vegetables. Since preserved duck, *Confit*, is hard to find outside France, I roast pieces of fresh duck and use it crisp, keeping some of the cooking fat and juices for later use. Once the beans and meat are cooked, I refrigerate them overnight so most of the fat is easy to discard and all the bones and gristle can be removed. Finally, I mingle all the elements and bake them together in a pot. Tomatoes, with their acid quality, seem to me essential. A *hachis* made with chopped garlic and lard can be added to the stew just before baking. If I need to thicken the sauce, I prefer to use crushed beans than the traditional goose, duck or pork fat. The crust on top is important as it seals in all the aromas. It is traditionally supposed to be delicately broken seven times, but three or four times seems enough, just so that bits of crisp crust are buried with the fragrant mixture.

Left-over *Cassoulet* freezes well and improves as it is re-heated. Since it requires quite a number of ingredients and takes time to prepare, I never make it for fewer than eight people.

As for dishes to accompany this splendid recipe, in Languedoc, asparagus and melon are served before a *Cassoulet*, and it is usually followed by a tossed salad. A lemon, raspberry or armagnac sorbet or a fresh fruit salad are the only desserts one can possibly contemplate after a *Cassoulet*.

—————— *Serves 10* ——————

FOR THE DUCK
4 pieces preserved duck, Confit *(see
    page 183)*
or 5 pieces fresh duck
*handful of rough sea salt or kosher
    salt*
3 teaspoons dried thyme
1 tablespoon dry white wine
salt and freshly ground black pepper

FOR THE BEANS
*2 lb (900 g) dried white haricot
    beans*
*1½ lb (675 g) unsmoked bacon
    shoulder joint*
*piece of rind from bacon, cut into
    1 inch (2.5 cm) pieces*
2 large onions, chopped
4 tomatoes, skinned and quartered
6 carrots, sliced
1 leek, thickly sliced
4 teaspoons dried thyme
3 bay leaves
2 cloves
4 cloves garlic, crushed
*4 fresh Toulouse sausages (or
    Cotechino, Salsietta or a good
    quality Hungarian sausage)*

8 oz (225 g) cured ham (optional)

FOR THE LAMB
1 tablespoon groundnut oil
*3 lb (1.4 kg) lean stewing lamb,
    shank or boned shoulder,
    trimmed and cut into 2 inch
    (5 cm) cubes*
3 onions, chopped
1 stalk celery, chopped
5 fresh or canned tomatoes, skinned
6 cloves garlic, crushed
3 bay leaves
1½ pints (900 ml) dry white wine
1 pint (600 ml) water

TO FINISH
1 clove garlic
5 teaspoons dried thyme
4 tablespoons dry white wine
*4–5 tablespoons chopped fresh flat-
    leaved parsley*
*4 oz (100 g) fresh breadcrumbs
    (preferably home-made)*
*1 tablespoon groundnut, olive or
    walnut oil or butter*
*2 cloves garlic, finely chopped
    (optional)*

If you have *Confit,* preserved duck, you do not need to season or cook it before adding it to the casserole. If you use fresh duck, rub the pieces with salt and thyme, cover and refrigerate overnight.

Soak the beans overnight in cold water. Drain and rinse then place in a pan, cover with fresh water, bring to the boil and boil for about 10 minutes, as directed on the packet. Leave to cool, then drain.

Place the beans in a large pot with the bacon, rind, vegetables, herbs, cloves and garlic. Just cover with water, bring to the boil, then lower the heat, cover the pot and simmer gently for about 1 hour. Add the sausages, cover again and continue to simmer for a further 30 minutes until the beans are soft but not creamy. Add the cured ham, if using, for the last few minutes of cooking. Remove from the heat and drain, reserving the stock for later use. Refrigerate the beans and meat and the broth.

Meanwhile, heat the oil in a frying pan. Pat the lamb cubes dry with kitchen paper, add to the oil and brown on all sides. Discard the fat, add a drop more oil and fry the onions and celery for 5 minutes. Add the tomatoes, garlic, bay leaves, wine and water and season with salt. Bring to the boil then simmer for 1 hour, uncovered. Remove the meat from the broth. Strain the broth through a sieve, pushing with a wooden spoon to squeeze out all the juices. Place the lamb back in the broth, cool then refrigerate.

Pre-heat the oven to gas mark 5, 375°F (190°C).

Pat the pieces of fresh duck dry with kitchen paper and roast in the oven for 1½ hours. Add the tablespoon of wine to the pan over a low heat and scrape the coagulated juices with a fork. Sprinkle with salt and pepper and reserve both the juices and the duck for later use.

Remove the lamb from the refrigerator and discard all the fat which will have congealed on the top. Remove the beans and meat from the refrigerator, slice the sausages, cut the bacon into 2 inch (5 cm) pieces and cut the cured ham into about 6 pieces.

Rub a large 8 pint (4.5 litre) earthenware or porcelain oven-proof casserole dish with a clove of garlic. Place half the beans in the bottom and sprinkle with a little thyme, wine and pepper. Add the pieces of lamb and the sliced sausages then add more beans. Add the pieces of cooked duck or *Confit* and cured ham and finally the remaining beans. Sprinkle a little salt and pepper on top then add the deglazed juices from the duck. Add enough of the cooking broth to cover the top of the ingredients and keep the rest at hand since you will add a little more later on as the juices evaporate, and the beans must remain moist as they cook. Sprinkle with the parsley then the breadcrumbs and sprinkle with oil. You may like to prepare everything up to this point then refrigerate until 2 hours before you are ready to serve.

Pre-heat the oven to gas mark 5, 375°F (190°C).

Place the Cassoulet dish in the top third of the oven and cook for 20 minutes. Pierce the golden crust on top three or four times with the back of a spoon but don't stir, and add a little broth on the edges of the dish so the beans remain moist. Reduce the oven temperature to gas mark 2, 300°F (150°C) and continue to cook for a further 1½ hours.

Just as you are ready to serve, you might sprinkle a little finely chopped parsley and garlic on top. Wrap the dish in a thick towel, bring it straight to the table and serve from the baking dish.

Notes

Today, local chefs in search of interesting variations prepare Cassoulet with lentils – tiny green lentils or brown ones – and also fresh and dried lima beans. I once tasted a Cassoulet made with salt cod, beans, anchovies and seasoned with saffron. Some cooks like to add a handful of chopped fresh mint leaves just before the final baking.

SIMPLE CASSOULET

This is a much simpler Cassoulet recipe which omits the lamb stew.

———————— *Serves 4–6* ————————

2¾ lb (1.2 kg) dried white haricot beans, soaked overnight	1 lb (450 g) salt belly of pork
1 large onion, chopped	12 oz (350 g) green collar of bacon
4 tomatoes, skinned and chopped	1 tablespoon oil
3 stalks celery, sliced	8 Toulouse sausages or Cotechino or
5 cloves garlic, chopped	Salsietta or good quality
2 bay leaves	Hungarian sausages
2 sprigs fresh thyme	1 × 4 lb (1.8 kg) duck, cut into
2 sprigs fresh parsley	8 pieces or 8 pieces Confit (see
	page 183)
	2 tablespoons chopped fresh parsley
	1 oz (25 g) breadcrumbs

Drain the beans and put them into a large pan with enough water to cover. Bring to the boil then cook rapidly for 10 minutes, skimming off any scum. Add the onion, tomatoes, celery, garlic, herbs, salt pork and bacon. Cover and simmer gently for 1 hour.

Meanwhile, heat the oil and cook the sausages until browned all over.

If using fresh duck, pre-heat the oven to gas mark 6, 400°F (200°C). Place the joints in a rack in a roasting tin and cook in the oven for 1 hour. Remove from the oven and reserve the duck fat. If you are using *Confit*, omit this stage.

Drain the beans, reserving the liquid. Remove the meat. Cut the bacon, pork and duck into large pieces. Cut the sausages into large chunks.

Pre-heat the oven to gas mark 6, 400°F (200°C).

To assemble the stew, spoon half the beans into a large casserole dish. Add the duck, bacon, pork and sausages then cover with the remaining beans. Pour in enough of the bean liquid to cover the beans, adding extra stock or water if necessary. Sprinkle with parsley then breadcrumbs, and drizzle the duck fat over the top, if liked. Bake in the oven for 1½ hours. The crust which forms on top should be broken into the stew every 30 minutes, without stirring. If the stew begins to dry out, add a drop of stock or water. Remove from the oven and serve from the cooking pot.

Note

Cassoulet is best prepared the day before serving as the flavours improve with re-heating and the fat can be removed. Re-heat at gas mark 6, 400°F (200°C).

ÉPAULE D'AGNEAU FARCIE AUX LÉGUMES ET AUX FRUITS

Catalan stuffed lamb shoulder

With its bustling squares, elegant palm trees and *Belle Époque* buildings, the lovely, lively city of Perpignan is the French capital of Roussillon. It is also very much a part of Catalonia, the ancient region which spreads from Valencia in Spain through Barcelona to Perpignan.

For the last seven centuries, the Arabic influence has transmitted a variety of surprising habits and tastes to the cooking of the region. Catalan foods are light and highly flavoured. Their fragrant *charcuterie* is prepared with dried, uncooked pork and seasoned with a variety of strong spices and herbs, marjoram being a particular favourite. There is a mingling of meats and fruits: goose or lamb with pears, chicken with garlic and lemon, rabbit with prunes and greengages. In pastries, there are accents of aniseed, lemon, almonds and honey. Beef is not cooked in the region, but pork is served in all kinds of ways, mainly with unripe fruits. Sauces are not thickened with egg yolks, butter, cream or flour, as they are elsewhere in France, but with honey and crushed almonds. In one day I was blessed by an instant education – visually, gastronomically and historically – on Catalan food by Eliane Thibaut-Comelade and a few of her friends. Her garden in the very centre of Perpignan grows the essentials: almond, lemon, orange, palm, fig trees and lots and lots of aromatic herbs. She prepared this lamb dish for us because it embodied all the characteristics and delights of Catalan cooking.

─────────── *Serves 6* ───────────

1 large shoulder of lamb, boned and
    flattened to a rectangular shape
few thin slices pork fat or streaky
    bacon
4 tablespoons olive oil
10 fl oz (300 ml) chicken stock or
    water

FOR THE STUFFING
1 tablespoon olive oil
1 thick slice stale bread
8 oz (225 g) meat from the centre of
    the lamb, chopped
8 oz (225 g) streaky bacon, chopped
3 oz (75 g) pigs' liver or chicken
    livers, chopped (optional)
1 oz (25 g) almonds, crushed
1 tablespoon snipped fresh chives
1 tablespoon chopped fresh
    marjoram or savory
2 tablespoons chopped fresh
    rosemary

1 tablespoon fennel seeds
1 clove star anise
6 cloves garlic, crushed
1 tablespoon rosemary honey
salt and freshly ground black pepper
1 tablespoon grated lemon rind

TO GARNISH
4 small purple globe artichokes,
    trimmed
12 tiny new potatoes
1 tablespoon olive oil
4 oz (100 g) wild or button
    mushrooms
6 small fleshy peaches, peeled and
    stoned
6 fresh figs, pricked with a needle
    (optional)
6 small dessert apples, peeled and
    cored
6 small pears, peeled and cored

Heat the oil and fry the bread until golden. Drain and place in a
bowl. Add the remaining stuffing ingredients and mix together by
hand or in a food processor or blender. The mixture should not be
too smooth. Spread the stuffing across the narrow part of the lamb
about 2 inches (5 cm) from the edges and roll it tightly so the
stuffing is enclosed. Sew it all along into a neat cylinder. Wrap the
fat or bacon round the meat and tie with string if necessary. Heat
the oil in a heavy-based pan and fry the lamb until browned on
both sides. Lower the heat, cover and cook for 20 minutes.

    Cook the artichokes and potatoes in boiling salted water for 5
minutes. Drain well, then arrange around the lamb, cover and cook
on a medium heat for 25 minutes, shaking the pan from time to
time so that the vegetables brown on all sides. Heat the oil and fry
the mushrooms for a few minutes, season with salt and pepper,

then add to the lamb with the peaches and figs and cook for a further 5 minutes. Add the apples and pears to the pan and simmer for a further 10 minutes. When everything is golden on all sides, add a little stock and heat through.

Remove the meat from the pan and discard the string. Cut the meat into thin slices and arrange on a warm serving platter. Arrange the fruits and vegetables around it. Stir the cooking juices in the pan well then spoon them delicately over the meat and vegetables and serve at once.

— LANGUEDOC —

AGNEAU À L'AIL

Roast lamb with creamy garlic and wine sauce

The region of Languedoc is a link between the eastern and western parts of southern France. I spent a day with Geneviève Cano, a Languedocienne. She talked about her household where five generations lived under the same roof. Every day the younger members of the family awoke to the chopping sound of the heavy cleaver against the thick board as parsley, garlic and *ventrèche* were pounded to make the *persillade* which would be used during the day to season meats, vegetables, soups and stews.

With *Agneau à l'Ail*, Geneviève served sliced potatoes sautéed to a crisp in goose fat and sprinkled with the beloved *persillade*, home-made *pain d'épice*, tiny goat cheeses drizzled with honey and almonds, and a basket of figs and dark red peaches, *pêches de vigne*, which her uncle had gathered in his vineyard. It was a glorious meal.

Goose fat is available in tins in many shops, but oil or butter can replace it as long as you use a good, firm garlic. The overwhelming quantity of garlic makes for a surprisingly gentle, nutty flavour; the garlic looses its force when cooked and its taste changes completely. Geneviève's young son explained to me all the ailments that garlic would cure, but I did not need any medicinal justifications to enjoy the sumptuous sauce.

154

——————— *Serves 6–8* ———————

5 lb (2.25 kg) leg of lamb, trimmed
14 cloves garlic, halved
salt and freshly ground black pepper
1 tablespoon goose fat, butter or
   olive oil

1 tablespoon dried thyme
30 cloves garlic, unpeeled
4 tablespoons cold water
1 pint (600 ml) dry white wine, still
   or sparkling

Pre-heat the oven to gas mark 5, 375°F (190°C).

Stab the lamb all over with a very sharp knife and insert the garlic halves into the meat. Sprinkle it with salt and pepper and rub it in with your hands. Spread the goose fat, butter or oil over the lamb then place the meat in a deep roasting tin and roast it fat side down for 30 minutes. Turn the lamb over, sprinkle the thyme over the top and arrange the unpeeled cloves of garlic around the meat. Cook for 10 minutes. Stir the garlic cloves so that they do not stick to the pan, pour in the water and cook for a further 30 minutes or until the lamb is cooked to your liking.

Transfer the lamb to a warm serving platter and keep it warm in the turned-off oven. Transfer the garlic cloves to a bowl, peel them then mash them with a fork. Drain the fat from the pan. Add the wine and stir, scraping the bottom of the pan to mix in all the lamb juices. If you use a sparkling wine, as Geneviève did, it will sizzle and make a frothy sauce. Stir in the garlic purée and cook for 1 minute. Season to taste with salt and pepper.

Slice the lamb and arrange it on a warm serving platter. Spoon a little of the garlic sauce over the top and serve the rest separately.

*P*ORC AUX *H*ERBES ET AUX *L*ÉGUMES

Pork roast seasoned with herbs and vegetables

Monsieur Joel Robuchon is France's finest palate, the most absolute reference for anyone interested in cooking, and the most rigorous and attentive of chefs. I saw him prepare the following recipe as he explained each of the important turning points of what was originally a simple home dish. There were no exotic or expensive ingredients – pork has always been enhanced by sage and juniper berries and is generally deglazed with wine. The technique was minimal but perfectly confident. But it is the sum of decisive gestures – marinating the meat with herbs and salt (so it would be permeated with flavours), browning it to crisp before final cooking (so the meat retains all its piquancy), salting it only after the surface is crisp and brown, adding a fine tuning of bitter and acid elements (vinegar, juniper berries, the green parts of the leeks), the coarse cutting of the onions and leeks (to give texture), the bones added to the meat as it simmers (to add taste), the rubbing instead of mincing of sage leaves (to enhance flavour) – which made Monsieur Robuchon's version unique. There is nothing dogmatic about vegetables or herbs – if there are no leeks, then fennel bulb thinly cut would do, savory could replace thyme – the only concern for him was to fix all the flavours, to preserve the texture of the vegetables and not to dilute the cooking juices, so the dish will explode with fresh flavours. I have prepared the following version inspired by Monsieur Robuchon very often and always with the same delight.

---------- *Serves 4* ----------

2–3 lb (900 g – 1.4 kg) pork
   roasting joint, trimmed and
   boned
4 cloves garlic, cut into slivers
2 teaspoons chopped fresh thyme
salt
2 tablespoons groundnut oil
a few beef bones (optional)
5 spring onions or 5 shallots, halved
3 tomatoes, skinned and coarsely
   chopped

4 leeks, white and 2 inches (5 cm) of
   green, trimmed and halved
2 teaspoons sugar
10 fl oz (300 ml) dry white wine
1 tablespoon red wine vinegar
5 juniper berries
freshly ground black pepper
2 teaspoons dried thyme
10 fresh sage leaves
2 tablespoons butter

Sprinkle the meat with the garlic, fresh thyme and salt, roll it and tie it into a neat cylinder. Wrap it in cling film and refrigerate overnight. If the roast is already rolled, sprinkle the salt and thyme on the surface and stud slivers of garlic into the meat.

When you are ready to cook, pat the meat dry carefully. Heat the oil in a heavy-based pan, add the bones and the meat and brown on all sides, uncovered, until slightly caramelised. Add the spring onions, tomatoes and leeks, sprinkle with sugar and cook, uncovered for about 10 minutes. Add the wine and wine vinegar and stir the coagulated juices with a wooden spoon. Sprinkle in the juniper berries and add a little salt to the vegetables (not much on the meat as it already had salt in the marinade). Sprinkle the roast generously with pepper; this is a highly tasty dish. Sprinkle in the thyme then rub and crush the sage leaves between your palms and add them to the pan. Stir well, cover and simmer for about 1½ hours, stirring from time to time.

Remove from the heat and discard the bones. Stir in the butter, cover and leave to rest for a few minutes before you slice so that the juices flow evenly through the meat. There should be a small quantity of fragrant sauce. Arrange the sliced meat on a warmed serving plate, pour over the sauce and arrange the vegetables around.

— **AUVERGNE AND THROUGHOUT FRANCE** —

POTÉE

Pork and bean stew

Most regions in France have a version of this dish. A chicken, half a pig's head, a breast of lamb, a piece of smoked streaky bacon, a *jambonneau*, pork spare ribs and most vegetables may be added to the smoked pork and the sausages.

Potée should be made in large quantities. It will keep refrigerated for a few days.

Serves 6–8

FOR THE VEGETABLES
1½ lb (675 g) dried white haricot
    beans
1 green cabbage, shredded
1 tablespoon butter
2 tablespoons oil
5 carrots, cut into 2 inch (5 cm)
    chunks
2 large onions, quartered
4 small white or pink turnips,
    quartered
8 cloves garlic
4 leeks, white parts only tied together
    with string
salt and freshly ground black pepper

FOR THE MEAT
green part of the leeks
3 bay leaves
1 tablespoon dried thyme
2 onions studded with 2 cloves
10 peppercorns
10 juniper berries
2 lb (900 g) lean streaky bacon
2 lb (900 g) piece of pork spare rib

2 lb (900 g) shoulder of pork, boned
    and rolled
piece of country ham (optional)
1 ham bone (optional)
a few Toulouse or boiling pork
    sausages

FOR THE VINAIGRETTE
1½ tablespoons white wine vinegar
6 tablespoons olive oil
1½ teaspoons Dijon mustard
2 tablespoons finely chopped fresh
    chives or coriander and chives
1 tablespoon chopped fresh flat-
    leaved parsley
1½ tablespoons finely chopped
    shallots
salt and freshly ground black pepper

TO SERVE
1 tablespoon chopped fresh parsley
1 tablespoon snipped fresh chives
2–3 different kinds of mustard
small bowl of sea salt
bowl of gherkins

Soak the haricot beans in cold water for 1 hour, or as directed on the packet. Drain, then place in a saucepan, cover with water and bring to the boil for 10 minutes. Lower the heat, cover and simmer for 1 hour. Drain and cool.

While the beans are cooking, bring a large pan of water (about 9 pints/5 litres) to the boil. Add the green parts of the leeks, the bay leaves, thyme, clove-studded onions, peppercorns and juniper berries. Boil for 10 minutes. Add all the meats except the sausages, return to the boil, lower the heat, cover and simmer for 1 hour.

Meanwhile, bring a saucepan of salted water to the boil, add the cabbage and return to the boil. Lower the heat then simmer for 10 minutes. Drain and rinse under cold water.

Heat the butter and oil and cook the carrots, onions and turnips for 10 minutes. Add the garlic and leeks and cook for a further 5 minutes until lightly browned.

Add the cabbage and browned vegetables to the meat and simmer for a further 10 minutes. Add the cooked beans, stir with a long-handled spoon and simmer for 10 minutes. Prick the sausages with a fork to prevent them from splitting and add them to the pot. Simmer for a further 20 minutes.

Place all the ingredients for the vinaigrette in a bowl and stir with a fork until well blended.

When ready to serve, remove and slice the meats and arrange them on a warm serving platter. Spoon a little of the broth over them, season with salt and pepper and sprinkle with a little parsley. Keep them warm. Arrange the beans and vegetables attractively on a warm serving dish, discarding the string round the leeks, and spoon a little of the broth over them. Sprinkle with salt, pepper and chives. Serve the platters of meat and vegetables with a tray containing the vinaigrette, mustards, salt and gherkins and a basket of crusty bread.

Note

A few crisp, spicy or garlic-flavoured Italian sausages can be sautéed in oil and arranged around the vegetables at the last moment. Left-over vegetables can be turned into soup or gratin, and left-over meats sliced and served cold with a well-seasoned vinaigrette or used to stuff chicken or a *Poche de Veau Farcie* (see pages 136–7).

MAGRETS DE CANARD

Duck breasts

The fattening of geese and ducks – one of the main activities in Gascony – is mainly done to produce the celebrated, silky *foie gras*. The drumsticks and thighs are cooked and preserved in duck or goose fat for *Confit* and used in winter in a variety of dishes, or they may be roasted. Bones, gizzard and neck are added to soups. Any left-over bits are turned into terrines and *Rillettes*.

But for decades that left many unused parts of the birds, and it took a brave musketeer, a modern d'Artagnan, André Daguin, the owner and chef of Auch's *Hôtel de France* to solve this problem.

Magret, in the southern dialect, means 'lean'. In a duck, the only lean part is the breast, the *magret*. It was always neglected because no one knew quite what to do with it. Some forty years ago, however, Monsieur Daguin discovered that barely-cooked duck breasts could compete with beef in a region where ducks were numerous and beef cattle almost non-existent. He proceeded to serve large sautéed or grilled duck *magrets* quite rare and skinless to his clients without whispering a word about where they came from.

Over the years *Magrets de Canard* have become the rage everywhere in France. They are prepared almost rare, sliced on the diagonal, but may also be grilled, poached or sautéed. They may be marinated in a mixture of salt, shallots, herbs and garlic overnight and served pink. They may be browned, deglazed with vinegar and honey then cooked with apple quarters and mushrooms or seasoned with lime juice and grated lemon rind. They may be served with potato chips or with white grapes, yellow peaches or wild, bitter cherries and their juices deglazed with a sweet dessert wine or a hearty red wine.

When Daguin cooked *Magrets de Canard* for us, he wrapped them in a huge spectacular shell of sea salt. The meat was served with a rich Béarnaise Sauce (see page 86) prepared with duck fat instead of butter, and accompanied with a celeriac purée and grilled aubergine. I have prepared this superb dish at home several

Opposite: MAGRETS DE CANARD

Château Chenonceaux, Loire

times, although I do not use duck fat for the sauce since I find it overwhelmingly rich. Curiously, all the duck flavours are sealed within the salt shell and no excess salt is left on the meat.

It is now possible to buy duck breasts in the supermarket. However, if you buy whole duck, remove the legs and thighs, which you can keep for another recipe or freeze for later, then cut down the breast along the breastbone on the side of the ridge. You will then be able to lift it in one solid piece away from the ribcage.

——————— *Serves 4* ———————

2 × 1 lb (450 g) duck breasts,
    boned and halved, skin on
coarsely ground black pepper
4 lb (1.8 kg) coarse sea salt or
    kosher salt

4 oz (100 g) plain flour
5 egg whites
3 tablespoons dried thyme
1 quantity **Sauce Aillade** (see
    page 89)

Trim any excess fat off the duck breasts and pat dry with kitchen paper. Using a sharp knife, score the skin at 1 inch (2.5 cm) intervals without piercing the flesh. Place the duck pieces in a heavy-based frying pan and fry without any oil over a medium heat for several minutes until the skin is crisp and brown. Sprinkle the top with pepper. Pour off and discard the fat. Remove the duck from the pan and tie the breasts together with string, skin side out.

Pre-heat the oven to gas mark 8, 450°F (230°C).

Mix together the salt, flour, egg whites, thyme and pepper in a large bowl and stir vigorously for 5 minutes. It is heavy work. Spread a piece of oiled kitchen foil in an ovenproof dish and pour in a thick layer of the salt mixture. Place the duck on the salt and cover with the remaining salt mixture. Press hard with both hands to shape a shell. Roast the duck in the centre of the oven for 17 minutes then remove it from the oven and stand it on a rack for 10 minutes.

Bring the dish to the table. Crack the white, hardened shell with a small hammer or a big heavy knife. The shell will open. Remove the duck breasts, cut and discard the string and brush off any bits of shell. Discard the skin and slice the meat diagonally into thin slices. Arrange them on a warm serving platter, sprinkle with pepper and serve with *Sauce Aillade* and a bowl of tossed green salad or a *Gratin Dauphinois* (see page 211).

RÔTI DE PORC AUX POMMES

Roast pork with apples, wine and spices

Once upon a time, when pigs roamed freely and fed on acorns and chestnuts, their meat needed little seasoning. Today fresh pork can be rather dull, so potent regional flavours are welcomed. I serve *Rôti de Porc* with a celeriac purée flavoured with some fresh apples. But you may like to serve it with sliced leeks or shredded cabbage simmered in butter, unpeeled boiled or sautéed potatoes, unpeeled cloves of garlic or plain boiled rice.

If it is possible, marinate the flat piece of pork overnight then roll and tie it into a roast. Pork meat is fat enough, so it should not be basted with its own juices but with milk, water, wine or cider.

Serves 4–6

FOR THE MARINADE
1 teaspoon sea salt
2 teaspoons dried thyme
5 peppercorns
2 teaspoons ground coriander
10 fl oz (300 ml) dry cider or dry
   white wine
1 tablespoon Calvados

FOR THE MEAT
2 lb (900 g) boneless loin or
   shoulder of pork
salt and freshly ground black pepper
2 tablespoons groundnut oil
1 tablespoon butter
few juniper berries, crushed
   (optional)

1 teaspoon ground coriander
   (optional)
1 teaspoon coarsely ground black
   pepper
3 tablespoons double cream

TO GARNISH
6 large cooking apples, 3 large
   quinces or 3 apples and 3 pears
juice of 1 lemon
2 small onions, very finely chopped
2 tablespoons butter
2 tablespoons sugar
½ teaspoon salt

Grind the salt, thyme, peppercorns and coriander in a mortar or in a blender then rub over the surface of the pork. Place in a bowl, pour over the cider or wine and Calvados, cover and refrigerate overnight.

Lift the meat from the marinade and pat dry on kitchen paper. Sprinkle with salt and pepper on both sides then roll it up and tie it into a neat cylinder shape.

Pre-heat the oven to gas mark 4, 350°F (180°C).

Heat the oil and butter in a heavy-based pan and fry the meat for a few minutes until golden on all sides. Place in a flameproof roasting tin about 3 inches (7.5 cm) wider than the meat and cook it in the oven for about 30 minutes, turning twice. Pour the marinade into the dish and cook for a further 1–1½ hours, basting the meat and adding a little more wine if it becomes too dry. The meat will caramelise and most of the juices will evaporate.

Meanwhile, peel, core and quarter the apples, quinces or apples and pears and sprinkle with lemon juice. Place them in a saucepan with the onions, dot with the butter and sprinkle with the sugar and salt. Cover and simmer over a low heat for 10–15 minutes until soft but not mushy.

Remove the meat from the oven and transfer the glazed golden roast to a warm serving platter. Cover and keep warm in the turned-off oven. If there is too little liquid in the roasting tin, add a little more wine. Cook the sauce over a high heat, scraping the coagulated juices. If you like a spirited sauce, add the juniper berries, coriander and pepper. Stir in the cream and simmer for a few minutes. Taste and correct the seasoning with salt and pepper.

Cut and discard the string from the meat. Slice it and arrange the pork in overlapping slices on a warm serving platter. Spoon the warm cream sauce over the meat so that each slice is coated and arrange the cooked apples round the edge of the platter. Extra sauce can be served in a sauce boat. If the apples have overcooked and become mushy, serve them separately in a shallow dish.

Note

I once tasted an interesting version made by Martine O'Jeanson in Tours. She stuffed each peeled and cored apple with a plump local Damas prune for a flavourful accompaniment.

LAPIN EN CIVET

Jugged rabbit simmered in herbs and red wine

Anne Majourel lives in Languedoc, in an old country-house hotel surrounded by green oaks, juniper and bay trees. There is a store room full of local produce, a well-stocked wine cellar (Anne's father is a *vigneron*), two bread ovens and a vegetable garden.

While I stayed at their hotel, *Les Demeures du Ranquet* Jean-Luc was busy gathering mushrooms from dawn until midday while Anne was sprinkling a garlic and minced parsley *persillade* on top of a stew, adding crushed fresh anchovies to a bowl of greens, filling halved tomatoes with a purée of potatoes and salt cod, *Brandade*.

She simmered a stew of wild boar flavoured with candied fruit, and cooked a platter of little grey snails *à la cévenole* with walnuts and anchovies. She served a duck liver perfectly cooked to brown outside and pink inside with her own home-made fig jam. She spread a thick layer of ratatouille on a pumpkin gratin, and made ravioli stuffed with chestnuts and anchovies and coated with a fragrant onion sauce. Late afternoon, with the light around us turning into a pale mingling of delicate lilac and blues, we spoke of many things: woman's place in the world, man's place in the kitchen, Protestant and Catholic culinary habits, Europe as friend or foe. We nibbled dried, rolled pigs' liver and thinly sliced purple artichokes as we sipped her father's wine. As the sun was setting, we both agreed that Montaigne must have been thinking of *Le Domaine du Ranquet* when he said our masterwork was to live well.

The following recipe is inspired by Anne. A basis of southern cooking, *civet* comes from the Latin word *cive*, onion. Traditionally, the blood of the animal or some crushed walnuts are used to thicken the sauce but she used bitter chocolate. I, for one, like to marinate the rabbit in red wine, orange rind and herbs overnight as I cannot easily find wild, herb-fed rabbit like Anne! I always cut the rabbit into small pieces so each piece is enriched with the cooking juices and I can add extra leg pieces if I wish. I serve it with polenta, noodles, tiny steamed potatoes or *millas*, a cornflour and milk dish fried in oil. To accompany, I choose shredded cabbage or sautéed carrot sticks.

——————— *Serves 4* ———————

1 × 4 lb (1.8 kg) fresh rabbit or
   back legs and saddle if frozen

FOR THE MARINADE
1 onion, chopped
1 strip of orange rind
4 cloves
1 sprig fresh thyme
1 sprig fresh parsley
1 pint (600 ml) hearty red wine

2 tablespoons groundnut or
   grapeseed oil
8 oz (225 g) streaky bacon, diced
8 oz (225 g) mushrooms, halved
   and quartered
1 large onion, sliced

salt and freshly ground black pepper
2 tomatoes, skinned, seeded and
   chopped or 1 teaspoon tomato
   purée
2 tablespoons plain flour
1 clove garlic, crushed
1 tablespoon chopped fresh or dried
   thyme
10 fl oz (300 ml) water or stock
1 tablespoon cognac
1 tablespoon red wine vinegar
1 tablespoon butter
1 square plain chocolate
1 tablespoon chopped fresh flat-
   leaved parsley
4 slices bread made into triangular
   Croûtons (see page 68)

Cut the rabbit into 8 pieces. Mix the marinade ingredients, pour over the rabbit and marinate overnight.

Heat a little of the oil and sauté the bacon then transfer to a bowl. Add a little more of the oil to the pan and sauté the mushrooms then add them to the bacon. Heat a little of the oil and sauté the onion until soft then transfer to a separate bowl. Drain the rabbit and pat dry on kitchen paper. Strain and reserve the marinade. Heat the remaining oil and sauté the rabbit on all sides; the pieces should be crunchy and almost caramelised. Season with salt and pepper. Stir in the tomatoes or tomato purée, sprinkle with the flour and stir well. Add the sautéed onions, the garlic, thyme, wine marinade and water. Bring to the boil, cover and simmer for 20 minutes until the rabbit is tender, stirring occasionally.

Transfer the rabbit to a plate. Boil the cooking juices for 5 minutes then rub them through a sieve and return to the pan. Add the bacon and mushrooms, the cognac, wine vinegar, butter and chocolate and stir until blended. Return the rabbit to the sauce and stir gently until heated through. Spoon on to a warm serving dish, sprinkle with the parsley and serve garnished with the Croûtons.

—— **THROUGHOUT FRANCE** ——

LAPIN À LA MOUTARDE

Sautéed rabbit seasoned with mustard, wine and herbs

Lapin à la Moutarde belongs to traditional home-cooking. It is a fragrant, light dish, easy to prepare, and is a staple on the menus of many country inns or city bistros. Serve it with sautéed vegetables, boiled potatoes, carrots, rice or fresh buttered pasta.

———————— *Serves 4* ————————

1 × 2–3 lb (900 g–1.4 kg) fresh rabbit or 2–3 back legs and 2 saddle pieces if the rabbit is frozen
salt and freshly ground black pepper
3 tablespoons groundnut oil
2 shallots or 1 onion, coarsely chopped
4 oz (100 g) streaky bacon, chopped
2 cloves garlic, chopped

2 carrots, sliced
2 leeks, white part only, sliced
1 tablespoon plain flour
10 fl oz (300 ml) dry white wine
2 bay leaves
3 teaspoons dried thyme
1 sprig fresh rosemary
2 tablespoons strong Dijon mustard
2 tablespoons chopped fresh flat-leaved parsley

Cut the rabbit into 8 pieces and pat dry on kitchen paper. Reserve the liver, if you are using fresh rabbit, and chop it coarsely. Sprinkle the rabbit with salt and pepper. Heat the oil in a heavy-based frying pan and sauté the pieces over a medium heat for about 10 minutes until golden on all sides. Remove to a side dish. Add a little more oil, if necessary, and sauté the shallots or onion, bacon, garlic, carrots and leeks for a few minutes, stirring well. Return the rabbit to the pan, sprinkle with flour and cook for 1 minute. Stir in the wine and herbs, bring to the boil, cover and simmer for 1 hour, stirring once or twice. Stir in the mustard and liver, if you have it, and season with salt and pepper. Simmer for a few minutes, check and adjust the seasoning and serve sprinkled with the parsley.

Note
In Provence, a handful of unstoned, firm, green olives and 2 chopped tomatoes are added for the last half an hour of cooking.

JAMBON À LA CRÈME

Ham slices baked in a fragrant sauce with mushrooms and shallots

Each region cooks ham in its own way, with cider, wine, broth or cream. A lovely, fragrant dish from Burgundy, this is easy to make and can be prepared in advance and re-heated for twenty minutes before the meal. *Jambon à la Crème* can be served with a crisp *Gratin Dauphinois* (see page 211), braised or steamed spinach, buttered pasta, steamed or sautéed new potatoes.

It is worth repeating the obvious here: although the ham will absorb the flavour of mushrooms, coriander and wine, a good quality ham is all-important. Bring the meal to the table in its cooking dish wrapped in a tea towel to avoid burnt fingers.

———————— *Serves 4* ————————

2 tablespoons groundnut oil
3 oz (75 g) butter
10 oz (275 g) mushrooms, thickly sliced
salt and freshly ground black pepper
5 × ¼ inch (5 mm) thick slices uncooked ham, whole or cut into 1 inch (2.5 cm) slivers
1 teaspoon ground coriander
1 teaspoon freshly ground black pepper

4 fl oz (120 ml) dry white wine
3 tablespoons coarsely chopped shallots or spring onions
15 fl oz (450 ml) double cream
1 tablespoon Dijon mustard
2 medium-sized tomatoes, skinned and diced
½ teaspoon freshly grated nutmeg
2 oz (50 g) Gruyère cheese, grated

Heat 1 tablespoon of the oil and 1 tablespoon of the butter in a frying pan and sauté the mushrooms for about 5 minutes over a high heat, tossing them from time to time with a wooden spoon. Sprinkle them lightly with salt and pepper then transfer them to a side dish.

Trim the ham and dry the slices or slivers on kitchen paper. Heat the remaining oil with 2 tablespoons of the butter and fry the ham until lightly browned on both sides. Sprinkle the top with the coriander and pepper, transfer to a covered dish and keep aside.

Pour the wine into the frying pan, scraping up all the coagulated juices. Add the shallots or spring onions and cook for 5
minutes over a high heat. Add the cream and season with salt and
pepper. Lower the heat and simmer gently for a further 5 minutes.
Add the mustard then taste and correct the seasoning. Add the
tomatoes, cover and remove from the heat.

Arrange two slices of ham (or half the slivered ham) on the
bottom of a buttered flameproof dish. Add the mushrooms and
their juices and top with the remaining ham. Pour over the cream
and shallot sauce, sprinkle with the nutmeg and cheese and dot
with the remaining butter. Grill under a warm grill for a few
minutes without letting the sauce boil. Serve warm.

Note

If you want a thicker sauce, knead together 1 tablespoon of butter
with 1 tablespoon of plain flour to make a *Beurre Manié*, stir it into
the warm wine and cream sauce and simmer very gently for 2
minutes.

CHARCUTERIE

Pork Specialities

· ·

French regional cooking is mostly founded on the pig. And whether pork is cooked as a fresh meat or turned into prepared, dried, salted, smoked or cooked *charcuterie*, every bit of it is good; *'Dans un cochon, tout est bon'*. Often referred to as *ministre* or *monsieur* – a secretary of state or gentleman – and fed on acorns, chestnuts, apples or potatoes, the pig has always been the most important animal on the farm. Today it remains an essential part of our gastronomy.

The word *charcuterie* comes from *chair cuite*, or cooked meat. It refers both to the art of making pork products, and to the shop in which they are sold. A pork butcher's shop offers different products. Some – like *pâté de campagne* (a coarse country pâté), saucissons and *jambon à l'os*, ham on the bone – are ready to be eaten; some – like *boudins, cervelas* and certain sausages – have to be cooked or at least heated. There are also fresh pork cuts for sale, like *poitrine fumée*, smoked cured streaky bacon, spare ribs, shoulder, pig's trotters and kidneys, and these form the heart of many traditional dishes. Finally, most *charcuteries* offer couscous, salads, stews, French fries, grilled chicken, *choucroute*, gratins and onion pies – all ready to eat. Such freshly prepared dishes cater not only for busy or single parents, or elderly people, but also for the local restaurants and brasseries which offer these *charcuterie*-made dishes on their menus.

Charcuterie products are immensely diverse but are always based on traditional recipes, whether they are prepared at home, in a shop or factory. Every province has its own *spécialités de la région*. Auvergne, Lyonnais, Pyrénées, Provence, Alsace and Brittany produce a variety of terrines and cooked, dry cured or smoked hams and sausages, all made to local recipes.

Sausages are traditionally prepared with coarsely or finely ground neck and shoulder of pork, although occasionally they are made with beef or lamb, as with *merguez*. They are seasoned with spices, pepper and herbs, and the recipe may include onions, garlic, chestnuts, pistachios or truffles according to the region. The finest sausages are always prepared by craftsmen, although some industrially produced products are of fairly high quality. Today the best pork products bear the *label rouge* which is an indication of the highest quality.

Lyon's famous sausages are *rosette* and *Jesus; saucisson de Lyon,* which is boiled and served with potatoes or wrapped in brioche dough; *cervelas* with its fine meat mixture; and the most celebrated in all France, *saucisson à l'ail*. Toulouse sausages are essential for Cassoulet; in the Jura they make flat *gendarme* sausages, *morteau* and *baudet* which are boiled in wine. There are fragrant, dry pigs' liver sausages in Roussillon and Corsica; delicate *roulade* which tastes a little like Mortadella; Auvergne's *saucisse sèche*; Alsace's smoked frankfurters; spicy *merguez* (delicious with couscous); and *andouilles* and *andouillettes* made from tripe. There are also *boudins blancs*, white sausages made with pork or chicken, eggs and cream; and *boudins noirs*, blood pudding prepared with rice, apples, onions, garlic and chestnuts.

In each region, sausages are fried, poached or grilled according to local taste and served with apples, chestnuts, potato purées, white haricot beans, lentils, braised cabbage or simply a pile of soft, golden onions.

Charcuterie is sometimes used in intriguing ways. On the Atlantic coast, a platter of raw oysters is served with crisp hot sausages, or *Crépinettes*, and white wine or Pineau. In Brittany, a fish is often stuffed with pork pâté, and some gourmands claim that crisp sliced bread spread with *Rillettes* and served with *café au lait* is the best of mid-morning snacks.

PLATEAU DE CHARCUTERIE
Platter of cooked pork meats

A *Plateau de Charcuterie* may be an extravagant display of *charcuteries* punctuated by a few salad leaves or by diced jelly. It may be amusingly formal: neat rows of sliced sausages and ham in semi-circles around a grand goose-shaped mould of *Rillettes*, or it may be simply an assortment of whole sausages piled on a wooden board with a heavy knife.

The offering will vary according to the occasion – a starter, a buffet or the best part of a meal – but whether it is a *Plateau* or a single *Assiette de Charcuterie* it will generally include sliced sausages and at least two kinds of thinly sliced ham: a dry cured ham from Bayonne, Savoie, Corsica or Auvergne, perhaps a smoked ham from Alsace or Brittany, or a few slices of excellent boiled ham, either *jambon à l'os* or *Jambon au Torchon* (see page 188). The *Plateau* may also include a *galantine*, a boned duck or chicken stuffed with a rich forcemeat and simmered in a fragrant broth, and a *roulade*, a pistachio-flavoured cooked sausage, with perhaps a plump garlic sausage. There will probably be a variety of *Rillettes* (see page 185), country pâtés and chicken liver mousses in their porcelain terrines, and finally a separate tray of mustards, gherkins, unsalted butter and a basket of bread. You will often see the cheeky term *Les Cochonnailles* appear on a menu instead of *Charcuterie*.

TERRINE DE CAMPAGNE
Crustless meat and herb pie

Pâtés and terrines were first made in medieval times and were served in exuberant displays. Today, bistros, brasseries and country inns offer guests a trolley packed with a variety of porcelain terrines with a jar of gherkins to accompany them. Starred restaurants serve as a starter slices of different terrines on the same plate, attractively garnished with watercress or salad leaves.

Both pâtés and terrines are easy to make at home and are consistently better than those that are available in the shops. A pâté is a mixture of pieces of veal, pork, poultry, fish, game or vegetables seasoned with herbs, spices, wine or brandy and baked in a pastry dough crust ('pâté' actually means crust). A terrine is a crustless pâté. It is basically made with the same ingredients and baked, and often served, in an earthenware or porcelain baking dish. Nowadays the names tend to be used interchangeably.

Whether it is a fancy terrine made with goose or duck liver, partridge or hare seasoned with truffles, marrow or pistachios, or a simpler version, the key element in this dish is the fine mingling of flavours and textures. Fragrant slices of chicken, ham, veal, pork, rabbit or duck – often marinated in brandy or wine – spread between layers of ground or chopped, highly seasoned meat, flavoured with a variety of herbs and spices, create the perfect combination for an interesting terrine. Eggs, bread or pork fat are added to bind the mixture together.

You can use a loaf tin to make this terrine, but if you enjoy home-made terrines, it is worth investing in a good quality glazed earthenware or porcelain terrine with a lid.

Pâtés and terrines are best chopped by hand if there is time so the juices do not escape, otherwise a food processor will do. They must be kept refrigerated for between two and seven days before they are served for all the flavours to develop fully. A terrine will keep for two weeks in the refrigerator. Serve them with country or wholemeal bread, a pot of butter, gherkins, pickled pearl onions and a tossed salad.

——————— *Serves 6* ———————

8 oz (225 g) pig or chicken livers
8 oz (225 g) stewing veal
8 oz (225 g) piece streaky bacon or
    shoulder steak
4 oz (100 g) pork shoulder, diced
8 oz (225 g) chicken breasts,
    skinned
1 1/2 teaspoons salt
1/4 teaspoon black, green or red
    peppercorns
2 teaspoons dried thyme
1 teaspoon dried sage
pinch of freshly grated nutmeg
10 juniper berries, coarsely ground

4 cloves garlic, chopped
1/2 teaspoon ground bay leaves
2 tablespoons brandy
2 teaspoons groundnut oil
2 onions, chopped
6 shallots, coarsely chopped
2 eggs
5 tablespoons dry white wine
20 thin slices streaky bacon or pork
    fat to line the terrine and cover
    the top
pinch of dried thyme
3 juniper berries, ground
3 bay leaves

Trim the meats, discarding any skin, gristle or extra fat. Slice the chicken breasts in half horizontally and set aside. Coarsely chop the livers and all the meats then mix with the salt, peppercorns, thyme, sage, nutmeg, juniper berries, garlic and ground bay leaves and stir the ingredients together. Sprinkle with the brandy and stir with your hands so that everything is coated with seasoning. Cover and leave to marinate overnight in a cool place.

Pre-heat the oven to gas mark 4, 350°F (180°C).

Heat the oil and fry the onions and shallots until soft. Stir into the marinated meat mixture. Place half the mixture in a bowl or a food processor and chop until fairly smooth then add the remainder and chop for a few seconds to obtain a coarser texture. Stir in the eggs and wine and mix together thoroughly.

Remove the rind from the bacon and stretch the rashers with the back of a knife blade. Line the bottom and sides of a 2 pint (1.2 litre) rectangular or oval terrine or mould with the strips of bacon or pork fat. Leave a little overhanging the sides. Spoon half the meat mixture into the terrine, arrange the chicken breasts on top then add the remaining meat mixture and smooth the top with the back of a spoon. Sprinkle with thyme and the juniper berries and arrange the bay leaves on top. Fold the bacon over the terrine and add some more slices of bacon or fat to cover the top, if necessary.

Place a piece of oiled foil on top and seal tightly. Put on the terrine lid if you have one. Place the terrine in a deep roasting tin and add enough hot water to come half way up the sides of the terrine. Bake in the oven for 1½–2 hours.

Remove from the oven, discard the foil lid and leave the terrine to cool for 1 hour. The juices will be clear and yellow and will circulate through the pâté as it cools, making the pâté mellow and fragrant. Cover the top with a piece of cardboard wrapped in foil or a piece of wood the size of your terrine top. Place a few tins on top to weigh the pâté down and make the texture firm and easier to slice. Leave to stand for 2 hours. Remove the tins, cover tightly and refrigerate for 2–3 days for the flavours to develop.

Remove from the refrigerator about 20 minutes before serving. Dip the bottom of the terrine in hot water, or dip a tea towel in hot water, squeeze it out then wrap the hot towel round the bottom and sides of the dish for a few minutes. Run a knife around the edge of the pâté and unmould on to a serving plate. Alternatively you can cut the pâté into ½ in (1 cm) slices and garnish with green salad, or serve directly from the terrine. Serve the terrine with gherkins and crusty bread and butter.

PÂTÉ CHAUD FAMILIAL

Veal pâté in a crust

Madame Monique Lansard of Chambéry is the acknowledged expert on the food of Savoie, a much underestimated cuisine, according to her. She regaled me with tales of the grand aristocratic dinners of the House of Savoie, when the duchy included much of northern Italy as well as Sardinia. In fact, Savoie voted to join the French republic as late as 1861. This dish reflects the richness of the gastronomic legacy with the use of candied lemon rind. The original recipe uses *cédrat*, citron, a large lemon-like citrus fruit which made its way up to the Alps from southern Italy. Madame Lansard also told me that another aspect of authentic Savoyard cuisine is the love of salty/sweet combinations with bitter notes. It's a far cry from the well-known clichés of cheese and potatoes.

Serves 6

1¾ lb (800 g) veal fillet, diced
4 fl oz (120 ml) white wine vinegar
4 fl oz (120 ml) water
4 oz (100 g) pork fat, finely
   chopped
5 oz (150 g) pork chop, boned and
   finely chopped
1 onion, finely chopped
a few sprigs fresh parsley, finely
   chopped
3 oz (75 g) candied lemon rind or
   citroen, coarsely chopped
salt and freshly ground black pepper

FOR THE PASTRY:

1 lb 2 oz (500 g) plain flour
a pinch of salt
6 oz (175 g) butter
3 oz (75 g) lard
5 egg yolks

FOR THE SAUCE:

2 oz (50 g) butter
2 tablespoons plain flour
1 pint (600 ml) beef stock
1 tablespoon red wine vinegar
2 tablespoons Madeira (optional)

Marinate the veal in the vinegar and water overnight.

    To make the pastry, place the flour and salt in a bowl and make a well in the centre. Add the butter and lard and work them into the flour until the mixture resembles breadcrumbs. Add 4 of the egg yolks and mix with your hands until the mixture comes away

A small church in Normandy

A sleepy village in Languedoc

from the sides of the bowl, adding a little water if necessary. Wrap in cling film and refrigerate until required.

Pre-heat the oven to gas mark 7, 425°F (220°C) and grease a baking tray.

Drain and dry the veal thoroughly. In a food processor, blend the fat, pork and the onion. Add to this paste the parsley, lemon rind, salt and pepper. Roll out the pastry on a floured board in a rectangular shape. Put one-third of the pork mixture in the middle and flatten it down, leaving a border of 1½″ all round. Then place half the cubed veal over the mixture and follow with another third of the pork mixture. Spread the other half of the veal on top of that and finish with a final layer of the remaining pork. Bring all the pastry edges up over the filling to cover it and seal the edges. Decorate with any left-over pastry cut into shapes. Brush with the remaining egg yolk and bake in the oven for 10 minutes. Cut a small hole in the top to release the steam. Reduce the oven temperature to gas mark 4, 350°F (180°C) and cook for a further 1 hour.

Meanwhile, make the sauce. Melt the butter, add the flour and stir until the mixture is golden. Gradually pour in the stock, stirring all the time to prevent any lumps forming. When the mixture comes to the boil, add the wine vinegar then turn down the heat and simmer for 20 minutes, stirring occasionally. Just before serving, season with salt and pepper and add the Madeira, if using. Serve the pie hot or warm accompanied by the hot sauce.

— LOIRE, SOUTH-WEST AND AUVERGNE —

GRILLONS

Crackling

Grillons start with the principle that everything – but everything – is good in a pig, goose or duck. Crackling in French has evocative names: *grattons, gratterons, frittons, chichons, griaudes, beursaudes, grillons*. They are the little crunchy bits left when preparing rendered pork fat while cooking belly pork, or the left-over meat and bones left from making *Confit* of duck (see page 183). These crisp, brown titbits of wing tips and neck or bits attached to the carcass are scooped out from the bottom of the cooling pan, drained and seasoned with salt and coarsely ground black pepper. If they are very uneven, they can be processed for a second in a food processor or blender, but they are a rustic treat and should remain coarse and crunchy. They can be spread on crisp toast rubbed with garlic and eaten with drinks. Sprinkled with red wine vinegar, parsley and garlic, they may be served hot with sliced apples or potatoes. Blended with a few eggs and fresh herbs they will fill a cooked pastry shell and make a savoury tart. Seasoned with thyme and freshly grated nutmeg, they can enliven an omelette. And stirred into plain dough, they will create a richly seasoned bread.

These crisp, tiny morsels of pork, duck or goose may also be covered with a layer of fat and stored in stoneware or glass jars like their soft cousins *Rillettes*.

TERRINE DE CANARD

Duck, ham and liver terrine flavoured with herbs, garlic,
shallots and cognac

A duck terrine may be cooked and served in an oval or rectangular baking dish. It must be made at least two days in advance, but it will keep covered for two or three weeks in the refrigerator.

Discard any nerves, gristle and any extra fat. If you cannot find duck liver, chicken livers can be used. Garnished with a few sprigs of watercress and served with a pot of fresh butter and a basket of country bread, it can make the centrepiece of a picnic, a buffet, a light summer lunch or a starter.

—————— *Serves 6* ——————

FOR THE DUCK
1 lb (450 g) duck (either magret,
    breasts, or boned thighs)
1 oz (25 g) salt
4 teaspoons dried thyme
2 bay leaves, crumbled
8 juniper berries
10 peppercorns
2 tablespoons cognac
4 fl oz (120 ml) Madeira, port or
    white wine
pinch of freshly grated nutmeg
4 cloves garlic, crushed
1 tablespoon grated orange rind
2 eggs
salt

FOR THE LIVER MIXTURE
1 tablespoon oil

4 oz (100 g) piece streaky bacon
1 duck liver or 3 chicken livers
3 thick slices boiled ham
3 tablespoons chopped fresh parsley
5 shallots, coarsely chopped
2 oz (50 g) pistachios or hazelnuts,
    shelled

TO ASSEMBLE
1 tablespoon duck fat
a few thick lettuce leaves
8 oz (225 g) thin strips of pork fat
    or slices of streaky bacon
3 bay leaves

TO GARNISH
few sprigs of flat-leaved parsley or
    watercress

Bone the duck, cut it into ½ inch (1 cm) pieces and place it in a bowl. Add the salt, thyme, half the crumbled bay leaves, the juniper berries, peppercorns, cognac and Madeira, port or wine. Leave to marinate for 1 hour, stirring once or twice. Stir in the nutmeg, garlic and orange rind. Blend in the eggs and season with salt.

Pre-heat the oven to gas mark 4, 350°F (180°C) and butter a terrine.

Heat the oil and sauté the bacon for a few minutes. Add the livers and sauté until sealed on both sides so they will have more flavour and will not shrink during the cooking of the terrine. Add the ham, parsley and shallots and stir for a few minutes then add the pistachios or hazelnuts.

In a separate pan, heat the duck fat and sauté the lettuce leaves for 1 minute.

Line the terrine with the thin strips of pork fat or slices of bacon. Spoon alternate layers of the duck mixture and the liver mixture into the terrine until all the ingredients have been used up. Hold the terrine with both hands and shake it so that the meats settle and the marinade penetrates throughout the dish. Arrange the bay leaves on the top then cover with the sautéed lettuce leaves. Cover with a piece of kitchen foil. Stand the terrine in a pan filled with water to come about 2 inches (5 cm) up the sides of the terrine. Cook in the oven for 1½ hours.

Turn off the oven, open the oven door and leave the terrine to cool in the oven for 30 minutes. Remove from the oven. Cover a piece of wood or cardboard the size of the top of the terrine with kitchen foil and place it on the terrine then place a couple of tins on top to weigh the mixture down. The cooking juices may overflow, so you can stand the terrine in a shallow dish so that you can collect the jellied juices and dice them to garnish the terrine. Refrigerate for at least 2 days to develop the flavours.

To unmould the terrine, dip the dish in hot water for a second or run a tea towel under hot water, wring it out and wrap it round the dish. Place a plate on top and turn over in one decisive gesture. Discard the bacon or fat and slice the terrine with a warm, sharp knife. Arrange a little of the diced jellied cooking juices around the terrine and garnish with the parsley or watercress.

Note

If you serve it straight from the cooking terrine, clean the top and sides with a damp cloth then use a spatula and a sharp knife.

*T*ERRINE DE *F*OIES DE *V*OLAILLE

Chicken liver terrine

Terrines and pâtés are pillars of *cuisine de ménage*, home cooking, because they are easy to prepare, keep for days in the refrigerator, and taste far better than anything one can buy.

Pâté and terrine-making is a wide field. There are delicate terrines made with sweetbreads, calf liver, fish, goose liver or vegetables. There are exotic pâtés made with chopped lamb, kidney fat, brown sugar, raisins, rum, lemon and pepper wrapped in a light pastry shell. There are potent terrines made with wild boar, partridge or hare.

But pâtés and terrines can also be prepared with simple, inexpensive ingredients and often need little preparation. This delightfully light terrine does not even need baking. Serve it in its terrine, wrapped in a fresh, white tea towel and presented with a basket of lightly toasted brioche or fresh country bread and a pot of unsalted butter.

—————— *Serves 4* ——————

10 oz (275 g) chicken livers, trimmed	*1 tablespoon butter*
salt and coarsely ground black pepper	*1 tablespoon groundnut oil*
pinch of ground coriander	*2 shallots, coarsely chopped*
1 teaspoon dried thyme	*2 tablespoons cognac or port*
1 bay leaf, crushed	*4 oz (100 g) butter, cut into pieces*
1 teaspoon juniper berries, crushed	*3 egg whites*
	8 oz (225 g) slices pork back fat
	3 large bay leaves

Wash the chicken livers under cold water then pat dry on kitchen paper. Sprinkle them with salt, pepper, the coriander, thyme, crushed bay leaf and juniper berries. Heat the butter and oil in a frying pan and sauté the chicken livers for 2–3 minutes. Add the shallots and cook for a further 2 minutes. Remove 3 livers and cut them in half. Sprinkle them with salt, pepper and the cognac or port, cover and leave to stand for 1 hour.

Place the sautéed liver and shallots in a food processor or

blender, add the butter and blend thoroughly. Taste and adjust the seasoning with salt and pepper if necessary. Whisk the egg whites until stiff. Gently fold them into the liver mixture.

Line the base and sides of a terrine with some thin slices of pork back fat reserving some for the top of the terrine. Spoon half the puréed mixture into the terrine, arrange the halved livers on top, then cover with the remaining mixture. Place the 3 bay leaves on top and cover with more fat. Cover with foil and the lid of the terrine if you have one. Refrigerate for 24 hours.

Remove the slices of fat from the top and serve directly from the terrine with a spoon dipped in hot water. Serve with lightly toasted brioche or country bread.

Note

A more conventional *Terrine de Foies* is prepared with the same quantity of chicken livers as streaky bacon, 2 eggs, spices and a little brandy, all coarsely chopped and baked for 2 hours in a covered terrine.

CONFIT DE CANARD
Preserved duck

Before refrigeration, different methods of preserving food were vital, and many ways were developed to preserve food while also enhancing the flavours of the products. Fruits, vegetables, meat and fish, for example, were dried for weeks or months. And in the process, plums turned into luscious *pruneaux*, dry cod became the spirited *morue*, dried mushrooms preserved within their brittle, delicate morsels the intoxicating essence of the forest. Salting was another common traditional method of preserving and improving. Preserving pork, turkey, rabbit, duck, goose or sausages in fat, however, is a method which has only ever been used in the south-west. *Confit* – meat preserved in fat – occupies a very special place in local gastronomy as the poultry fattened for *foie gras* acquires a superb texture and a fragrant taste in the process.

So although today duck can be frozen, vacuum-packed or tinned and the necessity to preserve it in this way has vanished, *Confit* remains more popular than ever. Duck *Confit* is more popular than goose because, as I was told by everyone in the south-west, duck is tasty, easier to handle and quicker to cook than goose. The duck starts to improve after one or two weeks as it matures and acquires its full flavour.

Pork, but more often duck or goose, *Confit* is used to enrich soups like *Garbure* (see page 60) or stews like Cassoulet (see page 146) and *Potée* (see page 158) to give a rich flavour. It can also be simply grilled, sprinkled with chopped fresh parsley and garlic and accompanied with sautéed potatoes, sautéed mushrooms, chestnut purée, braised cabbage, lentils or haricot beans. Slivered *Confit* is often served cold over a tossed green salad, seasoned with a walnut or olive oil dressing.

When you prepare *Confit*, you can buy separate duck legs and wings and a tin of fat (available in delicatessens), or buy a whole duck, cook and preserve the legs and wings and render the fat from the bird to prepare the *Confit*.

There are two schools of thought about cooking *Confit*. Most people simmer the meat for about two hours, while others cook it on a brisk heat for less than an hour and let it cool in the hot fat. Curiously, the latter duck seems to keep longer and better.

—————— *Serves 4* ——————

4 duck legs and 4 duck wings or
  2 ducks
5 tablespoons coarse sea salt or
  kosher salt
1 tablespoon coarsely ground black
  pepper
2 teaspoons dried thyme

1 teaspoon dried rosemary
3 bay leaves, crumbled
6 cloves garlic, studded with 6
  cloves
3 lb (1.4 kg) tinned duck or goose
  fat

If you prepare your own duck fat, remove as much fat as possible from the birds and cook it slowly on a medium heat until liquid. Pour it through a sieve into a jar and store for later use.

To prepare the duck, cut off the wing tips and separate the thighs and drumsticks. Mix together the salt, pepper, thyme, rosemary and bay leaves and rub all over the duck, patting with the palms of your hands. Place the duck pieces in a bowl with the clove-studded garlic cloves, cover and refrigerate for 24–48 hours.

Heat the prepared or tinned duck or goose fat in a large, heavy-based saucepan. Shake the pieces of duck and wipe off the excess salt. Pat the pieces dry on kitchen paper. Place the pieces of duck one at a time into the hot fat; they should be completely covered in fat. Cook for 45 minutes on a medium to high heat until the juices run mother-of-pearl pink when the flesh is pricked with a fork. Remove from the heat and leave to cool in the hot fat for 1 hour.

Remove the duck from the fat with a slotted spoon and pack the pieces in a wide glass, stoneware or porcelain storage jar. Cover with about 2 inches (5 cm) of melted fat then seal with a piece of muslin, a layer of coarse salt and finally a piece of thick kitchen foil. Store in a cellar or cool place or in the refrigerator for up to a year.

After 3 months, you may like to cook the duck again and store it in fat in the same way; its flavour will improve.

When ready to use a piece of *Confit*, remove it from the storage pot and shake off the excess fat. Place it in a dry frying pan skin-side down, and cook for 10 minutes on each side.

RILLETTES

A fragrant spread made with shredded meat seasoned with herbs

Rillettes can be made with goose, duck, rabbit, pork meat, or a mixture of all four. The meat is simmered with herbs and spices then shredded and potted under a layer of fat. There are many regional variations of *Rillettes*, but they are a Loire speciality.

Rillettes have a rough, silky quality, and it is the fat which supplies both the flavour and the texture. They are usually served cool, like terrines and pâtés, spread on crisp toast or sliced baguette. But they are also eaten with oysters on their shells, turned into a savoury tart or beaten into an omelette.

Rillons are about 4 inch (10 cm) cubes of pork neck, bacon, ham or goose cooked with spices and covered with melted dripping. They are sold in most *charcuteries* and served cold as a starter or warm with apples or potatoes.

RILLETTES DE CANARD

Duck Rillettes

In the south-west, duck or goose – including the bones and skin – are cooked in duck fat with pork belly, shredded and seasoned to become unctuous *Rillettes*.

─────── *Serves 4–6* ───────

1½ lb (675 g) belly of pork, cut into chunks	*1 pint (600 ml) water*
	3 bay leaves
2 lb (900 g) duck, including bones and skin, cut into chunks	*2 teaspoons dried thyme*
	salt and freshly ground black pepper

Follow the recipe for *Rillettes de Porc*, (see page 186) browning the pork then adding the remaining ingredients and simmering for at least 4–5 hours. Strain, discard the bones, shred the meats and season generously with salt, pepper and thyme. Store covered in a layer of fat.

RILLETTES DE PORC
Pork Rillettes

Pork *Rillettes* remain the most economical and the most frequently made. They are prepared from whatever pieces of pork are left over from making sausages, and may include some diced goose breast or rabbit. The proportions of fat and lean meat vary from equal quantities to half as much fat as lean, depending on the cook.

——————— *Serves 4–6* ———————

3 lb (1.4 kg) Pork neck, loin or belly
1 lb (450 g) pork back fat
1–2 pork bones (optional)
1 clove garlic, crushed
2 bay leaves
1 tablespoon chopped fresh thyme

pinch of freshly grated nutmeg
1 clove
10 fl oz (300 ml) dry white wine
10 fl oz (300 ml) water
salt and coarsely ground black
    pepper

Cut the meat and fat into 2 inch (5 cm) chunks and place them in a large saucepan with all the remaining ingredients and enough water and wine to cover. Bring slowly to the boil, stirring occasionally, then cover and simmer for about 4 hours, removing any scum on top from time to time. Most of the liquid will evaporate, but check the pan occasionally so that the meat does not stick and add a little water if necessary. Leave to cool.

Strain the mixture, reserving the fat. Taking a spoonful of meats at a time into a clean bowl, shred the meats with a fork in each hand and discard any bones or herbs. Season generously with salt, pepper and a little more thyme; *Rillettes* should be highly seasoned.

As the fat cools, stir as much of it as you want into the meat mixture and stir occasionally until cool. The texture should be rough, not too smooth or puréed. Spoon into glass jars or stoneware pots, cover with waxed paper or kitchen foil and lid if you have one. Keep in a cool place for 2 to 3 days before serving. If you pour about 1 inch (2.5 cm) of melted lard on top, the *Rillettes* will keep for 2 to 3 weeks. Serve with olives and gherkins.

RILLETTES DE LAPIN
Rabbit Rillettes

If you can find wild rabbit, fragrant with herbs, this dish will taste superb. However, it is still delicious made with ordinary rabbit. It will keep for a few weeks.

—————— *Serves 4* ——————

3 lb (1.4 kg) rabbit
1 lb (450 g) belly of pork
8 oz (225 g) pork fat
1 teaspoon dried thyme
2 bay leaves, crumbled
salt
6 tablespoons groundnut oil
2 lb (900 g) onions, sliced
1 lb (450 g) carrots, sliced

1 clove garlic
2 pints (1.2 litres) dry white wine
10 fl oz (300 ml) white vermouth
coarsely ground black pepper
1 tablespoon ground coriander
1 tablespoon chopped fresh chervil
1 teaspoon chopped fresh tarragon
enough rendered pork fat or lard to
    cover in a 1 inch (2.5 cm) layer

Remove the bones and gristle from the rabbit, pat it dry on kitchen paper and cut it into large cubes. Cut the pork and pork fat into large cubes. Place all the meats in a bowl and sprinkle with the thyme, bay leaves and salt. Heat the oil and cook the onions, carrots and garlic for a few minutes until beginning to soften. Add the meat and cook for about 10 minutes until everything is golden brown. Pour in the wine and vermouth, sprinkle with pepper and the coriander and bring to the boil. Cover and simmer gently over a low heat for 3–4 hours until the meat falls apart. Leave to cool.

Strain the mixture, place the meats in a bowl and return the liquid to the pan. With one fork in each hand, shred the meats; the texture should be rough, not puréed. Bring the cooking juices to the boil and add the chervil and tarragon. Simmer, uncovered, for a few minutes to reduce the quantity slightly then pour over the meats and stir well. Transfer the mixture to glass jars or stoneware pots. Heat the pork fat or lard and pour a 1 inch (2.5 cm) layer over the dish. Cover with kitchen foil and leave to cool then refrigerate for a few days. Serve with fresh walnuts sprinkled with red wine vinegar.

*J*AMBON AU *T*ORCHON

Ham cooked in a cloth

Ham can be prepared in many ways, rubbed and cured with sea salt, hung in a dark, airy room, or covered with ashes until it is dried and becomes *jambon cru* or *jambon de montagne*. It can also be smoked, preferably with fruit woods, or cooked in a good broth for a *Jambon au Torchon* or *Jambon de Paris*.

Jambon au Torchon is a wonderful product. Traditionally a handful of dried hay (preferably this year's crop) is spread at the bottom of the cooking pan to steady the ham as it cooks and impart its fragrant taste. I add a handful of herbs to flavour the broth instead.

This is an easy dish to prepare and it always tastes much more fragrant than when it is bought. The ham can be served cold as a starter or in sandwiches. It could also be used to prepare *Jambon Persillé* (see page 192), *Jambon à la Crème* (see page 167), *Poche de Veau* (see page 136), terrines and, of course, *croque monsieur*. Cooking time is about 20 minutes per lb (450 g) plus another 15 minutes.

———— *Serves 12–15* ————

8–12 lb (3.5–5.5 kg) uncooked,
   unsmoked ham or gammon
   labelled 'cook before eating' with
   or without bone
1 pint (600 ml) dry white wine
handful of dried breadcrumbs

FOR THE BROTH
2 carrots
2 onions each studded with 2 cloves

few sprigs fresh parsley
4 bay leaves
3 tsp dry thyme
2 tablespoons chopped fresh
   rosemary
10 peppercorns
1 teaspoon juniper berries
pinch of freshly grated nutmeg
bones and pork trimmings (optional)

Place the ham in a pan of cold water and leave to soak according to the instructions on the label, changing the water 4 or 5 times; the time will depend on the amount of brine injected into the ham. Brush the surface with a rough brush and rinse under cold water.

Bring a saucepan of water to the boil and add the broth ingredients, including the ham trimmings and bone you may have. Simmer the broth for at least 1 hour. Leave to cool. Wrap the ham in a large piece of clean cotton cloth or a double thickness of muslin and tie it into a bundle. Place a tea towel folded at the bottom of a large saucepan to prevent the ham from touching and sticking to the bottom of the pan. Place the ham on top and strain over the cold broth. Bring to the boil, skimming the broth twice with a slotted spoon. Lower the heat, cover and simmer for 2 hours. Add the wine and simmer for a further 30 minutes. The water should be kept just below boiling point or the rind may break. If the water evaporates too much, add a little more boiling water. Place a piece of board covered in kitchen foil and a few heavy tins on top to press it down and leave the ham to cool in the broth overnight.

The next day, discard the liquid and remove the wrapping cloth and string. Remove all the rind and part of the fat on top of the ham so that only about ½ inch (1 cm) of the fat remains. (Keep the rind and fat if you are likely to use them for a stew, a terrine or a *Potée*.) I like to rub dried breadcrumbs over the surface of the ham, pressing hard with both hands. Wrap the ham in a large clean cotton cloth and keep it refrigerated for at least 10 hours before using it so it will be firm and easy to carve.

Note

Professionals leave the rind on the ham – they have sharper knives than I do – and slice it with the ham. They only use breadcrumbs to cover the small *jambonneau*, the knuckle of pork, which is sold separately and cooked with lentils or beans.

CAILLETTES

Crisp meat and vegetable sausages

Whether they are called *gayettes, crépinettes, boulettes* or *caillettes*, each region makes its own version of what is basically a sausage without a casing.

They are prepared with a mixture made from a selection of: pig livers, chicken livers, rabbit, ham, bacon, kidneys, pigs' lungs, sweetbreads, pigs' head or pork. They may be enriched with chestnuts, diced celery, Swiss chard, sorrel, cabbage, spinach, olives, pistachios, garlic, dandelion leaves, parsley, basil or thyme. Some are shaped like a ball, others like an oval, flat sausage, and they are wrapped in a piece of caul or with thin slices of pork fat before being baked. They are stored in a jar covered with fat. When required, they can be served cold, or sliced, rolled in egg and breadcrumbs and fried or grilled.

Caillettes, which means 'little quails', is the version favoured in Provence. They are moulded into little balls, although you can also bake the mixture in a terrine. They are served warm with a bowl of bitter green curly endive, dandelion leaves or watercress seasoned with a sharp vinaigrette, or cold as a starter with toast, butter and a bowl of olives.

——— *Serves 4* ———

1 lb (450 g) fresh spinach leaves, frozen leaf spinach, or spinach and Swiss chard
2 tablespoons oil
2 tablespoons butter (optional)
1 onion, chopped
4 oz (100 g) streaky bacon, chopped
8 oz (225 g) chicken livers or pig liver, trimmed
1 tablespoon plain flour
8 oz (225 g) lean pork, chopped
4 teaspoons dried thyme
2 bay leaves, crumbled
4 cloves garlic, chopped
handful of sorrel leaves, coarsely chopped (optional) or juice of 1 lemon
5 tablespoons chopped, preferably flat-leaved, parsley
1 egg
salt and coarsely ground black pepper
16 sage leaves
1 lb (450 g) thin slices bacon or a piece of caul large enough to wrap the Caillettes

Pre-heat the oven to gas mark 5, 375°F (190°C).

If you are using fresh spinach, wash and dry it. Heat 1 tablespoon of the oil and the butter, if using, in a pan, add the greens, cover and cook for a few minutes until soft, stirring occasionally. Drain. If you are using frozen leaf spinach, thaw it and drain it throughly.

Heat the remaining oil and fry the onion over a low heat until soft. Add the bacon and sauté for a few minutes then transfer the mixture to a bowl. Sprinkle the liver with the flour and fry until crisp on all sides then add to the onion mixture. Sauté the pork for 15 minutes, sprinkle with the thyme and bay leaves and cook for a further 10 minutes. Stir in the garlic. Mix together the spinach, the onion mixture, the pork mixture and add the sorrel or lemon juice. Divide the mixture in half and add the parsley to one half. Place this half in a food processor or blender and process for a second so that it is coarsely ground. Remove from the processor and process the second half so that it is a little smoother. Stir the two mixtures back together, add the egg and season with salt and pepper. If you wish, fry a teaspoonful of the mixture in a little oil or drop it in boiling water so that you can taste it and adjust the seasoning if necessary.

Shape the mixture into little balls about 3 inches (7.5 cm) wide and place 1 or 2 sage leaves on top. Criss-cross 2 or 3 slices of bacon around each ball so that they will remain moist during baking and arrange them in a shallow ovenproof dish. Stand the dish in a roasting tin filled with a little water. Flatten the *Caillettes* slightly on the top with your hand and bake them for 45–50 minutes.

JAMBON PERSILLÉ

Ham in parsley, garlic and vinegar aspic

A must in Burgundy on Easter Sunday, *Jambon Persillé* is glorious in a buffet display, as a starter or as the centrepiece of a family summer meal accompanied with a tossed salad and a potato gratin.

I generally present *Jambon Persillé* in its bowl, this way I do not have to add gelatine and I think this gives a more interesting texture. If you do add the gelatine, it makes the shimmering dome easier to unmould and you can serve slices with a flat spatula and a spoon. The flavour will improve if it is refrigerated for at least a day, and it will keep, covered, for over a week.

———————— *Serves 8* ————————

FOR THE MEAT AND BROTH
3 lb (1.4 kg) uncooked, unsmoked ham or gammon or bacon shoulder joint
1 lb (450 g) veal bones or veal knuckle (optional)
2 onions
4 cloves
3 carrots
3 cloves garlic
1 stalk celery
5 black peppercorns
2 sprigs fresh tarragon

2 sprigs fresh thyme
1 pint (600 ml) dry white wine

5 tablespoons snipped fresh flat-leaf parsley
3 cloves garlic, crushed
3 shallots, coarsely chopped
3 tablespoons red wine vinegar
salt and freshly ground black pepper
1 oz (25 g) gelatine (optional)
1 egg white, lightly beaten

TO SERVE
2 teaspoons red wine vinegar

Remove the rind and most of the fat from the ham or bacon. Soak in cold water to remove the salt, if necessary. Place the ham and bones, if using, in a large pan, preferably not aluminium. Stud the onions with the cloves and add them to the pan with the carrots, garlic, celery, peppercorns, tarragon, thyme and wine. Add just enough cold water to cover the ham (about 2½ pints (1.5 litres)).

Opposite: JAMBON PERSILLÉ

Bring to the boil, cover and simmer for 2½ hours until the ham is soft enough to be pierced easily with a fork, skimming the top a few times during cooking. Remove from the heat and leave to cool in the fragrant broth for 1 hour.

Remove the ham from the stock, place it on a board and shred half the meat with one fork in each hand, and chop the remaining half into large chunks, discarding all the fat. Place it in a bowl and add the parsley, garlic, shallots and red wine vinegar and stir gently. Discard the bones and herbs from the stock. Remove the vegetables, chop or crush them with a fork and add them to the meat mixture. Spoon the mixture into a 2½ pint (1.5 litre) bowl or porcelain terrine.

Strain the stock into a saucepan, return it to a high heat and boil rapidly until reduced to 1½ pints (900 ml). Soak the gelatine, if using, in cold water for 2 minutes until softened. Whisk the egg white into the stock and gently bring to the boil, whisking all the time to incorporate all the impurities. Be sure to stop whisking before it reaches boiling point so that you do not break the crust. (See Consommé, page 73.) Leave to settle for 5 minutes. Line a sieve with muslin and strain the stock carefully then return it to the heat. If you have not used bones, you will need to add some gelatine. Whisk the gelatine into the hot broth until it dissolves. Taste and correct the seasoning with salt and pepper. Spoon the mixture over the meat. Press the mixture down with the back of a spoon, then add a little more stock, if necessary. Cover with a plate, place a few tins on top to weigh it down and refrigerate for about 24 hours. Pour any remaining stock into a bowl and refrigerate to use as a garnish.

Serve the *Jambon Persillé* from the dish, using two large spoons to serve. If you want to unmould it, dip the dish in hot water for a few seconds, or dip a tea towel in hot water, squeeze it out then wrap it around the bottom and sides of the dish for a minute. Run the tip of a knife around the bowl, place a large plate on top and unmould in one decisive movement. Spoon the reserved jelly, chopped, around the edge to decorate and sprinkle with the red wine vinegar. Dip a large knife or spatula into warm water and cut the dome into slices or wedges.

Opposite: GOUGÈRE WITH CASSIS (*see page 204*)

CHEESES

Les Fromages

Wits often like to muse over the fact that because France has more than 500 different kinds of cheese it must be a diverse and interesting country, and one which is sometimes quite difficult to govern. Lately, the rules imposed – or about to be imposed – by the new European market have created a great deal of anguish among the cheese-lovers of France. Would a bland industrial pasteurised type of cheese replace the vast range of cheeses made here for centuries? Fortunately, the same fear was shared by many traditional cheese-makers in Britain, Portugal, Spain, Italy and the Netherlands and diversity prevailed. The traditions of cheese-making remain strong, so although the rules are strict and numerous, fine quality cheese-making will endure.

France is the world's premier cheese producer with about 1,500,000 tons per year of cows', ewes' and goats' milk used either raw or pasteurised and turned into cheese by craftsmen on small farms, in co-operative dairies or large factories. Some of these cheeses are internationally famous, while others are not even known outside their own region, being made by a lone farmer, given no registered name and consumed entirely on the spot.

The metamorphosis of milk into cheese starts with the processing of the milk through the separating and treatment of the curd, moves through the careful ageing of the cheese (*affinage*) which is probably the most important step, and finally on to the packaging. It is a varied and patient process, and produces cheeses that differ in taste, texture and appearance.

The most popular cheeses in France remain Camembert, goat cheeses and Roquefort, but everyone has one or two favourites that no one else has ever heard of, and true gourmets regularly canvas both their local cheese shop and the countryside looking for new products as well as savouring familiar ones.

For the sake of clarity, I will say that according to their origin, preparation and shape, cheeses can be grouped into nine main families.

Les Pâtes Molles à Croûtes Fleuries

'Soft, creamy cheese with soft downy crusts', these are made with raw or pasteurised cows' or goats' milk and have a fat content of between 20 and 75 per cent. They have a creamy texture and a white or golden mould crust. It is the penicillium spread on the surface of the curd which gives the famous white fuzz (downy like a beautiful woman's cheek) of Camembert. The cheese will then ripen and be cured in cellars for two to four weeks to acquire its celebrated soft texture and delicate flavour.

The most famous cheeses in this family are: Brie, first made around the eighth century and prepared both in Meaux and Melun; Camembert, developed during the Revolution and probably the most popular cheese in France, always sold in its round wooden box; Neufchâtel, shaped as hearts, logs or rounds; Chaource; Carré de l'Est and Coulommiers.

These cheeses are at their best in autumn, winter and the beginning of spring because the cows have grazed on fields of flowers and new buds. This type of cheese does not keep very well. In fact, in France most people only buy one portion of Brie or half a Camembert to make sure the texture is *à coeur*, uniformly ripe and fresh. A good cheese merchant will always inquire when you are going to serve this cheese – lunch today, dinner tomorrow – so that it will be perfect when it is needed. Make sure the crust does not become reddish or wrinkly and that when you cut the cheese it is ivory throughout and neither chalky white nor too runny. Curiously in Normandy, Camembert is served soft, totally ripe but still firm, whereas in Paris it must be aged a bit longer so that it is slightly runny.

Wrap the cheese carefully and store it at the bottom of the refrigerator. Serve it with bread, ripe pears or figs. Although pasteurised industrially-made Camemberts may be good, unpasteurised craftsman-made Camembert is better, and imitations made far away from Normandy and sold in portions wrapped in plastic should only be used in cooking.

Les Pâtes Molles à Croûte Lavée

'Soft cheeses with a washed crust' have a stronger taste. Their curd is cut, stirred, matured in cool, moist cellars for over a month, and turned twice a week. The crust is brushed and may be washed with salty water, beer, cider, brandy or wine. The cheeses must be stored in a moist place wrapped in a towel moistened with salty water or wine. Autumn and winter are the best time to eat them.

The most famous members of this family are: Livarot, a very ancient type of cheese from Normandy with a red crust and one of the most pungent; Maroilles; Pont L'Évêque, a square, golden cheese also from Normandy; Munster, the most famous Alsatian cheese made in the same valley since the seventh century and sold in a pretty wooden box; Epoisse; and the glorious Vacherin Mont d'Or which is so creamy it must be eaten with a spoon.

Les Fromages de Chèvre

There are hundreds of types of goat cheeses made in Burgundy, Lyonnais, the Loire valley, Provence and the south-west. They come in all shapes: logs, tall cylinders, pyramids, tiny mounds. Apparently it was the Arab invasions of France during the eighth century which led to the breeding of goats in Poitou, hence the names of the most popular goat cheeses such as Chabichou and the tiny Chavignol which derive from the Arab word *chabli* for goat.

Goat cheeses originate mainly from wine-making and hilly regions, and the quality of the cheese is determined by the goats' feed: whether they graze on a dry hill, remain in a stable or feed in a rich pasture.

Goat cheeses are sold fresh, soft, dry, crumbly or very hard, and have either a bluish-white surface or are covered with ashes, herbs or spices. They may also be wrapped in a vine leaf, chestnut or plane leaves, or savory (*pèbre d'ane*). They may be sprinkled with white wine, olive oil or brandy.

The most famous goat cheeses are: Chevrotin which comes from different cities such as Chevrotin de Valençay, Chevrotin de Moulins; Chabichou; Chavignol; Picodon; Pouligny Saint Pierre; cylinder-shaped Sainte Maure from the Loire with a piece of straw in the centre; Selle sur Cher; Banon; Pélardon; and the tiny pungent *bouton de culotte*, the trouser button.

Serve goat cheeses from May to November when they are at their best. Fresh, as *fromage frais*, they are served soft and silky with a little cream and chives or with a drizzle of honey or marc brandy. When the texture is firmer, the taste becomes more intense and the crust begins to form and turn pale yellow. Then they are eaten for snacks or grilled on top of salad leaves as a starter or served at the end of a meal. Later when the cheese becomes very dry, shrivelled and pungent, it may be kept in olive oil with herbs in a glass jar then eaten with bread, served with a tossed green salad or stored for longer soaked in white wine or brandy.

Pâtes Persillées

The so-called 'parsleyed cheeses' are rich ivory-coloured cheeses which have blue or greyish-green streaks of mould running through them. They are made with cows' or ewes' milk. The most famous of all these cheese are Roquefort; Fourme d'Ambert; Bleu d'Auvergne; and the newest one, the creamy Bleu de Bresse.

Roquefort is the most prestigious. It was already being made from ewes' milk around the year AD 800 and was the first cheese to be given a specific AOC label (see page 201) to protect its quality.

The curd is made with natural rennet which is cut, crumbled and salted, then placed in perforated moulds and sprinkled with powdered rye bread which has been left to mould for three months (or sometimes with liquid penicillium). It is left to rest in chilled well-ventilated rooms for a few days then removed from the moulds and salted with sea salt on each side for a further week. The next stage involves piercing the cheese with long needles 'to let the cheese breathe' and stimulate the growth of the blue moulds by allowing the air to circulate within the cheese. It is then matured slowly in chilly, moist limestone cellars situated deep beneath the village which impart its characteristic blue colour. Finally, each cylinder is wrapped in tin foil so that the blue mould can spread more slowly while it matures for four months until it is unctuous, high in flavour, pale ivory in colour with blue-green veins. Hand-made Roquefort is firmer while machine-made versions are softer, dry and tend to be crumbly.

Roquefort and most blue cheeses hate both the cold and the heat and must be tightly wrapped in foil and stored at the bottom of the refrigerator. Remove them from the refrigerator about three hours before serving with a choice of breads, a pot of unsalted butter, walnuts, figs, pears or grapes. A strong red wine used to be the classic accompaniment to Roquefort, but recently a sweet Sauterne or Montbazillac, or a good port have become more popular as they offer an interesting counterpoint. Roquefort is good all year round.

Les Pâtes Pressées non Cuites

These cheeses, prepared with raw pressed curd, were first made by the Romans, and the tradition was carried on by the monks who continued to produce them for centuries in their *abbayes*. In fact, there are still about twelve *abbayes* making cheese today. These cheeses are made with pasteurised or raw ewes' and cows' milk. The curd is cut into tiny pieces, washed in lukewarm water and placed under a press to mature for between two weeks and a year, while it is brushed, turned and washed regularly.

The main cheeses of this type are: Cantal; Laguiole; Ossau-Giraty, a ewes' milk cheese from the Pyrénées; Reblochon from the Alps; Saint Nectaire which smells like hazelnuts or mushrooms; Salers; Mimolette which is French and not Dutch, as is often thought; Morbier from the Jura; and Tommes of all kinds, mostly from Savoie.

Under the amber-coloured crust of their huge moulds, Cantal, Laguiole and Salers – three famous cheeses from the Cantal region – are quite different, although they are made in basically the same way. In the high plains of central France Salers and Aubrac cows feed throughout the year on fresh clover, liquorice, gentian and blueberries. Salers, a more pungent type of Cantal, is made exclusively with the milk from brown-coloured Salers cows, which graze on hilly slopes. The cheeses each weigh 55 kg (121 lb) and must age for about a year. Laguiole is made on the Aubrac hills, in the south of the Cantal region, with the milk of the long-eyelashed, grey-coloured Aubrac cows.

Pâtes Pressées Cuites

These great wheels of mature, hard cheese require an enormous amount of milk for their preparation and are an important source of protein and calcium for families during the winter months.

The milk is heated then cooled and mixed with rennet so that the milk quickly curdles. The curd is then sliced into tiny pieces, stirred and heated for between half an hour and an hour, then left to stand for about three weeks, while it is washed, brushed and turned over regularly. It is the carbon gas released during the process which makes the holes in the cheese. By knocking against the crust of the cheese with his fist when the top is sufficiently rounded, the cheese-maker can judge whether the cheese has matured sufficiently. It can then be transferred to cool cellars to stop the production of the gas and to finish maturing.

In this Gruyère family, the finest cheese is the Beaufort, a cheese without holes which was first made by the Romans. The Comté from the Jura is a slowly-aged, delicate, fruity cheese with pea-sized holes and a yellow crust; the Emmenthal has larger holes and is most often used for cooking.

The label *grand cru*, generally reserved for fine wines, is also used for cheeses if they have been made with raw milk produced by cows fed only on fresh grass.

Hard cheeses taste good throughout the year and keep well wrapped in a tea towel lightly moistened with salty water or dry white wine.

Fromages Frais, Fromages Blancs

These fresh cheeses are neither pressed nor brushed but are simply the curd of cows' or goats' milk, pasteurised or raw, skimmed, whole or enriched with cream. Cream, honey, sugar, orange blossom, salt, pepper, garlic, fresh herbs, cumin, olive oil and brandy can all be added to flavour the cheese.

Petit-Suisse, Neufchâtel Frais and Boursin are drained and matured for a very short time and can be served, like fromage frais, with herbs, spices, raisins, chopped walnuts, minced onions, sugar or salt. There are also regional fresh cheese specialities like Brousse (which is similar to Ricotta); Crémets; Jonchées. Fontainebleau is made with fromage frais and single cream which is whipped then lightly wrapped in white muslin.

Because they are light, not too rich and not salty, they are popular on their own or to replace cream in sauces and some desserts. They can be used instead of Gruyère in gratins. They can have 40 per cent, 20 per cent or 0 per cent fat content, so, of course, the 0 per cent has become the best friend of all 'lean cuisine' fans.

Fromages Fondus

'Melted' or processed cheeses were first invented in the regions where *pâtes pressées cuites* like Gruyère are made. Often, Cantal, Emmenthal, Comté, Gruyère or even Roquefort and Bleus are used as the base for such cheeses which have become very popular, partly because they can be bought wrapped in individual portions.

They are prepared with a variety of crustless cheeses which are grated and mixed with milk, cream and sometimes spices, walnuts, ham, cumin, paprika or garlic. They can be spread on toast for snacks, cooked in gratins, used for *croque-monsieur* or cheese-burgers.

Les Fromages Forts

These fermented mixtures of cheese blended with local brandy or wine and flavoured with herbs or pepper are prepared in each region in a specific way. They are definitely an acquired taste. They offer a way to use left-over bits of cheese or cheeses which have hardened. They are strictly home-made products and need to be tasted with determination.

In the south, grated goats' cheese is moistened with brandy, pepper and herbs then aged in pots until it becomes the potent *Cachat* or *Brous*. In Burgundy, grated goats' and cows' cheeses are crushed and marinated with local marc brandy, thyme, bay leaves and vegetable broth then stored in a tightly-sealed crockery pot. Near Lyon, grated goats', cows' and Gruyère cheeses are mixed with fresh cheese, white wine and butter into a soft paste then kept for a fortnight before being spread on crisp toast or chicory leaves.

Appellation d'Origine Contrôlée

In a world where industrial products tend to prevail, supermarkets overflow with efficiently-packaged, inexpensive Danish-made Comté or Dutch-made Camembert, which may have their place in the market, but have nothing to do with the products prepared under the same name by skilled local craftsmen. So many countries chose to create a *marque* which a product could display to indicate and protect its origin and quality. Wine-growers, olive oil-makers, ham butchers and cheese-makers have therefore created their own *Appellation d'Origine Contrôlée*, and there are currently thirty-two cheeses able to boast the fact that they are AOC. For a cheese to qualify as AOC, it must conform to a specific series of quality controls relating to the region of origin, the soil, the climate, the type of animal, their breeding and feed, and the techniques of production. Each package of cheese must specify: the specific region from which the milk is collected; that the cheese is made from raw milk (although a few pasteurised cheeses are now accepted); that it is made by a precisely-defined traditional process; the size of each cheese; specific times spent draining and ageing the cheese before packaging; that it is wrapped where it is made; and the precise percentage of fat in each cheese.

COOKING WITH CHEESE

Cheeses are wonderful served as a *Plateau de Fromages*, but that is just the beginning. Spectacular multi-coloured trays of tiny rectangles, triangles and circles of cheeses covered with fresh herbs, cumin, raisins, minced walnuts and chopped olives make a splendid starter. Cheese is also an essential element of many cooked dishes such as soups, quiches, soufflés, omelettes, pies, gratins, salads and tarts. Camembert, Roquefort or hard cheeses can be wrapped in flaky pastry to serve with drinks. Grilled goat cheese can be served sprinkled with thyme and savory. And Gougères may be served plain or filled with Roquefort custard and pine nuts, or a nutmeg-flavoured Gruyère Béchamel sauce.

Cheese is a last-minute helper in the kitchen: a dot of softened butter and cheese to top a sizzling steak, a spoonful of Camembert, parsley, mushroom and cream stirred into a bowl of hot pasta, make a simple meal into a sumptuous one. Sliced cheese dipped in egg yolk and breadcrumbs then fried in hot oil with bits of *Magrets* (see page 160) turn a tossed green salad into a proper meal. Baked tomatoes filled with herb-flavoured goat cheese make a lively accompaniment to a roast. Celery and fennel coated with a cheese Béchamel make a fragrant gratin. In Savoie, *concoillote*, fresh curds, butter, white wine and garlic, are melted together and spooned over potatoes, while in the Auvergne, potatoes and cheese are transformed into the luscious *Aligot* and the lively *Truffade*, a mashed potato and cheese dish. To make baked potatoes into a nourishing lunch, scoop out the flesh and mix it with some rinded Cambembert, sprinkle with breadcrumbs and dot with butter before baking until melted and hot.

Finally for dessert there are many interesting offerings. There is a delicate layer of puff pastry covered with fresh cheese and berries sprinkled with mint; a tangy rosemary, honey-fresh cheese ice-cream; or for a healthy finale, baked apples filled with almonds and orange preserve served on a layer of fresh cheese.

———————— BURGUNDY ————————

GOUGÈRE

A savoury cheese choux pastry

There are no serious wine tastings in Burgundy without its best *faire valoir*: Gougère. And the ritual would charm the hardest heart: splendid, vaulted cellars, rich Burgundy wine served in the *impitoyables* – the huge round glasses with their narrow rim to capture the wine's splendid bouquet – and lots of warm, fragrant, golden Gougère puffs to nibble.

Gougère will enhance almost any wine – potent red, dry white or cool rosé – but it is particularly lovely served as an apéritif with kir (see page 266). Served as a large, golden ring with a tossed green salad, it makes a delicate luncheon dish or a pretty starter, and it is perfect as part of a warm buffet spread.

Gougère can be made as a large ring or as separate individual puffs. Dicing the cheese will give a more interesting texture. Generally one does not fill a Gougère, but they can be stuffed with a Béchamel Sauce (see page 83) flavoured with cheese or with a Roquefort and pine nut filling.

The only secret of making a fluffy Gougère is not to open the oven door before it is ready, and always to leave the Gougère in the oven for a few minutes after you have turned it off, so that it settles.

———————— *Serves 4–6* ————————

8 fl oz (250 ml) milk
2 oz (50 g) butter
4 oz (100 g) plain flour, sifted
3 eggs
½ teaspoon salt
pinch freshly ground black pepper
pinch freshly grated nutmeg

2 oz (50 g) Gruyère cheese, grated
   or finely diced
2 teaspoons Dijon mustard
pinch cayenne pepper (optional)

FOR THE TOPPING
2 tablespoons finely diced Gruyère
   cheese.

Pre-heat the oven to gas mark 6, 400°F (200°C) and butter a baking sheet.

Put the milk and butter in a saucepan and heat until the butter has melted. Bring to the boil then shoot in the flour all at once and stir vigorously with a wooden spoon until the mixture comes away cleanly from the sides of the saucepan. Beat the eggs into the mixture one at a time then season with the salt, pepper and nutmeg. Add the cheese and mustard. The batter should be very smooth and shiny. Taste it, and add a pinch of cayenne pepper or salt if necessary. Drop teaspoonfuls of the batter on the baking sheet at least 2 inches (5 cm) apart. Sprinkle with the topping cheese and bake in the oven for 20 minutes. Reduce the temperature to gas mark 4, 350°F (180°C) and bake for a further 10 minutes until well risen and golden brown. Do not be tempted by the delicious aroma to open the oven door as the Gougère is cooking.

Turn off the oven and leave the oven door ajar for a few minutes to allow the Gougère to settle. Transfer the Gougère delicately to a serving platter.

Note

When I don't entertain friends from Burgundy, I often add a tablespoon or two of Parmesan, dry goat or ewe cheese to the Gougère batter.

Alternatively, you can make one large Gougère by spooning large teaspoonfuls of dough on to a greased baking sheet, piling them on top of each other to form a plump ring with at least a 2 inch (5 cm) circle in the centre (you can sit a little tin cup in the centre to make a neat hole). Bake for 30 minutes at gas mark 6, 400°F (200°C) and 20 minutes at gas mark 4, 350°F (180°C).

FONDUE SAVOYARDE

Cheese, wine and kirsch fondue

This mountain dish was always the core of the *veillées*, those long evenings filled with singing and chatting, peeling chestnuts and shelling walnuts in Savoy villages.

Now, fondue is served in all ski resorts every night. Whether it is prepared with an assortment of cheese or with just Gruyère, it is the most convivial of dishes. Cold water and a little kirsch *eau-de-vie* are generally the best friends of the fondue, and chilled white wine its most dangerous companion.

True Savoyards say that the authentic version of the fondue (which is originally a Swiss dish) is the *berthoud*. The master *fromager-affineur*, Daniel Boujon, from Thonon-les-Bains, showed me the crucial difference. A *berthoud* is made exclusively from the French cheese Abondance. It is mixed with either white wine or madeira and is baked individually in small cast iron dishes. But when you prepare a fondue you will need long-handled forks as well as standard cutlery, and a tabletop heater to keep the fondue sauce warm in a flameproof dish.

———————— *Serves 4* ————————

3 cloves garlic, crushed
3 tablespoons butter
1½ lb (675 g) Gruyère cheese
 (without holes), shredded
1 pint (600 ml) dry white wine
3 teaspoons arrowroot
3 tablespoons kirsch
salt and freshly ground black pepper
pinch of freshly grated nutmeg

1 teaspoon bicarbonate of soda
about 8 slices stale or oven-dried
 bread, diced into 1 inch (2.5 cm)
 pieces.

TO FINISH
3 egg yolks
1 tablespoon butter
handful of diced bread

Rub a flameproof enamel or earthenware casserole dish with the crushed garlic cloves. Add 1 tablespoon of the butter then the cheese and about two-thirds of the wine. Reserve the remaining butter and wine to add as the sauce is cooking. Cook on a low heat, stirring with a wooden fork or spoon and lifting the mixture until all the cheese has melted and the sauce begins to bubble. Blend together the arrowroot and kirsch and stir it into the mixture with the salt, pepper, nutmeg and bicarbonate of soda. The fondue should have the consistency of a thick custard. Stir in a little more butter or wine as it cooks to maintain the correct consistency.

To serve, each guest spears a long-handled fork into a cube of bread and dips it into the fondue so that it is well coated then transfers it to their plate. Use a standard fork to eat the coated bread or you will burn your lips. You may like to serve a tiny glass of kirsch in the middle of the meal to make the fondue more digestible.

When most of the sauce has been eaten, add the egg yolks, butter and diced bread to the dish and stir for a few minutes. Serve with a large spoon to each individual plate.

Note

You may like to serve the warm mixture over hot sliced boiled potatoes, or for a grand treat, add a few tablespoons of cream then sprinkle the top of the fondue with a few shredded truffles if some come your way. In some villages, the pieces of bread are lightly dipped into kirsch before dipping into the fondue.

─── **THROUGHOUT FRANCE** ───

PLATEAU DE FROMAGES
Cheese board

A cheese board can be the most exuberant of displays or the most discreet of offerings. Everything depends on timing, situation, budget and which cheeses are in season. For most people, cheese is a blessing after a simple meal of soup, salad or omelette. When faced with a large family Sunday dinner (especially one which follows a large family lunch), I often arrange on the dining room table a large bowl of tossed green salad, a big platter of tiny steamed potatoes, a pot of unsalted butter, a pot of Brittany lightly salted butter, a basket of baguette, walnut, rye and wholewheat country breads, and as the core of the meal a sumptuous *Plateau de Fromages*. But at the end of a formal meal, if I decide to serve a cheese course, it will be either one splendid Vacherin in its large, round, wooden box, top crust removed, served with a spoon and spread on thin crisp slices of bread, or one large, single piece of Roquefort cheese served with walnuts, white grapes, rye bread, a sweet dessert wine or a mature port. For an informal dinner *en famille*, I serve a tiny *plateau* with two or three cheeses, a bowl of fruit and a pot of butter. If I am entertaining foreign friends or if I serve a buffet, then I'll prepare a formal *Plateau de Fromages*, offering a great diversity of choice.

Most restaurants offer a cheese board, but the best quality restaurants tend to have two-tier trolleys, *chariot de fromages*, or immense wicker trays covered with a huge variety of cheeses, usually including an extravagant display of local seasonal produce. It is an overwhelming sight. Most good restaurateurs deal with a reliable network of producers and maintain close ties with neighbouring cheese-makers who deliver their carefully made and perfectly mature products daily.

At home, a cheese board should include at least Camembert, Brie, Livarot and Roquefort. A formal *Plateau de Fromages* should offer at least one, preferably two or three, cheeses of each type (one Roquefort, two Bleus, a soft, a semi-dry and a pungent *chèvre*, for example), accompanied by at least two different wines and offered after the meat and salad courses and before the dessert. The

Barfleur, Normandy

fashion of cheese served with a tossed salad on the same plate is not yet quite acceptable; the vinegar and oil dressing of the salad is hard on the delicate flavour of the cheese.

The cheeses should be removed from the refrigerator and unwrapped at least an hour before serving and arranged on a vine or fig leaves or a plain paper doiley on a platter or flat wicker tray. Place a fork on the tray to hold the cheese, at least two cheese knives and a thin knife which has been held under hot water for a moment for serving Roquefort and Bleu cheeses.

Cut a cheese in such a way that every guest has a share of the crust, which they may eat or not according to taste. I think it is often the tastiest part. Cut soft, creamy cheese in triangles, goat cheese in slices, tiny goat mounds in halves. Start with the mildest of the cheeses then move on to the strongest, most pungent one. Accompany the cheese with a variety of good breads, a pot of quality unsalted butter, cider, a hearty red wine, dry white wine or a sweet dessert wine for your guests to choose. Cheese is eaten on an individual plate with a knife and with or without a fork.

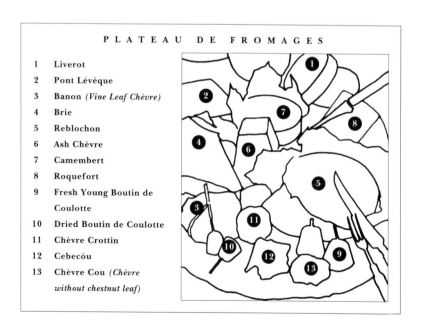

PLATEAU DE FROMAGES

1 Liverot
2 Pont Lévèque
3 Banon *(Vine Leaf Chèvre)*
4 Brie
5 Reblochon
6 Ash Chèvre
7 Camembert
8 Roquefort
9 Fresh Young Boutin de Coulotte
10 Dried Boutin de Coulotte
11 Chèvre Crottin
12 Cebecóu
13 Chèvre Cou *(Chèvre without chestnut leaf)*

Opposite: PLATEAU DE FROMAGES (*see page 208*)

How to Keep Cheese at Home

Apart from goat cheese or hard cheese like Gruyère, it is best to keep as little cheese as possible at home. Only buy what you need for two days. If you have a good cheese shop, buy only one or two pieces from a perfectly ripe cheese and serve it on the same day.

Wrap each cheese in its own paper and foil and leave it in the salad crisper at the bottom of the refrigerator. Add a piece of celery or the green leaves of a carrot to the package for extra moisture. Old-fashioned *gardemanger*, with their fine metal mesh, were wonderful for storing cheese in a cool, dark, well-ventilated place, and they can now be found again in specialist stores.

— LYONNAIS AND THROUGHOUT FRANCE —

Cervelle de Canut

Fresh cheese dessert

Cervelle de Canut is a lovely way to conclude a meal, something between a cheese and a pudding. You will need a rich type of fromage frais (Sainsbury's and Waitrose are good). The seasoning and herbs are very much a matter of personal taste.

——————— *Serves 4* ———————

1 lb (450 g) grainy fromage frais (20 per cent fat) or curd cheese
1 tablespoon cottage cheese
2 tablespoons olive oil
2 teaspoons red wine vinegar
2 tablespoons dry white wine
1 teaspoon marc brandy
salt and freshly ground black pepper

1 tablespoon chopped fresh flat-leaved parsley
1 tablespoon snipped fresh chives
1 teaspoon chopped fresh tarragon
2 cloves garlic, crushed
1 shallot or small onion, finely chopped
10 fl oz (300 ml) single cream

Beat the fromage frais or curd cheese and cottage cheese together then add the remaining ingredients and beat gently with a fork until well blended. The mixture should not be too smooth. Serve with crisp toasted bread.

GRATIN DAUPHINOIS
Potatoes baked in cream and cheese

Gratin Savoyard is traditionally prepared with potatoes, Beaufort cheese, a type of Gruyère, and meat broth, while *Gratin Dauphinois* uses milk or cream. Some add a layer of wild mushrooms, some a few thinly sliced turnips, some a piece of celeriac, or some sautéed leeks for an interesting texture.

Gratin Dauphinois is a splendid accompaniment, an easy way to be acclaimed for your culinary expertise with little effort. The potatoes should be served straight from the cooking dish when they are soft but not mushy.

———————— *Serves 4* ————————

2 cloves garlic, crushed
1 tablespoon butter
5 large firm, fleshy potatoes, thinly
    sliced
pinch of freshly grated nutmeg

salt and freshly ground black pepper
3 oz (75 g) Beaumont or Gruyère
    cheese, grated
10 fl oz (300 ml) single cream,
    warmed

Pre-heat the oven to gas mark 5, 375°F (190°C).

Rub an ovenproof dish with some of the garlic and butter. Pat the potatoes dry with kitchen paper or a towel but don't rinse off the starch. Season the potatoes with nutmeg, salt and pepper and mix with half the cheese and the remaining garlic. Spread the mixture in the ovenproof dish, pour over the warm cream and stir so that every potato is well coated with cream. Sprinkle with the remaining cheese and dot with the remaining butter. Bake in the oven for 1 hour. Place a loose piece of oiled foil on top to prevent the dish from becoming too brown and return to the oven for a further 30 minutes. Serve straight from the dish.

Note
I sometimes cook the potatoes and cream on top of the oven for 30 minutes then bake them in the oven for 30 minutes until crisp. Unsweetened condensed milk can be used instead of single cream.

SOUFFLÉ AU *FROMAGE*

Cheese soufflé

Contrary to its reputation, *Soufflé au Fromage* is not a temperamental creature. Prepared with a solid base which gives it flavour and body, and egg whites which provide the magical air bubbles, it is a reliable dish but, like all sensitive creatures, it does need to be understood and respected. The egg whites must be at room temperature and be stiffly beaten until truly glossy then folded into the base a little at a time, and you must not open the oven while it is cooking. Once you know the nature of the beast, taming it is child's play.

——————— *Serves 4* ———————

3 oz (75 g) Gruyère, Gruyère and
*   Parmesan or Gruyère and*
*   Pecorino cheese, finely grated*
10 fl oz (300 ml) milk
2 oz (50 g) butter
2 oz (50 g) plain flour

salt
cayenne pepper
pinch freshly grated nutmeg
4 egg yolks
5 egg whites

Grate the cheese an hour or so before making the soufflé so that it is slightly dry when you use it.

Pre-heat the oven to gas mark 6, 400°F (200°C) and butter a 2½ pint (1.5 litre) soufflé dish. Sprinkle with 2 tablespoons of the cheese. The egg whites must be at room temperature.

To prepare the sauce, bring the milk to the boil. Melt the butter over a low heat, stir in the flour with a wooden spoon and cook for 2 minutes, stirring continuously. Remove from the heat, gradually pour in the hot milk and stir until blended. Return to the heat and whisk vigorously for about 2 minutes until thickened. Season to taste with salt, cayenne pepper and nutmeg. The mixture should be quite thick and leave the sides of the pan. Remove from the heat and beat in the egg yolks one at a time. Mix in three-quarters of the remaining cheese. The sauce should be lukewarm. If it is too warm when the cheese is added, the cheese will melt too much.

Beat the egg whites with a pinch of salt until they hold soft peaks. Add 1 tablespoon of the whites to the pan to loosen the mixture. Delicately fold in half the remaining egg whites, cutting down and up towards the sides of the pan using a metal spoon or spatula. Add the remaining cheese then fold in the remaining egg whites.

Pour the mixture into the soufflé dish; it should be about three-quarters full. Smooth the top with a spatula. Reduce the oven temperature to gas mark 5, 375°F (190°C). Place the soufflé in the lower third of the oven and bake for about 25–30 minutes. Push a thin skewer into the centre and if it comes out clean, the soufflé is ready to serve at once.

DESSERTS

Les Desserts

•••••••••••••••••••••••••••••

It is along the Loire valley, in Alsace and in Normandy where desserts are taken the most seriously. But of course, every region has its own distinctive tastes. In Provence, it may be for a fresh goat cheese flavoured with honey, in Brittany a more substantial *far breton*, in Auvergne, a handful of fresh walnuts served with a piece of Cantal cheese, in the south-west a dish of pears, berries and prunes simmered in Sauternes wine and peppercorns.

Cakes, tarts and custards are definitely not everyday fare in France. During the week, most people tend to enjoy a platter of cheese and fruit at the end of a meal since we all know here that when dessert arrives on the table, one is no longer hungry and it is generally believed that a good meal does not need a rich ending. So dessert is either very light and fresh, or else it must stand out and be truly memorable.

On festive days and on Sunday, however, a stop at the pastry shop remains both an adventure and a must. Even if their eclairs, *mille feuilles* and *brioche mousseline* are not necessarily as airy as those in Paris, the smallest provincial town has bakers and pastry shops which offer staggering displays of local specialities as well as classic highly elaborate cakes. So much so that few home cooks in France dare challenge such professional creations. They would rather stick to *Gâteau de Savoie*, *Teurgoule* or *Gâteau Basque* because they can prepare them with their eyes closed. They can count on the seductive aroma drifting through the house and memories of past delights being summoned at the first bite. It is a known fact that with a *gâteau maison*, there is more than meets the eye.

Because elaborate desserts, considered the domain of the professional pastry chefs, and home or regional desserts are so very far apart, making pastry is no joking matter in a French home. It is a sensual way to evoke childhood pleasures, to show off, to make a grand statement, but it is not a casual activity like tossing a salad or making a *Daube*. So if you like Tante Cécile, you had better praise and finish her *Bavarois*, even if you think it is a bit of an *ètouffe-chretin*, a 'Christian smotherer'.

But times have changed and in the last decade, desserts at home and in restaurants have come back into the limelight. They help to balance the 'light food' which prevails in some circles and is still lingering in many starred restaurants. Whether it is called a *farandole* (a Provençal dance) of pastries, a 'dessert trolley', or '*le palais de Dame Tartine*' (a palace of goodies), an extravaganza of custards, sorbets, cakes and mousses concludes most restaurant menus. And because there is nostalgia for real flavours, for the taste of good butter, honey, fresh eggs and sharp, familiar fragrances, they tend to include many regional specialities and home desserts.

Now that industrially-made pastry, frozen and packed, is available everywhere in supermarkets and from the lorries that bring regular supplies even to the most remote of French villages, great, but simple, home-made desserts like *Clafoutis, Oeufs à la Neige, Madeleines* and the like are seductive again. A festive meal at home may offer a medley of chocolate mousse and *Pots à la Crème* but it may also have a *Pithiviers* or a plump *Baba au Rhum*.

Making pastry alone in one's kitchen remains a true challenge and the result must be worth the effort. The following recipes have been my trustworthy companions for the last few years.

Sweet wines and champagne are served with dessert, but coffee is taken after the meal, never with dessert and seldom at the dining room table. Chocolates and petits fours may be served with the coffee or after-dinner herb teas in restaurants or after an elegant dinner.

PÂTE BRISÉE

Pastry

This pastry is used for tartlet shells or *barquette* shells, which are oval with pointed ends.

——————— *1 quantity* ———————
This quantity makes enough pastry for
1 × 9 inch (23 cm) tart or 12 × 3 inch
(7.5 cm) tartlets

8 oz (225 g) plain flour	*½ teaspoon salt*
1 egg	*3 tablespoons water*
1 egg white	*4 oz (100 g) butter, cut into pieces*

Place the flour in a bowl and make a well in the centre. Add the remaining ingredients and use the fingertips to blend them gradually into the flour. Knead gently until smooth then roll into a ball, cover with cling film and refrigerate for at least 2 hours.

Grease the tartlet moulds with a little butter and arrange them on a baking sheet. Add a little flour to the dough if it is too sticky. Roll out the pastry on a lightly floured surface or between 2 sheets of baking parchment to about ¼ inch (5 mm) thick. Cut round or oval pieces slightly larger than the moulds, remove and discard the paper, if using. Lift the pieces on your rolling pin and unroll over the moulds. Fit the pastry on the bottom and edges of the moulds, pushing gently with the fingertips, then trim off any excess pastry around the edges. Make a pretty design along the edge, pushing the blunt side of a knife or the back of a spoon against the dough.

For unfilled, fully-baked shells: refrigerate the baking sheet and filled moulds for 1–2 hours so that the edges will not collapse as they cook.

Pre-heat the oven to gas mark 4, 350°F (180°C).

Prick the bottom of the pastry with a fork then bake the shells for about 10 minutes. Prick the bases again and push the dough back up with the back of a spoon if it has collapsed. Bake for a further 10–15 minutes until the shells have shrunk a little from the moulds and are lightly browned. Leave to cool then carefully remove from the moulds using a spatula.

For partially-cooked, filled shells: refrigerate the baking sheet and filled moulds for 1–2 hours.

Pre-heat the oven to gas mark 5, 375°F (190°C).

Prick the bottom of the pastry with a fork. Line the tartlets with a piece of buttered baking parchment or kitchen foil and fill with handfuls of baking beans, lentils or rice. Bake just below the centre of the oven for about 15 minutes. If the sides tend to collapse during baking, push them against the sides with the back of a spoon. The shell will shrink a little from the mould and brown lightly on the edges. Remove the baking beans and paper then return the moulds to the oven for a further minute. Leave to cool.

——— **THROUGHOUT FRANCE** ———

*P*ÂTE *F*EUILLETÉE
Puff pastry

If the weather is warm, make sure that your flour, butter, rolling pin and pastry board are well chilled before you start. A work surface can be chilled by standing a roasting tin filled with ice on the surface until you are ready to work.

——————— *1 quantity* ———————
This quantity makes enough for 1 × 9 inch
(23 cm) tart or 12 × 3 inch (7.5 cm) tartlets

8 oz (225 g) plain flour   *1 teaspoon salt*
8 oz (225 g) butter, softened   *4 fl oz (120 ml) cold water*

Place the flour in a bowl and make a well in the centre. Blend in 2 tablespoons of the softened butter. Add the salt and cold water and blend for 15 minutes until the dough is smooth and elastic. If the room is very warm, chill the dough for 15 minutes.

Roll out the dough on a lightly floured surface to a rectangle 8 × 15 inches (20 × 38 cm). Gently shape the remaining butter into a 4 inch (10 cm) square and place it on the centre of the dough. Fold the top third of the dough down over the butter, pressing the edges with your fingers. Fold the bottom third of the dough up over the butter, again pressing the edges with your fingers, to make a 5 × 8 inch (13 × 20 cm) rectangle of butter tightly enclosed in pastry. Turn the dough 90° to bring the seam to your left. Roll it out again, fold it and turn it in the same way, making sure the butter does not come through the dough as you roll it. Roll out and fold once again. Wrap the pastry in cling film and chill for 30 minutes.

Each rolling and folding of the dough is called a 'turn'. Make 2 more turns then chill for a further 30 minutes. Continue in this way until you have completed 8 turns in all.

Roll out the pastry on a lightly floured surface to about ⅛ inch (3 mm) thick. Cut into circles or rectangles slightly larger than the moulds. Gently press the pastry into the moulds and trim the edges. Chill for 30 minutes.

Pre-heat the oven to gas mark 8, 450°F (230°C) for 15 minutes.

Reduce the oven temperature to gas mark 4, 350°F (180°C). Bake the pastry moulds for about 15 minutes.

Note
Wrapped in a plastic bag or kept in a plastic container, puff pastry freezes well.

Variation
Flaky pastry, often used for *Pithiviers*, only requires 4 turns.

*P*ÂTE *S*ABLÉE

Sweet pastry

With its crunchy, buttery texture, *Pâte Sablée*, also known as *Pâte Sucrée*, is my favourite for *barquettes* and *tartelettes*. Even if it is a little more brittle and fragile than *Pâte Brisée*, it is well worth it. I use partially-baked tartlets for peaches, pears or custard and fully-baked shells for softer fruits such as strawberries.

—————— *1 quantity* ——————
This quantity makes enough for 1 × 9 inch
(23 cm) tart or 12 × 3 inch (7.5 cm) tartlets

8 oz (225 g) plain flour
2 oz (50 g) caster sugar
½ teaspoons salt

finely grated rind of 1 lemon
5 oz (150 g) butter, cut into pieces
2 egg yolks

Place the flour in a bowl and make a well in the centre. Add the remaining ingredients and use the fingertips to blend them gradually into the flour. Knead gently until smooth then roll into a ball, cover with cling film and refrigerate for at least 2 hours.

Grease the tartlet moulds with a little butter and arrange them on a baking sheet. Roll out the pastry on a lightly floured surface or between 2 sheets of baking parchment to about ¼ inch (5 mm) thick. Cut round or oval pieces 1 inch (2.5 cm) larger than the moulds, remove and discard the paper, if using. Lift the pieces on your rolling pin and unroll over the moulds. Fit the pastry on the bottom and edges of the moulds, pushing gently with the finger-tips, then trim off any excess pastry around the edges. Make a pretty design along the edge, pushing the blunt side of a knife or the back of a spoon against the dough.

Refer to the recipe for *Pâte Brisée* (see page 217) for baking instructions.

CRÈME PATISSIÈRE

Pastry cream

This thick custard sauce is the traditional filling for most pastries. It must be made a day in advance, and it will keep in the refrigerator for two days. It can be flavoured with chocolate, coffee, lemon or orange liqueur. It is perfect for éclairs and *Choux a la Crème* and can be used to coat the pastry crust in a tart or to fill a puff pastry cake such as *Pithiviers* (see page 226).

—— *Makes 1 pint (600 ml)* ——

1 pint (600 ml) milk
1 vanilla pod, cut in half
   lengthways
5 egg yolks
4 oz (100 g) caster sugar
pinch of salt
2 tablespoons plain flour
1 tablespoon cornflour

2 tablespoons Grand Marnier,
   cognac, kirsch, orange blossom
   water, coffee, chocolate, vanilla
   essence, almond essence, anise,
   rum or liqueur, or to taste
1 teaspoon butter, melted, or cream
3 tablespoons single cream
   (optional)

Place the milk and vanilla pod in a saucepan and bring to the boil. Remove from the heat, cover and keep warm.

Meanwhile, whisk the egg yolks, sugar and salt for about 5 minutes until the mixture turns frothy and pale yellow. Blend in the flour and cornflour. Discard the vanilla pod and gradually pour the hot milk into the egg mixture, stirring constantly. Return the mixture to the saucepan over a medium heat and gradually bring to the boil, stirring continuously so that the custard does not stick to the bottom of the pan. When it reaches boiling point, lower the heat and beat vigorously for 2 minutes then remove from the heat and continue to beat for a few seconds. Stir in the liqueur or flavouring, pass through a sieve into a bowl and keep stirring until the custard has cooled. Add the melted butter or cream on the top to prevent a skin forming. Refrigerate until required. You can stir in the tablespoonfuls of cream if the custard is too thick.

CRÈME ANGLAISE
Vanilla custard

This light custard sauce requires a little patience, and should be prepared a day in advance. It will keep for several days in the refrigerator. It is used as a base for *Oeufs à la Neige*, ice-cream, or to accompany *Gâteau de Savoie* (see page 237), *Marquise* (see page 230) or *Bavarois* (see page 248). It can be flavoured with vanilla, caramel, coffee, chocolate, orange, lemon, ginger, aniseed or a fruit liqueur. It should be made in a stainless steel saucepan.

—— *Makes 1 pint (600 ml)* ——

1 pint (600 ml) milk
1 vanilla pod, cut in half
  lengthways (optional)
6 egg yolks
5 oz (150 g) caster sugar
pinch of salt
2 tablespoons butter

finely grated rind of 1 orange or
  lemon, or to taste, or 3 teaspoons
  orange blossom water, strong
  coffee or cocoa powder or 3
  tablespoons brandy, rum, Grand
  Marnier or kirsch

Place the milk and vanilla pod and seeds, if using, in a heavy-based saucepan, bring to the boil then remove from the heat, cover and keep warm.

Place the egg yolks in a bowl and gradually work in the sugar and salt, whisking vigorously for about 5 minutes until the mixture is smooth and pale yellow. Gradually stir in the hot milk then return to the pan over a low heat and stir gently for 6–10 minutes without allowing the custard to reach simmering point. All the froth will disappear and the custard will be thick enough to coat the back of a spoon.

Remove from the heat, add the butter and chosen flavouring and continue to stir for a few minutes. Strain into a cold bowl and stir until the custard is cool, standing the bowl over a pan of ice cubes to speed up the process, if necessary. Cover and refrigerate until ready to serve. If lumps appear, process in a blender.

CRÈME CHANTILLY

Whipped cream flavoured with brandy,
chocolate, coffee or orange

Chantilly is famous for lace, china and its horse racing track but most of all for Chantilly cream. My mother learnt how to make Chantilly cream the day before her wedding, and decided to serve green salads and bowls of Chantilly cream at every meal. It was only after a month that she reluctantly introduced an omelette into her menu.

Chantilly is festive, versatile and easy to prepare. It can be flavoured with vanilla, cocoa powder, brandy, rum, coffee, candied ginger or orange peel. Seasoned with salt, it is used as a garnish for soups, or served with asparagus, steamed fish, or fish terrines.

Chantilly cream must be prepared at least one hour in advance and you must make sure all the ingredients are very cold. It will keep for about a day if it is covered and refrigerated. Discard the drops of liquid in the bowl as you serve.

—— *Makes 1 pint (600 ml)* ——

10 fl oz (300 ml) double cream, chilled
4 tablespoons cold milk
2 tablespoons icing sugar, sieved
1 teaspoon vanilla essence
1 tablespoon iced water

1 tablespoon rum or brandy liqueur or 3 oz (75 g) plain chocolate melted with 1 tablespoon water or 1 tablespoon instant coffee powder or 1 tablespoon finely shredded candied ginger or orange peel

It is much better to use a hand wire whisk since it will take no more than 3 minutes. If you use an electric whisk or a blender, start at a low speed and increase the speed after 1 minute.

Mix the cream and milk in a large, cold bowl as the mixture will double in volume. Whip the cream, moving the whisk around the bowl and lifting as you whisk to add as much air as possible, until the cream forms soft peaks. Add the sugar, vanilla essence and water and continue to whisk until very stiff. Stir in your chosen flavouring, cover and refrigerate for 1 hour.

*B*ARQUETTES DE *F*RUITS
Fruit tarts

Nothing is more inspiring than a platter of glittering fruit tartlets. The oval moulds are called *barquettes* because they look like little boats. The round *moules à flan* with a loose base are my favourite as they unmould easily.

The tartlets can be made with *Pâte Brisée* or *Pâte Sablée*, which I prefer even though it is a little more fragile. The *Crème Patissière* can be omitted and the pastry brushed with glaze or sprinkled with sugar and biscuit crumbs with fruits on top. For strawberries, grapes, raspberries, cherries, pineapple, oranges or lemons, tart shells should be totally cooked to avoid soggy crusts. For poached fruits such as pears, apricots, plums, peaches or for custard, they should be partially cooked (see page 218).

Frozen or tinned fruits must be properly drained. The fruits can be whole, halved or sliced and arranged in slightly overlapping circles. Well-drained cooked fruit should be arranged cut side down, but fresh fruit cut side up so the base doesn't become soggy.

Apricot glaze is used for apricots, pears and peaches while redcurrant glaze is traditionally reserved for red berries. I often use them interchangeably. Allow one or two tartlets per person.

———— *Serves 4–6* ————

1 quantity Pâte Sablée *(see page 220) or* Pâte Brisée *(see page 217)*
5 fl oz (150 ml) Crème Patissière *(see page 221) flavoured with 2 tablespoons brandy, orange blossom water or fruit liqueur*

10 fl oz (300 ml) redcurrant jelly or apricot jam
1 tablespoon sugar
1 tablespoon kirsch (optional)
1½ lb (675 g) strawberries, hulled and halved

Prepare the pastry and let it cool. Prepare the pastry cream, stir in your chosen flavouring and let it cool.

Butter the individual tartlet moulds and arrange them on a baking sheet.

Opposite: BARQUETTES DE FRUITS

Roll out the pastry on a lightly floured surface or between 2 sheets of baking parchment to about ¼ inch (5 mm) thick. Cut round or oval pieces 1 inch (2.5 cm) larger than the moulds, remove and discard the paper, if using. Lift the pieces on your rolling pin and unroll over the moulds. Fit the pastry on the bottom and edges of the moulds, pushing gently with the fingertips, then trim off any excess pastry around the edges.

Make a pretty design along the edge, pushing the blunt side of a knife or the back of a spoon against the dough. Refrigerate the baking sheet and filled moulds for 1–2 hours so that the edges will not collapse as they cook.

Pre-heat the oven to gas mark 4, 350°F (180°C).

Prick the bottom of the pastry with a fork then bake the shells for about 10 minutes. Prick the bases again and push the dough back up with the back of a spoon if it has collapsed. Bake for a further 10–15 minutes until the shells have shrunk a little from the moulds and are lightly browned. Leave to cool then carefully remove from the moulds using a spatula. (Remember that some fruits only need the shells to be partially cooked, see page 224).

To prepare the glaze, pour the jelly or jam into a saucepan, add the sugar and stir over a low heat until the mixture begins to froth and turn sticky and smooth. Stir in the kirsch, if using. Paint a little glaze on the inside of the pastry shells and reserve the rest.

Just before the meal, spread about ½ inch (1 cm) of *Crème Patissière* in the pastry shells and arrange the strawberries, stem down with the largest fruit in the centre and the smallest ones at the edges. Warm the reserved glaze to lukewarm and spoon it delicately over the fruit. Serve at once or refrigerate for an hour or so. Sprinkle with a little icing sugar before serving, if liked, or let them shine in their glaze.

Note

If you are using pears, apricots, cherries or plums, poach them in a sweet syrup for about 5 minutes then leave them to cool in the liquid. Drain them carefully. Use partially-cooked pastry shells, glazed and filled with *Crème Patissière*. Top with the sliced fruit and brush with the remaining glaze. Bake for a further 5 minutes.

Opposite: MARQUISE AU CHOCOLAT (*see page 230*)

PITHIVIERS

Flaky pastry cake with almond cream filling

This cake originated in the city of Pithiviers but is now offered in most patisseries throughout France. According to Madame Jacqueline Pilloy, winner of the 1992 Confrérie du Gateau Pithiviers' competition, the original confection was a sweet dense sponge cake made with ground almonds and decorated with glacé cherries and angelica strips (see page 228). In time this recipe was to be overshadowed by the more elabrate flaky pastry version which follows.

There are several stages to preparing this recipe, observe them closely for a perfect *Pithiviers*.

———— *Serves 8* ————

FOR THE PASTRY
7 oz (200 g) plain flour
6 oz (175 g) butter, softened
1½ teaspoons salt
5 tablespoons cold water
5 oz (150 g) butter, chilled

FOR THE CRÈME À PITHIVIERS
5 oz (150 g) ground almonds

4 oz (100 g) caster sugar
2 egg yolks
3 oz (75 g) butter
2 tablespoons rum

FOR THE GLAZE
1 small egg, beaten
2 tablespoons icing sugar
juice of 1 lemon

First, prepare the pastry. Place the flour and softened butter in a food processor and process at low speed for 1 minute. Add the salt and cold water and blend for a second then transfer to a bowl and knead for 1 minute until the pastry is smooth. Shape into a ball, cover and chill for 1 hour.

Place the cold butter between two sheets of waxed paper and tap it with a rolling pin to soften it a little. Flour the dough and the work surface. Roll out the pastry to a rectangle 6 × 18 inches (15 × 46 cm). Dot the top two-thirds of the pastry with pieces of butter. Fold the bottom unbuttered third up over the butter, pressing the edges with your fingers. Fold the top third of the pastry down, again pressing the edges with your fingers. Turn the pastry 90° to bring the seam to your left. Roll it out again, fold it and turn it in the same way, making sure the butter does not come through the pastry as you roll it and sprinkling with a little flour to prevent it sticking. Roll out and fold once again. Wrap the pastry in cling film and chill for 30 minutes.

Make 2 more turns then chill for a further 30 minutes.

For the *Crème à Pithiviers*, mix together the ground almonds, sugar and egg yolks with a wooden spoon then blend in the butter and rum to a smooth paste. Refrigerate until ready to use.

Butter a baking sheet.

Remove the pastry from the refrigerator and roll it into 2 × 8 inch (20 cm) circles. Place one circle on the baking sheet and brush the edges with beaten egg. Spoon the *Crème à Pithiviers* into the centre. Place the other circle of dough on the top and press the edges together firmly. Scallop the edges with the back of a knife and brush the top with beaten egg. Puncture a few holes in the crust to let the steam escape during baking. Chill in the refrigerator for 30 minutes.

Pre-heat the oven to gas mark 6, 400°F (200°C) for 10 minutes.

Brush the surface of the cake with a little beaten egg. Reduce the oven temperature to gas mark 5, 375°F (190°C) and bake for 15 minutes. Reduce the temperature again to gas mark 4, 350°F (180°C) and bake for a further 15 minutes.

Mix together the icing sugar and lemon juice and brush it over the top of the cake. Bake for a further 5 minutes until glazed and golden brown, reducing the oven temperature again if it browns too quickly.

'*L E V R A I*' *G Â T E A U* *P I T H I V I E R S*

Almond sponge cake

In the following recipe which comes from Madame Jacqueline Pilloy, she uses a professional bitter almond essence to intensify the flavour, but if you can't find it, the normal almond essence will do. The traditional decoration of glacé cherries and angelica strips is absolutely *de rigueur* for the authentic version!

—————— *Serves 6* ——————

7 oz (200 g) caster sugar
4 eggs
4 oz (100 g) unsalted butter, softened
7 oz (200 g) ground almonds

1 teaspoon almond essence (or 1 drop if using the professional variety)
5 oz (150 g) icing sugar, sifted
1 tablespoon water
angelica strips and glacé cherries to decorate

Pre-heat the oven to gas mark 4, 350°F (180°C) and grease and line an 8 inch (20 cm) cake tin.

Beat the sugar and eggs together in a large bowl until pale and doubled in size; it is easier if you use a hand mixer. Add the butter and mix thoroughly. Add the almonds and almond essence and mix again. Pour into the prepared tin and bake in the oven for about 45 minutes until the top is golden and a knife inserted in the centre comes out clean. Turn out and allow to cool completely.

Sift the icing sugar into a small bowl and add the water very gradually, using just enough to make the icing stiff but spreadable. Ice the cake thinly and decorate with the cherries and angelica.

GÂTEAU AU CHOCOLAT
Bitter chocolate cake

This is a deliciously moist, creamy cake with a soft crust on the top. Add only the minimum amount of sugar for the best flavour. I sometimes add two tablespoons of cocoa and a tablespoon of strong coffee for a more powerful flavour. Serve with a bowl of thinly sliced oranges or with a lemon-flavoured *Crème Anglaise* (see page 222).

8 oz (225 g) plain unsweetened chocolate	*2 tablespoons Grand Marnier (optional) or 1 tablespoon finely grated orange rind*
1½ tablespoons water	*1 teaspoon cocoa powder*
6 eggs, separated	*1 tablespoon thinly shredded candied orange rind*
8 oz (225 g) caster sugar	
8 oz (225 g) butter, softened	
1½ oz (40 g) plain flour	

Break the chocolate into small pieces and place it in a heatproof bowl with the water over a pan of gently simmering water. Leave to melt for 20 minutes without stirring.

Pre-heat the oven to gas mark 2, 300°F (150°C). Butter a 10 inch (25 cm) cake tin, sprinkle with a little caster sugar then shake off any excess.

Whisk the egg yolks and sugar until pale yellow and the mixture trails off the whisk in ribbons. Add the lukewarm, melted chocolate then blend in the softened butter and the flour. Add the Grand Marnier, if using, or orange rind. Beat the egg whites until stiff then delicately fold them into the mixture with a metal spoon, lifting the mixture as much as possible. Pour into the prepared tin and bake in the centre of the oven for about 1½ hours. The cake will be about 2 inches (5 cm) high and as you touch it, it should feel very soft, almost runny, under a light crust. Remove from the oven and leave to cool in the tin. Turn out only when it is thoroughly cold as it will have become firmer and be easy to cut with a warm, sharp knife. Serve sprinkled with the cocoa and scattered with the shredded candied orange rind.

MARQUISE AU CHOCOLAT
A light, moist chocolate dessert

This sumptuous dessert – which is, in fact, a glorified chocolate mousse, is easy to prepare and requires no baking. It is always served sliced on individual plates which have been coated with Chantilly cream, apricot purée or a custard flavoured with coffee, lemon, bitter chocolate, pistachio, aniseed or orange. Restaurants find it so very fashionable that in France it hardly seems worth serving it at home, although the range of colours and flavours in this recipe make it worthwhile! It must always be refrigerated for twenty-four hours before serving. The dark chocolate should be as bitter as possible; Sainsbury's or Waitrose Continental are good brands as they have 78 and 72 per cent cacao respectively.

——————— *Serves 4–6* ———————

FOR THE MOUSSE

8 oz (225 g) plain unsweetened chocolate
1–2 tablespoons strong black coffee
6 oz (175 g) butter, cut into pieces
3 eggs, separated
4 oz (100 g) icing sugar
pinch of salt
grated rind of 1 orange or 1 piece thinly slivered candied orange rind

TO DECORATE

1 quantity Crème Anglaise *(see page 222) flavoured with*
2 tablespoons Grand Marnier and grated rind of 1 orange
2 tablespoons thinly slivered candied orange rind (optional)

Line a 1 lb (450 g) loaf tin with cling film.

Break the chocolate into small pieces. Place the chocolate and coffee in the top of a double boiler or in a bowl over a pan of gently simmering water. Leave to melt, stirring occasionally. Remove from the heat. Add the butter, egg yolks, icing sugar, salt and orange rind then return to the heat until the butter has melted. Leave to cool slightly. Taste to check and correct the flavour, if necessary.

Beat the egg whites until they hold soft peaks. Delicately fold half of them into the chocolate mixture, then fold in the remainder until the mixture is smooth. Pour the mixture into the prepared tin, cover with kitchen foil and refrigerate for at least 24 hours.

Prepare the *Crème Anglaise* and stir in the liqueur and grated orange rind. Leave to cool then refrigerate.

Half an hour before serving, remove the *Marquise* and custard from the refrigerator. Dip the loaf tin into a bowl of hot water for a second, cover the top with a flat plate and unmould the mousse with one decisive movement.

Use a long, warm knife to slice the *marquise* into ½ inch (1 cm) slices and arrange them in the centre of dessert plates. Spoon a little *Crème Anglaise* around the *Marquise* and garnish with the slivers of candied orange rind. Alternatively, unmould the *Marquise* whole on to a serving dish and surround with the *Crème Anglaise*.

Note

For a more chocolatey flavour, I often add 2 tablespoons of cocoa powder to the melted chocolate.

TARTE AUX CERISES À LA FRANGIPANE

Bitter cherry and hazelnut custard tart

Tarte aux Cerises à la Frangipane is a spirited dessert, especially when the custard is made with hazelnuts rather than almonds. When using fresh cherries, they must be stoned, a delicate job, then poached in a wide saucepan so most of their juice evaporates. I think frozen or tinned *griottes* or *bing* cherries are the best for this recipe as they are ready-stoned and have a strong, pungent taste, but you can try it with any well-flavoured sour cherries.

—————— *Serves 4–6* ——————

1 quantity Pâte Sablée *(see page 220) or* Pâte Brisée *(see page 217)*
2 lb (900 g) sour cherries, stoned

FOR THE FILLING
4 oz (100 g) hazelnuts or almonds
4 tablespoons butter

2 oz (50 g) caster sugar
2 eggs

FOR THE GLAZE
3 tablespoons redcurrant jelly
1 tablespoon icing sugar
1 tablespoon kirsch

Butter a 10 inch (25 cm) loose-bottomed flan ring.

Prepare and chill the pastry. Roll it out on a lightly floured board and use to line the flan ring. Prick the base with a fork then refrigerate for 1–2 hours. Pre-heat the oven to gas mark 4, 350°F (180°C). Bake the dough for about 20 minutes until fully baked and golden. Leave to cool on a rack.

If you are using fresh fruit, place them in a wide pan with a little water and simmer for a few minutes until most of the juices have evaporated. Remove them from the pan with a slotted spoon and leave to drain, reserving the juice. If you use frozen, tinned or bottled cherries, drain them thoroughly and reserve the juice.

To prepare the filling, finely grind the nuts in a food processor. Add the butter and sugar and process for 1 minute. Add the eggs and process for a few seconds until blended.

Pre-heat the oven to gas mark 5, 375°F (190°C).

Place the redcurrant jelly, icing sugar and cherry juices in a saucepan, bring to the boil and simmer, uncovered, until thick, stirring occasionally. Add the kirsch and simmer for a further 1 minute. Spread a thin coating of the warm glaze on the bottom of the cooked shell. Spoon the cool filling over it. Arrange the cherries on top of the custard, stem sides down. Brush the remaining glaze over the top. Place in the oven for about 15 minutes until the cherries have softened a little. The custard will pop up around them and the glaze will shine evenly on top. Cool on a wire rack then serve with a wide spatula and a large spoon.

———————————— GERS ————————————

SABLÉS À L'ARMAGNAC
Armagnac biscuits

When Madame Lydie Dèche of the Domaine de Millais made these biscuits, all the ingredients came from the family's farm and armagnac production. But I have successfully prepared these at home without homemade Armagnac and cream from my own herd of dairy cows!

——————— *Makes about 36* ———————

10 fl oz (300 ml) double cream
8 oz (225 g) caster sugar
8 oz (225 g) plain flour
3 tablespoons armagnac

Pre-heat the oven to gas mark 7, 425°F (220°C). Butter a baking sheet.

Mix together all the ingredients until the mixture is smooth and fairly stiff. Place teaspoonfuls of the mixture on the prepared baking sheet 3 inches (7.5 cm) apart since the biscuits will spread as they cook. Turn the oven temperature down to gas mark 5, 375°F (190°C). Place the biscuits in the centre of the oven and bake for about 10–15 minutes until golden. Remove from the oven and cool on a wire rack. Store in an air-tight tin.

Note
A few raisins marinated in armagnac for a few hours and drained can be placed on top of each little *sablé* before baking.

GÂTEAU BASQUE

Rich pastry cake with bitter cherry or Crème Patissière filling

Biarritz may boast about its grand palaces and its bold and graceful surfers, but for me *Gâteau Basque* remains its ultimate claim to fame. *Gâteau Basque* is considered both a pie and a cake, and it is prepared in many different versions throughout the Basque country. It may be filled either with cherry jam, prune purée, a brandy-flavoured *Crème Patissière* or with a mixture of cherry preserve and *Crème Patissière*. My favourite filling is bitter cherry jam flavoured with a spoonful of kirsch and the juice of a lemon.

———— *Serves 4–6* ————

FOR THE PASTRY
10 oz (275 g) plain flour
1 egg
1 egg yolk
½ teaspoon salt
5 oz (150 g) caster sugar
finely grated rind of 1 lemon
5 oz (150 g) butter, cut into pieces

FOR THE FILLING
6 tablespoons bitter cherry jam
juice of 1 small lemon
1 tablespoon kirsch

FOR THE ALTERNATIVE CREAM
  FILLING
1 quantity Crème Patissière *(see page 221) flavoured with orange blossom water, rum or brandy*

FOR THE ALTERNATIVE PRUNE
  FILLING
12 oz (350 g) prunes, stoned
10 fl oz (300 ml) strong tea

FOR THE GLAZE
1 egg yolk, beaten
1 teaspoon milk

First, make the pastry. Place the flour in a large bowl and make a well in the centre. Add the egg, egg yolk, salt, sugar, lemon rind and butter. Gradually blend the flour into the other ingredients until the pastry is soft and smooth. Dust with a little flour, cover and refrigerate for a few hours or overnight.

Select your filling. For the cherry filling, mix together the cherry jam, lemon juice and kirsch. For the custard filling, prepare the *Crème Patissière* and leave it to cool. For a custard and jam filling, prepare half quantities of these two fillings. For a prune filling, simmer the prunes in the tea for about 30 minutes until soft. Strain and purée the prunes, add a little of the tea to make the desired consistency.

Butter an 8 inch (20 cm) cake tin.

Divide the pastry into two, one part slightly larger than the other. Roll out or pat the largest piece of pastry into a 9 inch (23 cm) circle and use it to line the bottom and sides of the prepared cake tin. Spoon your chosen filling into the centre. Roll or pat the second piece of pastry into an 8 inch (20 cm) circle. Place it over the filling and fold the edges of the large circle over the top, pressing all round with your fingers to seal the pastry and prevent the filling from leaking out. Beat the egg and milk and brush over the top. Make light criss-cross lines on the top with the tines of a fork and make 2 incisions with a sharp knife to let the steam escape as it cooks. It is a rustic-looking cake. Chill in the refrigerator for 30 minutes.

Pre-heat the oven to gas mark 7, 425°F (220°C) for a few minutes then lower the temperature to gas mark 5, 375°F (190°C).

Bake the cake for 40–45 minutes until golden brown. Run a sharp knife around the edge then let it cool in the tin for 15 minutes. Carefully remove from the tin and finish cooling on a wire rack. It will become a little firmer as it cools. Lift delicately and place on a serving platter.

—— **NORMANDY AND LOIRE** ——

*L*ES *C*RÉMETS

Fresh cream hearts

These are as popular in Normandy as they are in the Loire. They are made in heart-shaped moulds with draining holes or in a plain colander lined with a piece of muslin. They should be prepared a day in advance and served coated with fresh cream or with a purée of fruits.

———— *Serves 4* ————

1 pint (600 ml) double cream
7 fl oz (200 ml) soured cream
1 tablespoon finely grated lemon rind
1 teaspoon caster sugar
4 egg whites

TO DECORATE
10 oz (275 g) fresh or frozen berries
3 oz (75 g) caster sugar
juice of 1 lemon
2 tablespoons single cream
8 oz (225 g) raspberries or strawberries

Line individual perforated moulds or a colander with a piece of muslin.

Whisk the cream until it forms soft peaks then gently stir in the soured cream, lemon rind and sugar. Whisk the egg whites until stiff then fold them into the cream mixture. Pour the mixture into the prepared moulds and stand them in a deep plate so that they can drain. Refrigerate overnight.

Purée the fruit, sugar and lemon juice in a food processor or blender, adding a little more sugar or lemon juice to taste.

When you are ready to serve, invert the *Crémets* on to individual plates, top with single cream and spoon a little fruit purée around them. Serve the fresh berries on a flat platter and the rest of the fruit purée in a sauce boat.

Note

I sometimes use a mixture of cream cheese, cottage cheese, and double cream for *Crémets*, choosing the proportions to make a pleasing texture.

GÂTEAU DE SAVOIE
Light sponge cake

This dome-shaped cake is served as a dessert or a tea-time *goûter*, or snack. It is often sliced and may be offered with stewed fruits, tangerines or prunes preserved in armagnac (see page 255), ice-cream, sorbets, light custard, fruit purée or a warm chocolate sauce. The cake is best prepared in a fairly large quantity in a 4 pint (2.25 litre) dome-shaped mould, and made a day in advance.

———————— *Serves 8* ————————

8 oz (225 g) caster sugar
7 eggs, separated
5 oz (150 g) plain flour
4 oz (100 g) cornflour, arrowroot
   or potato flour

1 teaspoon grated lemon rind
1 tablespoon lemon juice or orange
   blossom water
1 teaspoon icing sugar

Pre-heat the oven to gas mark 4, 350°F (180°C). Butter a 4 pint (2.25 litre) dome-shaped mould and dust with a little flour.

Reserve 2 tablespoons of the sugar. Beat the egg yolks and gradually add the remaining sugar until the mixture is pale yellow and frothy. Whisk the egg whites until they form soft peaks then add the reserved sugar and whisk again until stiff. Blend the flour with the cornflour, arrowroot or potato flour. Fold a tablespoon of the egg whites and a tablespoon of the flours alternately into the egg yolks, lifting to let as much air as possible into the mixture. Fold in the lemon rind, the juice or orange blossom water. Pour the batter into the prepared mould; it should only be three-quarters full. Sprinkle with the icing sugar. Place it on a baking sheet and bake in the oven for 40–50 minutes until a skewer inserted into the centre comes out clean. If the top of the cake reaches the top of the mould and begins to brown, cover it with a moist piece of kitchen paper. Remove from the oven and leave to cool in the mould for 10 minutes before turning out. Leave to cool before slicing. If you do not use it at once, store the cake wrapped in kitchen foil; or it freezes perfectly.

TARTE AUX POMMES

Classic apple tart

Tarte aux Pommes is eaten everywhere in France and there are many different approaches to making it. Most of the tarts are open, but the apples may be diced, quartered or sliced; they may be cooked on a pastry shell sprinkled with sugar or sliced almonds, or spread on a layer of thick apple sauce. Sometimes it is made with a paper-thin, flat layer of pastry covered with apples. It is served warm and feels more like the evocation of a tart than the real thing.

The following recipe makes a classic apple tart. The pastry is partially cooked so that it is set and does not become soggy. The apple sauce is then spread over the pastry case and topped with a pretty concentric arrangement of sliced apples. If you use cooking apples, make sure you choose a variety that remain firm when cooked. If you like to try different variations, you can use twice as much apple sauce for a mellow texture, replace the apricot jam with Seville marmalade for a sharper flavour, or add toasted almond flakes on top before you cook it. Serve at room temperature or barely warm, never chilled.

——————— *Serves 4–6* ———————

1 quantity Pâte Brisée *(see page 217)*

1½ lb (675 g) dessert apples such as Cox's

FOR THE FILLING
1½ lb (675 g) cooking apples such as Bramleys
4 tablespoons butter
5 oz (150 g) caster sugar
3 tablespoons apricot jam
1 tablespoon Calvados or rum
grated rind (optional) and juice of 1 lemon

FOR THE GLAZE
4 tablespoons apricot jam, sieved
2 tablespoons caster sugar

TO SERVE
bowl of Crème Chantilly *(see page 223) or double cream*

238

Pre-heat the oven to gas mark 4, 350°F (180°C). Butter a 10 inch (25 cm) flan ring.

Roll out the prepared pastry on a lightly floured surface and use to line the flan ring. Prick the base with a fork. Bake in the oven for about 5 minutes then leave to cool.

Peel and core the cooking apples and chop them coarsely. Place them in a saucepan with 1 tablespoon of the butter and simmer over a low heat for about 15 minutes, stirring occasionally, until soft. Add 3 oz (75 g) of the sugar, the apricot jam, Calvados or rum and 2 tablespoons of the butter and stir until well blended. Taste and add a little of the lemon juice or a little more jam or Calvados, if necessary, and the lemon rind, if using.

Peel and core the dessert apples and slice them thinly. Toss with the lemon juice then sprinkle with half the remaining sugar.

To make the glaze, warm the sieved apricot jam with the sugar over a low heat for about 3 minutes, stirring gently until melted. Remove from the heat.

Spread a little of the warm glaze on the base of the cold shell. Cover the remainder and keep it warm for later use. Spoon the apple purée into the pastry shell and arrange the raw apples in concentric circles on the top, starting in the centre and overlapping the slices as you go. Sprinkle with the remaining sugar and dot with the remaining butter.

Bake in the oven for 20 minutes. Lower the oven temperature to gas mark 3, 325°F (160°C) and bake for another 20 minutes until the apples are soft and lightly browned. Place on a rack to cool and spoon the reserved warm glaze over the top. Serve with the Chantilly or double cream.

GRATIN DE FRUITS AU SABAYON

Sabayon and fruit gratin

Raspberries, redcurrants or cherries, orange, grapefruit or tangerine are essential to the dish for their sharp flavour and their juices. All fruit must be fresh and ripe, but you can use frozen berries. When I have a good variety of red fruits I use orange juice. If the fruits lack flavour, I simmer a sweet wine for twenty minutes, then sprinkle the fruits with grated orange or lemon rind.

———————— *Serves 4–6* ————————

FOR THE FRUIT
8 oz (225 g) raspberries
1 large orange
1 juicy pear
2 apricots or 1 peach or 2 plums or
* 1 additional pear*
8 oz (225 g) strawberries, halved
juice of ½ lemon
few mint leaves, finely chopped

FOR THE SABAYON
3 egg yolks
pinch of salt
3 tablespoons caster sugar
8 tablespoons orange juice,
* Marsala, champagne, dry white*
* wine or sweet white wine and the*
* juice of 1 lemon*
1 tablespoon demerara sugar
2 tablespoons flaked almonds
* (optional)*

Spread the raspberries in the bottom of the individual ramekins or gratin dish. Peel and remove all the pith and membrane from the orange. Peel and core the pear. Peel and stone the other fruits. Cut the fruit into thick slices. Scatter the fruit in the dishes and sprinkle with the lemon juice and mint. Place the egg yolks, salt, sugar and orange juice or wine and lemon juice in the top of a double boiler or in a heavy bowl placed over a large pan of simmering water. Whisk the mixture vigorously for at least 10 minutes until it is thick and frothy. It should be creamy and warm to the touch and double its size. Pour over the fruit. Sprinkle with the demerara sugar, and flaked almonds, if using, and grill for about 3 minutes until golden brown on top. Serve with fresh berries or sorbet.

Opposite: GRATIN DE FRUITS AU SABAYON

TARTE AUX POMMES NORMANDE

Rustic Normandy apple tart

Monique Piat's beautiful half-timbered auberge overlooking the Valley d'Auge in the heart of Normandy is surrounded by a rich variety of apple trees. We prepared this apple tart, which seems to be the original apple tart Eve intended to offer to Adam. No custard, no compote, no glaze, just lots of apples standing straight and close together, 'like a group of little soldiers', said Monique. We used twenty apples for a tart prepared for about eight people. This tart is often called *Bourdelot* locally, although the term is also used for a whole apple wrapped in pastry and baked. You can serve the warm tart with a bowl of double cream.

——————— *Serves 4* ———————

½ quantity Pâte Sablée *(see page 220)*
2 lb (900 g) firm, tart apples

juice of 1 lemon
1 egg white
1 tablespoon brown sugar

Prepare the pastry then chill for 1 hour. Core and quarter the apples, leaving them unpeeled. Sprinkle with the lemon juice to prevent them from browning. Pre-heat the oven to gas mark 7, 425°F (220°C). Butter a 9 inch (23 cm) shallow cake tin.

Roll out the pastry on a lightly floured surface to a circle slightly larger than the tin and use to line the base of the prepared cake tin, leaving a little pastry up the sides. Brush the base with the egg white. Reserve a few of the apple pieces. Arrange the remaining apples in concentric circles round the tart on one of their cut sides and pressed tightly against each other so they stand firmly. Slice the reserved apples and insert the slices between the gaps so that the cooked apples will remain in a tight mass. The apples will stand about 2 inches (5 cm) above the pastry shell. Sprinkle with the brown sugar. Fold the sides of the pastry in and gently fold into a neat, plump roll around the edges. Bake in the oven for 40–50 minutes, until the apples are soft and golden. Serve lukewarm.

Opposite: TARTE AUX POMMES NORMANDE

CRÊPES NORMANDES

Thin crêpes filled with apples and flavoured with Calvados

Crêpes offer the simplest and cheapest of desserts – but surely one of the most delicious. Every region of France prepares crêpes in its own individual way. The batter may be flavoured with aniseed, lemon, rum, armagnac, or orange blossom water, as in Roussillon; the crêpes may be spread with local salted butter, as in Brittany, or filled with a variety of jams, honeys, walnuts or whipped cream. But whether they are served at the end of a meal or as mid-afternoon snack, they seem to be the ultimate crowd-pleaser for all ages.

For me, *Crêpes Normandes* served with a sharp local cider or a sweet dessert wine are the top of my list of favourites. They can be prepared in advance – always a wonderful point for a hostess – and heated just a few minutes before serving.

Serves 4–6

FOR THE CRÊPES
4 oz (100 g) plain flour
2 eggs
¼ teaspoon salt
4 fl oz (120 ml) milk or beer
4 fl oz (120 ml) water
2 tablespoons butter, melted, or
   1 tablespoon oil and 1 tablespoon
   butter, or a piece of pork fat to
   cook the crêpes

FOR THE FILLING
1½ lb (675 g) crisp, sharp apples
   such as Granny Smith

2 oz (50 g) soft brown sugar
1 tablespoon butter
1 tablespoon lemon juice
grated rind of 1 lemon

TO DECORATE
4 tablespoons redcurrant jelly
4 tablespoons water
juice of 1 lemon
1 tablespoon Calvados

Pour the flour into a bowl and make a well in the centre. Beat the eggs lightly then add the salt. Blend the eggs into the flour then whisk in the milk or beer and water and the melted butter or oil. The mixture does not have to be perfectly smooth. Cover and leave to rest for at least 1 hour.

Peel, core, and slice the apples and place in a saucepan with the sugar, butter, lemon juice and lemon rind. Cover and simmer over a low heat for about 20 minutes until soft, stirring occasionally.

When you are ready to cook the crêpes, stir the batter well; it should be smooth like custard. For quicker results, you can use two small pancake pans about 5 inches (13 cm) in diameter. Grease the pans before cooking each crêpe by adding a little piece of butter, or by rubbing the pan with a piece of muslin dipped in oil and wrapped round a fork, or with a piece of pork fat on a fork. Very little fat is needed after you have cooked the first few crêpes.

Heat and grease the pan. Pour in 2 or 3 tablespoons of batter, turning the pan so that the base is evenly coated in batter. After 1 minute, the edges of the crêpe will begin to brown and detach from the pan. Shake the pan gently to detach the crêpe, then toss it or turn it with a spatula and cook the other side for 1 minute. Stack the cooked crêpes on top of each other on a platter as you cook them.

Butter a shallow baking dish.

When all the crêpes are cooked, place a tablespoon of cooked apple in the centre of each crêpe and roll it like a fat cigar. Place the crêpes side by side in the baking dish in a single layer. Dot with a little butter and cover with kitchen foil. You can prepare to this point in advance and refrigerate.

Pre-heat the oven to gas mark 4, 350°F (180°C) about 30 minutes before serving.

Re-heat the crêpes in the oven for 20 minutes.

Mix the redcurrant jelly, water and lemon juice in a small saucepan and stir over a medium heat for a few minutes until blended. Remove the foil from the crêpes and pour half the mixture over them. Return to the oven for a further 5 minutes. Remove from the oven, sprinkle with the Calvados and pour over the remaining redcurrant sauce. Serve directly from the baking dish with a spatula and a large spoon.

Note

Some regions have interesting versions such as crêpes stuffed with sliced, poached pears or quince which are flavoured then flambéed with pear liqueur or pear brandy.

— **PARIS AND THROUGHOUT FRANCE** —

CRÊPES SUZETTE

Orange butter crêpes flambéed in brandy

Long live the Suzette who inspired such a glorious dish. Although the finished dessert is theatrical, it follows a simple process; crêpes are made in advance, flavoured with orange butter, sprinkled with warm liqueur, ignited and served. It is better if the crêpes and the orange butter are prepared, covered and refrigerated overnight. This makes the crêpes easier to handle and the orange butter more piquant. You must make sure the sauce in the chafing dish is very hot when you add the crêpes and that they are thoroughly heated before serving them.

This is a very rich and heady dish not intended for children or timid souls. I allow two or three crêpes per person and I never prepare more than ten or twelve crêpes at a time as the dish cannot be made properly and with the necessary dramatic quality for a larger group.

———————— *Serves 4* ————————

FOR THE CRÊPES

4 oz (100 g) plain flour
¼ teaspoon salt
2 eggs
10 fl oz (300 ml) milk, beer or
  water
1 tablespoon butter or oil
butter or oil to cook the crêpes

FOR THE ORANGE BUTTER
grated rind of 1 lemon
grated rind of 1 orange
3 tablespoons icing sugar, sieved

2 tablespoons orange juice
4 oz (100 g) butter, softened
2 tablespoons Grand Marnier,
  Cointreau or Curaçao

FOR THE SAUCE
3 tablespoons butter
3 tablespoons caster sugar
juice of 1 orange
2 tablespoons cognac
2 tablespoons Grand Marnier or
  Cointreau

To make the batter, mix together the flour, salt, eggs, milk, beer or water and oil or butter and stir for a few minutes until thoroughly blended. Cover and leave to stand for at least 1 hour so the batter has the consistency of a light custard.

To make the orange butter, place the lemon and orange rinds in a bowl and sprinkle with the sugar and orange juice. Blend in the butter and liqueur with a fork to make a soft paste. Cover and refrigerate.

Heat and grease a pancake pan. Pour in 2 or 3 tablespoons of batter, turning the pan so that the base is evenly coated in batter. After 1 minute, the edges of the crêpe will begin to brown and detach from the pan. Shake the pan gently to detach the crêpe, then toss it or turn it with a spatula and cook the other side for 1 minute. Stack the cooked crepes on top of each other on a platter as you cook them, putting greaseproof paper between each one. Cover and refrigerate overnight.

Remove the crêpes and orange butter from the refrigerator an hour before serving. Spread each crêpe with a small teaspoon of orange butter. Roll them or fold them in quarters into triangles.

Depending on the size of your pan, you may need to cook the crêpes in 2 batches, so use a proportion of the ingredients, if necessary. Heat the butter for the sauce in a large chafing dish or frying pan, sprinkle with the sugar and let it brown slightly. When the bottom is coated with a light caramelised sauce, add the orange juice and stir until hot. Start heating the rolled or folded crêpes, adding them two or three at a time, turning them in the sauce with a spatula and a pair of tongs and pushing them to the outside of the dish when they are ready. Sprinkle with the cognac and Grand Marnier or Cointreau. Ignite, if you wish, basting the pancakes until the flame dies, although you do not have to go through this dramatic gesture. Holding each folded crêpe with two spoons or spatulas, turn it delicately in the warm sauce. Serve the crêpes on warm dessert plates and spoon a little hot sauce over them.

Note

Originally *Crêpes Suzettes* were made with tangerines instead of oranges; it's worth trying.

CRÈME BRULÉE

Creamy custard topped with crisp caramel

An all-time favourite, this unctuous, delicate dish is easy to serve as it is presented in its cooking dish. It originates in the French West Indies and is, in fact, a variation on *Crème Anglaise*. It can be prepared in one dish or in individual ramekins. At the *Mère Poularde* restaurant in Normandy, I sampled a predictably rich version using twelve egg yolks to a litre of cream.

————— *Serves 4–6* —————

1 pint (600 ml) double cream	2 teaspoons cornflour
3½ fl oz (100 ml) milk	2 tablespoons grated orange rind or
2 vanilla pods, halved	finely chopped candied orange
5 egg yolks	rind
4 oz (100 g) caster sugar	3 oz (75 g) demerara sugar

Pre-heat the oven to gas mark 2, 300°F (150°C). Butter a large ovenproof dish or individual ramekins.

Bring the cream, milk and vanilla pods to the boil in a saucepan. Remove from the heat, discard the vanilla pods, cover and keep to one side. Blend the egg yolks, sugar, cornflour and orange rind. Stir in the hot cream and whisk vigorously. Pour the mixture into the prepared dish or dishes; it should only be about 1 inch (2.5 cm) deep. Place the dish or dishes in a roasting tin filled with water to come about 1 inch (2.5 cm) up the sides. Bake in the oven for 30 minutes until the cream is set but not too firm. Leave to cool then refrigerate for 2 hours.

Pre-heat the grill. Sprinkle the cream with the demerara sugar and grill for a few seconds so the top is covered with a golden crust. Serve lukewarm or cold.

Note
You may like to add a few raspberries, sliced strawberries or 2 Seville orange slices to the bottom of the dish before pouring in the custard.

—— **THROUGHOUT FRANCE** ——

BAVAROIS À L'ORANGE

Moulded cream dessert flavoured with orange liqueur

A royal dessert served on grand occasions, this is nevertheless quite easy to prepare at home. In fact, it is a mixture of *Crème Anglaise*, *Crème Chantilly* and gelatine blended together and chilled until firm so that it can be unmoulded. In cold weather, you may need less gelatine than in summer. A ring mould with a hole in the centre – whether it is plain or fluted – is necessary to ensure an even cooling of the mixture and for a homogeneous texture.

A Bavarois can be flavoured with orange, hazelnuts, almonds or fresh fruit purée, and these will also add texture to the custard. It is served with *Crème Chantilly* (see page 223), *Crème Anglaise* (see page 222), *coulis de fruits*, fruit purée, or fresh fruit.

———— *Serves 6* ————

almond or groundnut oil for
  greasing
1 pint (600 ml) milk
5 egg yolks
4 oz (100 g) caster sugar
pinch of salt
1 teaspoon cornflour
1/4 oz (10 g) gelatine
3 1/2 fl oz (100 ml) orange juice
3 tablespoons orange liqueur
2 tablespoons grated orange rind

1 pint (300 ml) whipping cream,
  chilled

TO SERVE
3 oranges, thinly sliced
1 candied orange rind, cut into thin
  slivers
10 fl oz (300 ml) double or
  whipping cream, whipped, or
  fruit purée

Grease a 10 inch (25 cm), 2 inch (5 cm) deep ring mould with almond or groundnut oil.

Heat the milk in a saucepan. Place the egg yolks in a bowl and gradually work in the sugar and salt, whisking vigorously for about 5 minutes until the mixture is smooth and pale yellow. Gradually stir in the hot milk then return to the pan over a low heat and stir gently for 6 to 10 minutes without allowing the custard to reach simmering point. All the froth will disappear and the custard will be thick enough to coat the back of a spoon. Remove from the heat and stir in the cornflour.

Soak the gelatine in the orange juice for 10 minutes. Stir into the warm custard with the orange liqueur and orange rind until well blended. If it is not smooth enough, rub through a sieve then leave to cool.

Whip the cream until stiff. When the custard is cool but not cold, place the whipped cream on top and, using a large spoon or spatula, gently bring the mixture on top of the cream. Continue to lift and fold the mixture, turning the bowl so that it is evenly blended with your left hand.

Spoon the mixture into the prepared mould and cover with a piece of kitchen foil. Holding it with both hands, tap the mould lightly on a table to make sure it is tightly packed. Place in the coldest part of the refrigerator overnight or for at least 4 hours.

Dip the mould in a bowl of hot water for a second or dip a tea towel in hot water, wring it out then wrap it around the mould. Run a sharp knife round the edge. Place a plate on top of the mould and turn it over to unmould the Bavarois with a decisive movement. Arrange the sliced oranges around the edges and the candied orange on top. You may offer a bowl of whipped cream or a bowl of fruit purée with the Bavarois. An unmoulded Bavarois can be refrigerated for a few hours.

*B*ABA AU *R*HUM

Moist, plump cake flavoured with syrup and brandy and filled with fruit or cream

All we know about this cake is that it was invented and brought to France by Louis XV's father-in-law. It is one of the most popular desserts in France. Small, plump Babas oozing with rum and syrup are part of every bistro's dessert offering; and wrapped in their little pleated paper cases, they are a staple of every *patisserie* window display.

When the dough is baked in the shape of a large ring, the cake is called a Savarin in memory of the famous gourmet Brillat Savarin. A few raisins steeped in Malaga wine or rum, diced candied fruits or a few drops of orange blossom water may be added to the dough. Choose a light custard, fresh fruit or fruit compote to fill the centre of a savarin, if you wish. This recipe makes enough for 1 Savarin or about 8 Babas. Savarins and Babas freeze well. If you are making a Savarin, choose either the fruit or the orange filling. You will not need a filling for the Babas.

——————— *Serves 6* ———————

FOR THE BABAS OR SAVARIN
1 oz (25 g) fresh or ½ oz (15 g)
dried yeast
6 tablespoons warm milk
8 oz (225 g) strong plain flour
pinch of salt
2 tablespoons caster sugar
2 eggs, lightly beaten
4 tablespoons melted butter

FOR THE SYRUP
8 fl oz (250 ml) water
juice of 1 lemon or 1 orange
5 oz (150 g) caster sugar
4 tablespoons rum, kirsch or Grand
Marnier

FOR THE FRUIT FILLING
ALTERNATIVE
2 apples, peeled, cored and sliced
2 pears, peeled, cored and sliced
juice of 1 lemon

FOR THE ORANGE FILLING
ALTERNATIVE
4 oranges, peeled and thinly sliced
2 tablespoons Grand Marnier
1 tablespoon lemon juice
2 tablespoons sugar

FOR THE GLAZE
4 tablespoons apricot jam, sieved
1 tablespoon sugar
juice of 1 lemon

TO DECORATE
4 glacé cherries
1 quantity Crème Chantilly (see
    page 223)
glacé fruits
few slivers of angelica
few flaked almonds

To make the dough, blend the yeast and milk together with 2 tablespoons of the flour and leave to stand in a warm place until frothy. Place the remaining flour in a bowl with the salt and sugar and make a well in the centre. Pour in the yeast mixture, blend in the flour and knead for a few minutes. Knead in the eggs, one at a time, then the melted butter. Knead well for about 10 minutes until the dough is soft, elastic and sticky like a thick batter. Cover with a damp tea towel and leave to rise in a warm, turned-off oven for about 20 minutes until doubled in size.

Lightly butter a ring mould or individual moulds.

Punch down the dough and place it in the mould or divide it between the individual moulds so that they are about half full. Leave in a warm place to rise for 40 minutes.

Pre-heat the oven to gas mark 5, 375°F (190°C).

Bake in the oven for about 25 minutes for a Savarin or 15 minutes for Babas until a knife or thin skewer inserted into the centre comes out clean. Leave to cool on a rack for a few minutes then unmould and leave to cool. If the cake sticks to the mould, wrap it in a piece of kitchen foil for a few minutes. The steam produced will make it easy to turn out.

To make the syrup, bring the water, lemon or orange juice and sugar to the boil and boil for about 3 minutes until thick. Leave to cool then add the liqueur. Prick the top of the Savarin with a fork and slowly spoon the syrup over the cake so that the cake is fully impregnated. Baste the cake until most or all of the syrup has been absorbed. It should be very moist but not totally soggy. Just before serving, remove excess syrup with a spoon or bulb baster. If you are preparing individual Babas, you can immerse them in syrup then drain them on a rack.

For the fruit filling, simmer the apples, pears and lemon juice over a low heat until soft. Reserve.

For the orange filling, place the orange slices in a bowl and sprinkle with the Grand Marnier, lemon juice and sugar. Cover and reserve.

To prepare the glaze, heat the apricot jam, sugar and lemon juice in a small saucepan for about 1 minute, stirring until smooth and liquid.

Spoon the glaze over the tops of the Babas or Savarin. Place a glacé cherry or a dot of *Crème Chantilly* on top of each Baba, or decorate the top of a Savarin with glacé fruits, slivers of angelica and flaked almonds. Press them down gently then brush with another light coating of glaze. Spoon the chosen filling into the centre of the Savarin and serve with the *Crème Chantilly*. If you have chosen a fruit filling, you may like to decorate the top of the Savarin with fresh berries.

Note

I sometimes use strong tea instead of water to prepare a more fragrant syrup. Before being soaked in syrup, the cake can be wrapped in foil and refrigerated for 2 weeks or frozen for even longer. Thaw the cake thoroughly then warm it for 5 minutes in a moderate oven before pouring over the lukewarm syrup.

GÉNOISE

Iced sponge cake with cream filling

This glorious sponge cake is generally cut in half, filled with butter cream, spread on top with a thin layer of apricot jam then covered with a rich icing or a garnish of candied fruits. Génoise cake also makes the most versatile of bases and can be cut into small squares or triangles and covered with icing to become *petits fours*.

I like Génoise covered with a light icing, slivered almonds or bitter chocolate shavings. I fill it with a layer of *Crème Bourdaloue*, jam, or a light chocolate mousse.

Tightly wrapped in foil, it will keep in the refrigerator for a week. It also freezes well, but must be thawed slowly.

——————— *Makes 1 × 9 inch (23 cm) cake* ———————

FOR THE CAKE
5 eggs
5 oz (150 g) caster sugar
3 oz (75 g) butter, melted
5 oz (150 g) plain flour
1 teaspoon grated lemon rind

FOR THE CRÈME BOURDALOUE
  FILLING
10 fl oz (300 ml) milk
1 egg
2 egg yolks
5 oz (150 g) caster sugar
2 oz (50 g) rice flour or arrowroot
4 oz (100 g) ground almonds

2 oz (50 g) butter
1 tablespoon kirsch

FOR THE GLAZE
3 tablespoons apricot jam
1 tablespoon rum
6 tablespoons water

FOR THE ICING
5 oz (150 g) icing sugar, sieved
1 egg white

TO DECORATE
2 squares plain chocolate, scraped to
  make shavings

Pre-heat the oven to gas mark 4, 350°F (180°C). Butter a 9 inch (23 cm) cake tin then dust with a little flour and shake off the excess. The eggs should be at room temperature and the melted butter lukewarm when you begin.

To make the cake, place the eggs and sugar in a bowl and whisk for about 5 minutes until very fluffy and pale yellow and the mixture trails off the whisk in ribbons. Alternatively you can use a food processor. Don't overbeat the mixture or it will become dry.

Bring a saucepan of water to the boil. Place the bowl containing the egg mixture over the water and beat the mixture vigorously for a few minutes until the mixture is warm to the touch. Remove from the heat and continue to whisk for about 3 minutes until cool, thick and pale yellow. It should double in bulk. Stir in the melted butter, then whisk in the flour and lemon rind a little at a time, lifting the batter upwards so that it is smooth and homogeneous. Pour the mixture into the prepared cake tin and bake it in the centre of the oven for 25–35 minutes until golden brown. A finger pressed on the surface will not leave a print or a knife inserted into the centre will come out clean. The cake will only rise by one-third. Remove from the oven and leave to cool for 10 minutes before unmoulding upside-down on to a rack to cool completely. The bottom of the cake will become the top and provide a smooth surface which will be easy to ice.

To make the *Crème Bourdaloue* filling, heat the milk in a saucepan. Beat the egg, egg yolks and sugar in a bowl then slowly stir in the flour or arrowroot and ground almonds. Pour in the hot milk and mix well then pour the mixture into the saucepan. Bring to the boil, stirring, then reduce the heat and simmer for about 2 minutes, stirring until the mixture is very thick. Remove from the heat and stir in the butter and kirsch. Leave to cool.

To make the glaze, simmer the jam, rum and water in a small saucepan for a few minutes until thick then rub through a sieve.

To make the icing, place the icing sugar in a small bowl and make a well in the centre. Gradually blend in the egg white, a little at a time, until the mixture is thick, smooth and soft.

Slice the cake in half horizontally, fill with the *Crème Bourdaloue* and sandwich together. Spread a thin layer of glaze over the top and sides of the cake and leave to dry for a few minutes. Pour the icing delicately over the cake and allow it to spread gracefully like butter on hot toast. Leave it to dry. Sprinkle with the chocolate shavings.

GLACE À L'ARMAGNAC ET AUX PRUNEAUX

Prune ice-cream flavoured with armagnac

The area around Agen in south-west France is renowned for its succulent prunes, which are puréed for desserts, stuffed for sweetmeats, served with roast meat and macerated in the other local product, armagnac.

In Auch, capital of Gascony, the celebrated chef of the *Hôtel de France*, André Daguin made this luscious dessert for us with the ease and vigour of a true musketeer. He topped it with a marinated prune on a dessert plate coated with a light vanilla custard.

I would advise you to prepare the Prunes in Armagnac at once, since they need to marinate for several weeks. You will use them also with cakes, on stewed fruits, in fruit omelettes, or in tiny glasses as a mid-afternoon snack or to complete a meal. They will keep for a year. Remember to use a wooden spoon to remove the prunes and to close the jar tightly after each use. For the fastidious gourmand, Bas-Armagnac is the best.

———————— *Serves 4–8* ————————

FOR THE PRUNES
10 fl oz (300 ml) strong tea
3 oz (75 g) sugar
12 oz (350 g) extra-large prunes, stoned
1 pint (600 ml) armagnac

1 clove

FOR THE CUSTARD
1¾ pints (1 litre) milk
10 egg yolks
10 oz (275 g) caster sugar

Prepare the tea, stir in the sugar then leave to cool. Soak the prunes overnight in the tea then drain them carefully. Place the prunes in a glass jar, cover with the armagnac, add the clove and stir. The prunes should not rise to the surface. If they do, add a little more armagnac. Close the jar tightly, turn it upside down and keep it in a cool, dark place for at least 4 weeks.

Place the milk in a heavy-based saucepan, bring almost to the boil then remove from the heat, cover and keep warm.

Place the egg yolks in a bowl and gradually work in the sugar, whisking vigorously for about 5 minutes until the mixture is smooth and pale yellow. Gradually stir in the hot milk then return to the pan over a low heat and stir gently for 6–10 minutes without allowing the custard to reach simmering point. All the froth will disappear and the custard will be thick enough to coat the back of a spoon. Remove from the heat, cover with a piece of greaseproof paper and leave to cool.

Measure 10 fl oz (300 ml) of prunes and armagnac and coarsely chop the prunes to make a moist mixture. Stir this into the cold custard. Pour the mixture into an ice-cream maker and process until firm and creamy. Alternatively, pour into a freezer tray and freeze until firm, removing from the freezer and whisking several times during freezing. Unmould on to a platter lined with a folded napkin so that it will not slip as you cut it. Garnish each serving with a prune in armagnac.

Note

The proportions of armagnac and prunes can obviously be altered to suit personal taste.

WHERE DO YOU STAND?

A *gourmand* eats well but a little too much.
A *gourmet* is a delicate expert.
A *goinfre* eats with avidity.
A *glouton* eats excessively.
A *goulu* eats too quickly.

Opposite: GLACE À L'ARMAGNAC ET AUX PRUNEAUX
(*see page 255*)

*T*RUFFLES

Chocolate truffles

Home-made chocolate truffles are delicious. They are perfect as a gift for anyone. Enjoy truffles in small quantities as they have a very powerful chocolate flavour. Use a good quality bitter chocolate such as Sainsbury's or Waitrose's Continental Chocolate which have 78 and 72 per cent cacao respectively.

—— *Makes about 70 truffles* ——

2 egg yolks
4 oz (100 g) icing sugar, sieved
4 fl oz (120 ml) double cream
2 oz (50 g) butter, softened
1 lb (450 g) plain unsweetened chocolate, grated
3 tablespoons Calvados or cognac (optional)

FOR THE COATING
8 oz (225 g) plain unsweetened chocolate, grated
1 tablespoon strong black coffee
1–2 tablespoons cocoa powder

Place the egg yolks and half the sugar in a bowl and beat until pale yellow. In a separate pan, beat the cream, butter and remaining sugar over a low heat and bring to the boil. Place the bowl containing the egg and sugar mixture over a pan of gently simmering water, stir in the warm cream and grated chocolate and stir until smooth. Add the brandy, if using, remove from the heat and whisk until lukewarm.

Line a small baking tin with baking parchment. Pour in the cool chocolate mixture, fold the parchment over the top and refrigerate for 4 hours. Dust your hands with a little sieved icing sugar and roll the chocolate mixture into small walnut-sized balls. Refrigerate again until firm.

Place the unsweetened chocolate and the coffee in a bowl over a pan of simmering water and stir. Lightly roll each truffle in the melted chocolate then in cocoa powder. Refrigerate for 48 hours and store them in an airtight tin.

Opposite: TRUFFLES

CROUSTADE

Filo pastry with apple filling flavoured with armagnac

This famous dessert from south-western France is filled with apples or prunes flavoured with armagnac. It is prepared in many ways and has many names – *Croustade, Pastis, Tourtière* – and was clearly inspired by the Arab tradition still evident in the region.

At her lovely auberge in St Martin d'Armagnac, I helped Pierrette Sarran make this exquisite *Croustade* for us and I found the process memorable but quite awesome as she whispered, 'Mireille, the dough must be as thin as a bride's veil'. Pierrette kneaded 2 lb (900 g) of flour, 3 eggs, 5 fl oz (150 ml) of water and a pinch of salt to a dough which she refrigerated overnight. Then she expertly stretched the dough over a huge table swathed in a cotton cloth until it was paper thin.

As Pierrette also told me that it takes at least thirty or so attempts to make a perfect dough, I strongly recommend that you use frozen filo pastry, although I would never dare to mention this to Pierrette; it could be the end of a friendship.

The pastry is always cut with sharp scissors rather than a knife. Prunes marinated in armagnac (see page 255) or poached quinces can be added to the sliced apples, if you wish.

─────────── *Serves 8* ───────────

FOR THE FILLING
1 large apple, peeled and thinly
  sliced
3 tablespoons armagnac

FOR THE PASTRY
10 oz (275 g) filo pastry, thawed
4 oz (100 g) butter
2 oz (50 g) caster sugar

Marinate the apple in the armagnac for a few hours. Alternatively, you can sprinkle the apple with armagnac as you assemble the pastry.

Pre-heat the oven to gas mark 6, 400°F (200°C). Butter a baking sheet.

Unroll the pastry and keep the sheets covered with a damp tea towel to prevent it from drying out while you are working with the rest of the pastry. Melt the butter and add the sugar. Lay one sheet of pastry on the baking sheet and brush generously with the butter and sugar mixture. Lay a second sheet on top, brush with butter and sugar then lay a third sheet on top and brush again. Arrange the apple slices in a thin layer over the pastry, avoiding the corners. Lay another sheet of pastry on top at an angle so that it creates a star shape. Brush it with butter and sugar, then lay two more sheets directly on top, brushing each time. Don't press the pastry as the sheets will stick together as they bake. Bake in the oven for about 10 minutes until crisp and golden brown. Serve lukewarm cut into wedges with sharp scissors.

Note

Sometimes, orange blossom water is added to the armagnac.

— SOUTH AND THROUGHOUT FRANCE —
GELÉE DE COINGS
Quince jelly

There is nothing more intoxicating than the fragrance of ripe quinces in a room. I love quinces as an accompaniment to meats, baked on their own, in a tart, marinated in wine, made into jam and jelly. The fruits must always be very ripe, yellow-coloured and without spots.

—— *Makes about 2 lb (900 g)* ——

3 lb (1.4 kg) quinces   *about 2 lb (900 g) sugar*

Peel and quarter the quinces. Remove the core and pips and discard the stems. Place in a large saucepan, cover with cold water, bring to the boil, cover and simmer for about 1 hour until the fruit is very soft.

Line a sieve with 2 layers of muslin and stand it over a bowl. Strain the mixture through the sieve and let it drain for 2 hours. Do not press the fruit or the jelly will be cloudy. Reserve the fruit.

Measure the juice and pour it into a preserving pan or large saucepan. Add 1 lb (450 g) sugar for each 1 pint (600 ml) of juice. Heat gently, stirring until the sugar dissolves. Bring to the boil and boil rapidly for 15–30 minutes, skimming the foam from the top during cooking if necessary, until the jelly reaches setting point. This is 220°F (104°C) or when a spoonful of cool jam on a saucer wrinkles when pressed. Pour the sticky liquid into warm jars, leave to cool then cover tightly.

Note

The fruits left over after you have prepared the jelly can be used to prepare *Pâte de Fruit*. Rub them through a sieve. Weigh and add the same weight of sugar. Cook over a medium heat for about 15 minutes, stirring with a wooden spoon, until the mixture pulls away from the sides of the pan. Spread about 1 inch (2.5 cm) thick over an oiled baking sheet, sprinkle with coarse sugar and leave uncovered, for 4 days. Cut into small squares, sprinkle with sugar and wrap in baking parchment. Store in an airtight tin.

HOME BEVERAGES

Boissons de Ménage

—— **PROVENCE AND THROUGHOUT FRANCE** ——

VIN CHAUD

Hot spiced wine

Cold wine beverages have always been popular in France. *Vin cuit*, a traditional spiced wine, used to be served in Provence on Christmas night with the 'thirteen desserts', including nuts and oranges, and for Epiphany with the *Gâteau des Rois*. It was made with the fresh must of crushed muscat grapes boiled rapidly to one-third of their volume and flavoured with coriander, cloves and orange rind then enhanced by a small glass of brandy. Today, as must is not readily available, *vin cuit* has been replaced by *Vin d'Orange* (see page 264), port or a sweet dessert wine.

Mulled wine, *Vin Chaud*, however, remains a favourite in most homes in all regions of France. It is recommended in winter after a bracing walk – or before one. It is the best thing to prevent a cold, to cure a cold and to forget a cold.

————— *Serves 6* —————

6 oranges

8 oz (225 g) sugar

3 tablespoons boiling water

2 pints good red wine

2 bay leaves

Peel the rinds carefully from the oranges so that no pith is attached and place them in a bowl. Sprinkle with the sugar and pour over the boiling water. Stir well, cover and leave to stand for 40 minutes. Extract the orange juice.

Place the wine and bay leaves in the top of a double boiler or in a saucepan and heat gently. When the wine is warm, stir in the orange rinds and syrup then discard the orange rinds and bay leaves. Add the orange juice and continue to heat until very hot.

CAFÉS

The French spend a great deal of time in cafés. We sit outdoors and sip a *diabolo menthe*, a refreshing mixture of sparkling water and mint syrup, to get a bit of sun after a long day in the office. We sit indoors to savour a *thé citron*, lemon tea, and three croissants after a long walk through the rainy streets. We run to a café when we want to finish a book or when we feel at a loss and want to observe how others live, dress, quarrel. We go there to meet a daughter after school so she can complain, wonder and giggle over a foamy hot chocolate and a *croque madame*, a slice of bread topped with ham, grated cheese and egg and grilled until bubbling.

People talk and read and show off in cafés. Young executives indulge themselves with *un sérieux*, a draught beer, and read their faxes. Students spend the afternoon over *petits noirs*, espresso or filter coffee, and intense conversation. Tourists ask for *café crème*, and once more wonder where the cream is when they are presented with a pot of espresso and a pot of warm milk, while the waiter declares once more that's the way it has always been. Local shopkeepers come for a quick break, a *grand crème*, double espresso, warm milk, and a pile of *tartines*, slices of buttered baguettes. Pampered grandmothers sit and chat over madeleines and *liégois*, chocolate or coffee topped with whipped cream. Exotic beauties order *citron pressé*, made with fresh lemon juice. Lovers order *double express* and ignore it to continue their dreams, their anguish, their bliss, their discoveries. Elderly men sip their bitter *Suze* and feel nothing changes. The French spend a great deal of time in cafés.

VIN D'ORANGE

Orange wine

Many people still love to boast about the wine or the liqueur they prepare at home. It is economical, you know exactly what goes into it, and there is that magical element of witchcraft in the making which is so exciting. Not only that, but these concoctions of fennel, thyme, sage, coriander seeds, juniper, fruits, brandy and wine are always supposed to have some medicinal virtues.

Orange wine is very popular in the south of France. It is generally prepared in February when the bitter Seville oranges are in season. If bitter oranges are unavailable, you can make it more fragrant by adding the juice of a lemon and the rind of an orange. It is served chilled as an apéritif or as a dessert wine.

Makes about 10 pints (5.5 litres)

5 Seville oranges or 7 oranges and the rind of 1 oven-dried orange
rind of 1 lemon
2 pints (1.2 litres) brandy (45% alcohol content)

6 pints (3.4 litres) red or rosé wine
2 lb (900 g) sugar
2 vanilla pods, split in half

Wash the fruits and cut them into small pieces, discarding only the pips. Place them in a large glass jar with the lemon rind, brandy, wine, sugar and vanilla pods, close tightly and leave in a cool, dark place for about 6 weeks, stirring every few days. Strain, pour into bottles and store in a dark cupboard.

BURGUNDY

CRÈME DE CASSIS

Blackcurrant liqueur

Blackcurrant berries and leaves were traditionally infused in herb teas to cure fever, plague and lingering digestive problems. Today, blackcurrants are made into jams, sweets, fruit purées, syrups, liqueur and Crème. Although it is prepared commercially, it is very easy to make at home. It is also easy to use at home, in Kir drinks, sorbets, in fruit purées, salads, and compotes.

— *Makes about 3 pints (1.75 litres)* —

1½ lb (675 g) ripe blackcurrants   *2 lb (900 g) sugar*
2 pints (1.2 litres) good red wine   *10 fl oz (300 ml) brandy*

Rinse the berries under cold water, crush them coarsely and place them in a large glass jar. Pour in the wine, cover and leave to stand for 2 days.

Rub through a sieve into a saucepan and add the sugar. Bring to the boil, stirring with a wooden spoon, and simmer for 5 minutes. Leave to cool, strain again and stir in the brandy. Pour into bottles, seal and store in a cool place. It will keep for years.

— BURGUNDY AND THROUGHOUT FRANCE —

KIR

Wine and blackcurrant apéritif

The drinking of kir began decades ago when city workers started the day with an invigorating glass of white wine and added a little Crème de cassis to sweeten it. Blackcurrants grow alongside the vineyards in Burgundy, and in the 1950s the formidable Canon and Mayor of Dijon turned both into a national fashion and gave his name, *le Kir*, to the old *blanc cassé*.

The best wine for kir is a Bourgogne Blanc Aligoté, but you can also prepare it with champagne for a 'Royal'. Prepared with red wine it is a 'Cardinal'. Variations on the kir theme are made with blackberry, raspberry or strawberry and even peach liqueurs.

──────── *Serves 1* ────────

1 glass dry white wine, chilled

1 teaspoon Crème de Cassis *(see page 265)*

Mix together the wine and cassis and serve chilled.

266

RATAFIA D'ORANGES

Spiced orange liqueur

Ratafia, Riquiqui, Carthagène, Pineau – all these superb home drinks were, and often still are, prepared just after the *vendange*, the grape harvest, with the must newly crushed and blended with local cognac, armagnac or marc brandy and stored for at least a year in wooden barrels. They are the *vignerons'* treasures.

However, there is a Ratafia which is easier for us to prepare. It is also made with armagnac, cognac or marc brandy, but it can be flavoured with cherries, muscatel grapes, apricots, orange blossom, juniper, jasmine flowers, angelica, pomegranates, apricot and peach stones or aniseed.

In Provence and in the south-west, where they love the bitter taste of Seville oranges, they prepare the following version.

— *Makes about 2½ pints (1.5 litres)* —

6 oranges or 2 Seville and 4 sweet
   oranges
rind of 1 lemon
6 oz (175 g) sugar

3 sticks cinnamon
2 pints marc brandy, armagnac or
   cognac

Peel the rinds carefully from the oranges and the lemon so that no pith is attached. Cut it into thin strips and place in a saucepan. Extract the orange juice; you should have about 10 fl oz (300 ml). Pour over the rinds, bring to the boil for a few seconds then remove from the heat and leave to cool.

Add the sugar, cinnamon and brandy and stir until the sugar has dissolved. Pour into glass jars, close tightly and store in a cool, dark place for 2 months. Strain the Ratafia and discard the rinds. Return to clean bottles, seal and store for a further month before tasting.

Note

If the oranges do not yield 10 fl oz (300 ml) of juice, you can add extra orange juice.

INDEX